"Proper theological method is essential to [...] of Christian Theology: A Basic Introduction, [...] how this is the case. I heartily recommei.. ..i.. book for those who desire greater theological awareness and formation, and for those who want the church to know and enjoy the same."

—**Jason K. Allen**, president, Midwestern Baptist Theological Seminary

"Simply stated, *The Method of Christian Theology* is a splendid book. Rhyne Putman, one of the truly outstanding young evangelical theologians of our day, has given us a masterful introduction to the task of doing theology for the church. Blending head and heart, this engaging and illuminating volume provides guidance, clarity, and insight for pastors, students, and all who are interested in the work of Christian theology. It is a genuine delight to recommend this excellent work, which should be essential reading for ministerial students and seminarians across the country."

—**David S. Dockery**, president, International Alliance for Christian Education, and distinguished professor of theology, Southwestern Baptist Theological Seminary

"In *The Method of Christian Theology*, Rhyne Putman has provided the church with an accessible, user-friendly introduction to one of theology's perennial questions: What is the best way to study and articulate Christian doctrine? Rather than some dry discussion of ethereal issues, though, this book engages the heart, soul, and hands as well as the mind as Putman seeks to form Christlike theologians through their systematic handling of God's Word. This book should be used in any classroom or church setting in which the topic of conversation centers on theological method. I cannot recommend it highly enough."

—**Matthew Y. Emerson**, professor of religion and dean, Hobbs College of Theology and Ministry, Oklahoma Baptist University

"Far too often, theological method is treated as little more than the preliminary material at the beginning of a systematic theology textbook. But the 'how' of theology is closely related to the 'what' of theology—to the glory of the 'Who' of theology. Rhyne Putman has written a great introduction to theological method that understands that theologians are worshipers and that theology rightly understood is as much doxological as it is academic. *The Method of Christian Theology* will be an essential resource for theology students and a challenging-but-edifying refresher for pastors and other ministry leaders. Highly recommended."

—**Nathan A. Finn**, provost and dean of the university faculty, North Greenville University

"Putman provides an important introduction to a wide array of often neglected areas in theological method, highlighting the necessary academic depth and grounding, while also exploring a wide array of topics. He also identifies potential pitfalls, providing prudent advice for readers concerning various available methods. The overall goal is a balanced approach that speaks to issues of both the head and the heart. While introducing the essentials, the book is easily readable. Highly recommended."

—**Gary R. Habermas**, distinguished research professor
of apologetics and philosophy, Liberty University

"When I think of Rhyne Putman, what comes to mind is a trusted scholar who can speak deep truths to regular people. There seems to be a large gap in the theological reading realm between popular-level books and those books only read and understood by trained theologians. Dr. Putman is able to speak to both ends of the spectrum, providing a middle-level approach that is so greatly missing. Pastors, seminary students, and church members desiring to take a deeper step into theological reading will all benefit from this book."

—**Dean Inserra**, lead pastor, City Church, Tallahassee, FL

"A homeowner does not get excited by talking about the foundation of a house; neither does a Christian by talking about theological method. But both are vital, and to get them wrong could prove disastrous. As a reliable and tested guide, Rhyne Putman has given a clear and enjoyable introduction to theological method that is grounded in Scripture, attuned to the Christian tradition, aware of contemporary issues, and geared toward the church to help Christians faithfully know their blessed God and proclaim his glorious gospel. I highly recommend this work for church leaders, students, and all Christians who desire to think rightly of their triune God and all things in relation to him."

—**Oren Martin**, assistant professor of Christian theology,
The Southern Baptist Theological Seminary and Boyce College

"Evangelical Christians have neglected theological method for generations—and that is a harmful neglect. Rhyne Putman offers a serious consideration of theological method that will make a lasting mark in evangelical theology. This is a major contribution to theological discussion."

—**R. Albert Mohler Jr.**, president,
The Southern Baptist Theological Seminary

"Rhyne Putman is to be commended for this faithful guide to theological method. It is wisely conceived, crisply written, clearly organized, and judiciously presented. Students will find it to be a helpful, thoughtful, and enjoyable textbook."

—**Christopher W. Morgan**, dean and professor of theology, California Baptist University

"Dr. Putman has contributed to discussions about theological method at a high level. He now uses his expertise in this field to provide pastors and students with a sophisticated but accessible introduction to the conversation. I especially like how he emphasizes that theologians must develop their minds and their hearts. Readers will find this text academically helpful and spiritually edifying."

—**David Rathel**, associate professor of Christian theology, Gateway Seminary

"Faithful theological method is God-centered: it takes the Bible seriously as the revelation of the triune God, reflects on God's work throughout church history, and is sensitive to God's continued work in the world. Rhyne Putman lays out such a method in a way that helpfully contributes to both the academy and the church."

—**Brandon D. Smith**, assistant professor of theology and New Testament, Cedarville University, and editorial director, Center for Baptist Renewal

"Ethicist Jeffrey Stout once complained that preoccupation with method is like clearing your throat: 'it can go on for only so long before you lose your audience.' But Rhyne Putman understands that to speak of theological method is already to be engaged in the task of theology itself. As such, he never risks losing his audience. Instead, Putman distills his broad knowledge of theology, exegesis, tradition, and philosophy into a readable and, most crucially, usable manual on how to do theology. This volume will now be my go-to textbook on theological prolegomena."

—**R. Lucas Stamps**, associate professor of Christian studies, Anderson University

"'Show me the way to go home.' Rhyne Putman probably didn't have the lyrics to this song in mind when he was writing this book, but he could have. A method is a way of doing something, and his book provides everything newcomers to Christian theology need to embark on their way home—back to God, for whom our hearts are restless until they find rest in him. It also provides precious practical help along the way—the preparation, procedures, and practices pilgrims and disciples need for understanding, formulating, contextualizing, and even preaching doctrine. Anyone interested in interpreting Scripture for knowing God will benefit from the clear signage Putman provides along the way."

—Kevin J. Vanhoozer, research professor of systematic theology, Trinity Evangelical Divinity School

"Rhyne Putman deals directly with what is often neglected in the doing of theology. He recognizes that what one thinks about the nature of theology and how one is prepared for the task determines how one does theology. This book calls us to envision theology as disciple-making. Putman knows that how one conceives of God and his work in the world will determine how they themselves live in the world. It is for this very reason that he says Christian theologians must have both the right heart and head in order to be good theologians. And Putman embodies both throughout the book. Complex ideas and skillful conclusions are drawn with engaging instruction and pedagogical virtues to equip the student for situating, articulating, and proclaiming their theological convictions. *The Method of Christian Theology* is excellently written for the beginning theological student."

—Keith S. Whitfield, provost, Southeastern Baptist Theological Seminary

"A Christian can either steer straight or drive woefully astray, immediately and for life, depending on his or her method of thinking about God. Addressing this seminal crisis, Rhyne Putman makes accessible to novice theologians the high purpose and proper method for a Christian disciple's theology. Putman is among the keenest, most judicious, and most engaging writers today, and every professor would do well to require *The Method of Christian Theology* as a primary text. While once helping introduce theological method to evangelicals, I now heartily commend this more accessible volume."

—Malcolm B. Yarnell III, research professor of theology, Southwestern Baptist Theological Seminary

THE METHOD OF

CHRISTIAN

THEOLOGY

THE METHOD OF

CHRISTIAN

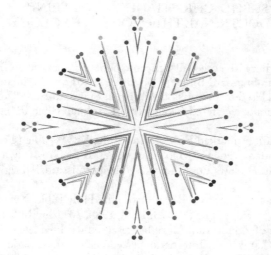

THEOLOGY

A BASIC INTRODUCTION

RHYNE R. PUTMAN

B&H
ACADEMIC
NASHVILLE, TENNESSEE

Published by B&H Academic
Nashville, Tennessee

ISBN: 978-1-5359-3333-9

DEWEY: 230
SUBHD: CHRISTIANITY--DOCTRINES /
DOCTRINAL THEOLOGY / THEOLOGY

Cover design by Mark Karis. Cover illustration by naqiewei/iStock.

Printed in the United States of America

2 3 4 5 6 7 8 9 10 VP 26 25 24 23 22

For
Bennett Roberts Putman,
my only son.

Love God.
Love people.
Change the world for King Jesus.

CONTENTS

Acknowledgments   *xiii*

Abbreviations   *xvii*

Introduction: Method Matters   1

Part One: Principles   7

1   Defining Theology and Its Tasks   9

2   Doctrine and Truth   23

3   Doctrine, Worldview, and Disciple-Making   43

4   The Theological Disciplines   67

Part Two: Preparations   85

5   A Heart Prepared for Christian Theology   87

6   A Mind Prepared for Christian Theology   101

Part Three: Procedures   119

7   Scripture and Its Interpretation   121

8   Tradition and Christian Theology   139

9   Philosophy and Christian Theology   163

10   Experience and Christian Theology   177

11   A Procedure for Theology   195

Part Four: Practices   221

12 Contextualizing Doctrine   223
13 Writing a Theological Research Paper   241
14 Preaching a Doctrinal Sermon   263

Conclusion: Doctrine That Makes Disciples   *283*
Bibliography   *285*
General Index   *306*
Scripture Index   *314*

ACKNOWLEDGMENTS

In his "Letter to an Aspiring Theologian," Kevin Vanhoozer gave what may be the best job description of a theologian ever put into human language: "Theology is neither a nine-to-five job nor a career. To know and speak truly of God is a vocation that requires more than academic or professional qualifications. The image you should have in mind is not the professor with a tweed jacket, *but rather the disciples who dropped everything to follow Jesus.* Becoming a theologian means following God's Word where it leads with all one's mind, heart, soul, and strength."[1] Here I must express gratitude to many disciples who have gone before me, dropped everything to follow Jesus, and poured into my life and ministry so I could do this work.

I must express gratitude to the trustees at New Orleans Baptist Theological Seminary, who granted me a full-year sabbatical in a financially trying time so I could work on this project. Dr. Norris Grubbs, the provost at New Orleans, advocated for me at every step along the way. Even though he is an Ole Miss fan—no one in this fallen world is perfect—he is a great friend and servant leader. James K. Dew, the ninth president of NOBTS, has been a constant source of encouragement and support, even in my transition back to Williams Baptist University. I am so thankful for him; his sweet wife, Tara; and the rest of the Dew Krewe.

---

[1] Kevin J. Vanhoozer, "Letter to an Aspiring Theologian: How to Speak of God Truly," *First Things*, August 2018, https://www.firstthings.com/article/2018/08/letter-to-an-aspiring-theologian, emphasis mine.

xiv

ACKNOWLEDGMENTS

My church family at First Baptist Church, Kenner, Louisiana, was a rock for me during the global pandemic that changed all our lives in 2020. I thank God for the nearly four years I spent shepherding them. Deacons like Johnny Barlow, Wesley Bouler, Bob Carjaval, John Dryden, Jeff Farmer, Bob Frechette, Boyd Guy, Scott MacCord, Danny Moore, Dwight Mulholland, Bart Neal, Jim Parrie, Jason Robles, Chris Screen, Chuck Simmons, Tyler St. Amant, Steven Whatley, and Russell Wright held my arms up during this time and enabled me to keep up pastoral ministry and finish projects like this one. I thank Jesus for this dear church family: the Allens; the Amiris; the Armstrongs; the Barlows; Carolyn Bennett; Jerry Berry; Marlene Bertucci; Susan Boffone; the Bonners; the Bordelons; Todd Boudreaux; the whole Bouler clan; the Brukettas; the Calvins; Bunny Carrone; the Chateaus; Shantrice Coleman; Richard and Nancy Cox; the Crafts; Josh Crown; Ruby Dayberry; Denise Demars; Josie Dennis; Mary Helen Driver; the Drydens; the Dupres; Eddy Eyo and Lynlee Morgan; the Farmers; all the Farnsworths and James Falvey; the Faucheux family; the Frechette family; Betty Gambino; the Godbolds; Jenny Gullo; the Guys; Kelli Hardesty; the Hardins; the Hihars; the Hinkles; the Horns; the Johnsons; the Kelly family; the Kierans; the Killians; Pat Kruse; the Lancasters; Barbara Lee; Jason Lemoine; Gary Lewis; Mary Ellen Logan; the MacCords; the Martins; the McCleskeys; the Michels; the Mohrs; the Moores; the Morrows; the Mulhollands; the Neals; Donna Nesbit; the Newsoms; the Parrie family; the Pizzolatos; the Poes; the Quackenbushes; the family of Jillian Quarles; Sal Randazzo; Patty Riedlinger and her late husband, Gary; Rose Roberts; the Robleses; the Rollinses; the Russells; the Salathe family; the Screens; the Shirleys; the Simmonses; the Skaggs; Carol Stamm; the Telschow family; the Twiggs; the Vickrey family; the Wallers; the Westmans; the Whitehorns; the Wiedmans; and the Whitlows. Pastors Cody Killian, Nathan Michel, and Clint Newsom are among the finest men I have ever had the pleasure of serving with in my time of ministry.

It is a great pleasure to work alongside the fine team at Williams Baptist University, including but not limited to Joy Norman, Marvin Schoenecke, Brett Cooper, Doug Walker, Angela Flippo, Robert Foster,

Walter Norvell, Amber Grady, Kay Lynn Bennett, Tracy Henderson, and
Taylor Baker.

I would not be in this seat, writing a project on theological method,
were it not for the men who taught me systematic theology over the
years: my first systematic teacher and the president of Williams Baptist
University, R. Stanton Norman; mein Doktorvater, Robert B. Stewart;
and other teachers and colleagues at NOBTS, like Jeffrey B. Riley, Rex
Butler, Lloyd Harsch, Page Brooks, Michael Edens, and Tyler Wittman.

I am also heavily indebted to those who never instructed me in the
classroom but who nevertheless had a significant role in shaping my theological mind: Millard Erickson, David Dockery, Timothy George, Kevin
J. Vanhoozer, Alister E. McGrath, Gregg Allison, R. Albert Mohler Jr.,
Bruce Ashford, N. T. Wright, Michael Bird, Malcolm Yarnell, and the
late, great James Leo Garrett. The user-friendly writings of Andrew
David Naselli provided a model for how I wanted to lay out my recommended procedure for studying systematics.

This book would not be what it is without the insights and helpful
feedback of friends like Adam Harwood, Keith Whitfield, Christopher
Morgan, Brandon Smith, Trevin Wax, and Nathan Finn. I am especially
grateful to Chris Thompson and Jim Baird, who initially encouraged me
to take up this project.

Of course, I could not do this without the love and support of my
parents, Glen and Diane Putman; my in-laws, Collin and Marcia Elder;
my children, Ben and Annie; and my incredible wife, Micah Danielle. I
have dedicated this book to my firstborn, my one and only son, Ben. He
is not yet a disciple, nor is he old enough to appreciate this book, but my
most desperate prayer for him is that one day he will become a disciple-
making disciple sold out for God's Word and God's people. I love you,
son! Change the world for King Jesus!

Soli Deo Gloria
Rhyne Putman
Williams Baptist University
August 4, 2020

ABBREVIATIONS

ANF	*The Ante-Nicene Fathers: The Writings of the Fathers down to A.D. 325.* Vol. 3, *Latin Christianity: Its Founder, Tertullian*, edited by Rev. Alexander Roberts and James Donaldson. New York: Charles Scribner's Sons, 1903.
AT	Descartes, René. *Oeuvres de Descartes.* Rev. ed., edited by Charles Adam and Paul Tannery. 12 vols. Paris: J. Vrin/ C.N.R.S., 1964–1976.
JETS	*Journal of the Evangelical Theological Society*
NIDNTTE	Silva, Moisés, ed. *New International Dictionary of New Testament Theology and Exegesis.* 2nd ed. 5 vols. Grand Rapids: Zondervan, 2014.
NPNF[1]	*Nicene and Post-Nicene Fathers Series 1.* Edited by Alexander Roberts, James Donaldson, Philip Schaff, and Henry Wace. 14 vols. Peabody, MA: Hendrickson, 1994.

INTRODUCTION

Method Matters

First-year theology students normally enjoy debating hot-button theological topics like the doctrine of creation, predestination and free will, the miraculous spiritual gifts, the covenants, and the timetable for Christ's return, but they rarely muster the same enthusiasm for *theological method*. After all, time spent in the classroom on methodology can feel like an extended discussion of the syllabus. Talk about method may be a necessary evil, but we need to get through it quickly so we can move on to the juicy stuff.

Before we can get into all that excitement, we must first talk about theological method, or what is otherwise known as *theological prolegomena*. (Say it with me: *pro-le-gom-e-na*. Now say it three times fast.) The singular term, *prolegomenon*, which literally means "a word spoken beforehand," is a critical introduction to a topic or field of study. As a critical introduction to theology, theological method explores the definitions, the tasks, the sources, and the processes of Christian theology. Method addresses foundational questions like: What is theology? What do theologians do? How can they do it better? How should I study theology? And what use does theology serve for the people to whom I am called to minister?

Everyone who thinks about God has a method for approaching this subject matter, though few people stop to think about the way they reach their conclusions. How one defines theology, sees its task, and uses its sources will shape the final product of doctrine, for better or worse. In the words of Gordon Spykman (1926–1993), "Show me your prolegomena, and I will predict the rest of your theology."[1] When handling the things of God revealed in his Word, our method matters. Wise and faithful theological methods usually lead to true doctrines that bless and grow the people of God. Inattention to method can lead to false doctrines that wreak havoc on the church.

The history of doctrine provides us with numerous examples of destructive theologies that began with fundamentally flawed methods.

- Less than a hundred years after Jesus, a group of religious intellectuals who called themselves the Gnostics began *carelessly mixing pagan philosophy with Scripture*. Claiming to have hidden knowledge of the spiritual realm, they rejected the one true God, the goodness of his creation, and the incarnation of Jesus.

- Later that century, a popular teacher named Montanus claimed to speak on behalf of the Holy Spirit, offering "new prophecies" to anyone who would listen. Many exited orthodox churches to be part of this leader's movement. Montanus encouraged his followers to reject marriage and sex, to fast regularly, and to seek martyrdom. Many religions follow the pattern of Montanism today, emphasizing *religious experience over and against the written Word of God*.

- Modalists denied the doctrine of the Trinity by asserting that the Father, the Son, and the Holy Spirit are one and the same person. Modalists were also known as the "Father-sufferers" (patripassianists) because they taught that the Father died on the cross. Modalists *ignored a large portion of biblical texts* that clearly distinguish between the persons of the Trinity and *opted for an overly simplistic answer to a difficult question*.

---

[1] Gordon Spykman, *Reformational Theology: A New Paradigm for Doing Dogmatics* (Grand Rapids: Eerdmans, 1992), 40.

- Arius, an elder from Alexandria, set off a theological world war in the fourth century when he declared "there was a time when the Son was not." Armed with *an overly literal approach to Scripture*, Arius took Paul's description of Jesus as the "firstborn over all creation" (Col 1:15) to mean Jesus was literally the first person God created. Created by God, Jesus is less than truly God and incapable of saving us from our sin.

Each of these historical heresies was unique, but they all shared a common thread: *inattention to proper ways of thinking about God and interpreting Scripture*. None of these teachers rightly divided "the word of truth" (2 Tim 2:15). Closer attention to theological method may have helped them avoid these dangerous doctrines.

Disciples of Jesus today face similar challenges and threats from heretics, but we also live in a time unlike any other in human history. Thanks to our interconnected global culture, we are met every day with conflicting perspectives about what it means to be a human being, how we are to relate to one another, and why the world is the way it is. Anyone with a smartphone and a social media account can act like an authority on any subject. We are rich with information but poor in wisdom. How do we make wise decisions about what is true? How can we who claim to follow Jesus avoid the mistakes of the past or keep from making new ones? How can we have confidence we are properly understanding God's Word and living in obedience to it? Once more, theological method matters.

The interest in theological method has intensified over the last few decades. More books have been written on the subject in the last half century than any other time in the history of the church. So, why write another when the market seems so well saturated? What could possibly be offered from another outing on the topic? Even though a prolegomenon is meant to be an "introduction" to a subject matter, many of the works that bear this name are inaccessible to those who are not already specialists entrenched in the field. Oftentimes, books on theological prolegomena are technical works written by theologians for other theologians and their doctoral students. Furthermore, few of the books written about method offer their readers an actual procedure for doing theology.

Most books in the genre of theological method read more like a "philosophy of theology" than *methodology*.

My primary goal here was to create a user-friendly book on method that upper-level undergraduates and first-year seminary students could read alongside their systematic theology textbooks, an introduction that really could be the "first words" read when diving into the incredible world of academic theology. I am not trying to reinvent the wheel here or display my cleverness. I only sought to take the best elements of the great works written over recent years in theological method and share them with pastors and teachers in training. Second, I hope pastors and church leaders can benefit from the resources provided here as a way of enriching their preaching and discipleship ministries.

By writing this book, I desire to serve those whom God has called "to equip the saints for the work of ministry, to build up the body of Christ, until we all reach unity in the faith and in the knowledge of God's Son, growing into maturity with a stature measured by Christ's fullness" (Eph 4:12–13). The calling God has placed on pastors is no picnic, but know-how in the area of theological method can make them more effective in "speaking the truth in love" (Eph 4:15) and preventing their people from being "blown around by every wind of teaching" (Eph 4:14).

Theological Method for Christian Disciple-Makers

This book explores theological method as it relates to the Great Commission (Matt 28:18–20). My end goal is not to sustain the academy but to develop a group of students passionate about Christian truth and reaching the nations for King Jesus. Theology is both a guide for Christian mission and an essential part of it. I am convinced the study of theological method can help us be more effective disciple-makers in the various ministry contexts to which God calls us.

This book begins where many other works in theological method linger—the *principles of theology*. In chapter 1, we will look at various definitions of the term *theology* and describe the tasks of systematic theology. The second chapter tackles a more controversial topic: the nature of doctrine and its function in the life of the church. Chapter 3 explores the role of theology in disciple-making, especially in the way theology shapes the Christian worldview. I conclude this section with a chapter about the relationship between the various theological disciplines.

The next section of the book, *preparations*, deals with the character of the theologian. Chapter 5 is about spiritual preparation for studying Christian theology. Here, I compare and contrast theology in the flesh with theology in the Spirit. Chapter 6 is about having a mind prepared for the study of Christian theology. It explores the tension between faith and reason, the nature of Christian knowledge, and the need for intellectual virtues in studying Christian doctrine.

We next move to the *procedures*. Chapter 7 is an exploration of the nature of Scripture and its interpretation, highlighting the way we read the Bible as the Word of God so that we can know God. The three chapters that follow (chapters 8–10) explore how other "authorities" like tradition, philosophy, and experience serve Scripture in theological method. This section concludes with a concrete, replicable process for students working their way through a doctrinal topic.

I wrote the final section of this book—*practices*—especially for students. Chapter 12 addresses teaching Christian doctrine in a way that is faithful to Scripture and fitting to one's ministry context. Chapters 13 and 14 explore the two main "deliverables" of the academic study of Christian theology: (1) academic papers and (2) doctrinal sermons taught in the life of the local church. Oftentimes we who are theology professors assign our students papers to write but give little or no concrete direction for how to write them. Building on the procedural level laid out in the previous section, chapter 13 details how to pick a theological topic, how to narrow the focus of the paper, how to research, how to outline the paper, and how to make arguments. In chapter 14, I address two different ways doctrine can be preached or taught in a local church setting.

PART ONE

Principles

*Understanding the nature of
Christian theology and its tasks*

Defining Theology
and Its Tasks

I pray that the God of our Lord Jesus Christ, the
glorious Father, would give you the Spirit of wisdom
and revelation in the knowledge of him.

—EPHESIANS 1:17

What is theology? The commonly given short answer, though not necessarily the most precise or helpful one, is that theology is "the study of God." After all, *theology* draws its name from two Greek words: *theos*, meaning "God," and *logos*, which means "word," "reason," or "speech." In contemporary usage, we usually associate the suffix *-ology* with the study or science of something. One may think of **theology** as the "study of God" in much the same way biology is the study of living organisms, cultural anthropology is the study of human cultures, and bracketology is the study of college basketball tournament schedules. We do, in fact, study theology to learn about God.[1]

But this description is thin and somewhat misleading. The so-called study of God is categorically different from any other science. God cannot be seen through a telescope or observed in a petri dish. No theologian studies God as a detached or neutral observer, nor can we ever "master" the only "subject matter" who knows us better than we know ourselves. In some ways, the idea of "studying" God is like Harry Potter studying J. K. Rowling or Atticus Finch researching Harper Lee. Like Abraham, Isaac, and Jacob, we are merely created characters in the divine drama God is writing through our lives. We only *know* this God because he purposely makes himself known to us.

Theology must be more than an intellectual novelty, an academic program, or a lucrative career option. (Just trust me on that last one.) Theology begins and ends with the God who created us, loves us, and knows us better than we know ourselves. When pursued properly, the study of theology can help us strengthen and affirm our personal faith, equip the body of Christ, reach the nations with the gospel, smash the idols of our culture, and find deep, lasting satisfaction in the rewards of serving our eternal King.

Yet before we can achieve these marvelous ends, we must learn how to come into theology in the right way, to take the right first steps. That is the duty of theological method. Before we can set about detailing the business of theology, we must first describe what it is theology does. How one defines theology will shape the way one practices theology.

How Has Theology Been Defined?

Though the word *theology* appears nowhere in Scripture, the Bible is a very theological book—or better stated, a library of theological books. God did not choose to inspire a systematic theology textbook, but as

---

[1] As Thomas Aquinas explained, "The object of the science [i.e., a field of study or knowledge] is that of which it principally treats. But in this science, the treatment is mainly about God; for it is called theology, as treating of God. Therefore, God is the object of this science" (*Summa Theologica* 1.1.7).

Bruce Ashford and Keith Whitfield astutely observed, the Bible (1) anticipates the task of systematic theology, (2) provides the narrative framework for theology, and (3) provides the trajectory for the theological task.[2]

Scripture anticipates the task of theology in providing the content of theology, in calling people everywhere to love its principal object of study, and in shaping the way we think about God's world. Every biblical author wrote "ad hoc theology" with doctrinal and practical instruction directed toward circumstances in Israel or the early church. Christian theologians work to interpret these context-specific messages, to reconstruct the belief system behind them, and to apply them to the needs of the church today.

The Bible may anticipate theology, but the formal development of theology as a discipline took more time. Christians and non-Christians alike have used the term *theology* in several ways throughout history.[3] One of the earliest known uses of *theologia* is found in the works of Plato, where the philosopher used it unfavorably to describe pagan myths about the gods.[4] Plato rejected the "theological" stories of Greek poets who characterized the gods like the crazy guests on a daytime talk show, always "warring, fighting, or plotting against one another."[5] Aristotle also dismissed the ancient "theologies" or mythologies that used the gods to explain natural phenomena.[6] Greek philosophers later described their respective philosophies of religion as theologies, a use that resonated with the earliest Christian theologians.[7]

---

[2] Bruce Riley Ashford and Keith Whitfield, "Theological Method: An Introduction to the Task of Theology," in *A Theology for the Church*, 2nd ed., ed. Daniel L. Akin (Nashville: B&H Academic, 2014), 3–17.

[3] See Frank Whaling, "The Development of the Word 'Theology,'" *Scottish Journal of Theology* 34 (1981): 289–312.

[4] Plato, *The Republic* 2.379a.

[5] Plato, 2.378c.

[6] Aristotle, *Meteorologica* 2.353b. Elsewhere, Aristotle used the term *theologia* positively to describe the study of things related to the divine. See Aristotle *Metaphysics* 6.1026a.

[7] Whaling, "The Development of the Word 'Theology,'" 290–92.

For the first eleven centuries of the faith, Christian thinkers predominantly used the word *theologia* to describe the Christian doctrine of God.[8] Today, we specify this use of the term as *theology proper*. **Theology proper** is a specific category of Christian doctrine that explores the existence, essence, attributes, and activity of God. Theology proper bears some family resemblance to the way Greco-Roman philosophers approached the philosophy of religion, but the God Christian theologians speak of is not "the god of the philosophers."[9] He is the triune God who has "spoken to us by his Son . . . the radiance of God's glory and the exact expression of his nature" (Heb 1:2–3).

The earliest Christian theologians appropriated the term *theologia* to describe Christian doctrine and their defense of the faith. The first Christian theologies were responses to heretical theologies. The teachings of heretics forced orthodox Christians to explain their own beliefs.[10] Justin Martyr (c. 100–c. 165) offered apologetic responses to Jewish and Greek critics of Christianity.[11] Second- and third-century theologians Irenaeus (c. 130–c. 202) and Tertullian (c. 155–c. 240) wrote theological treatises in response to the heresies of groups like the Gnostics, who denied the incarnation of Christ and the goodness of creation.[12] The late-second-century theologian Clement of Alexandria (c. 150–215) wrote

---

[8] David K. Clark, *To Know and Love God: Method for Theology*, Foundations of Evangelical Theology (Wheaton, IL: Crossway, 2003), 34–37.

[9] Blaise Pascal, *Pensées and Other Writings*, trans. Honor Levi (New York: Oxford University Press, 1992), 172.

[10] See Harold O. J. Brown, *Heresies: Heresy and Orthodoxy in the History of the Church* (Peabody, MA: Hendrickson, 2003), 42. For this reason, Brown called heresy "the stepmother of orthodoxy" and a specific heresy like Gnosticism "the stepmother of systematic theology."

[11] *The First Apology* and *The Second Apology* are defenses of Christian belief addressed to Roman rulers and authorities. Justin responds to Jewish criticism of Christian doctrine in *Dialogue with Trypho*.

[12] The major extant works of Irenaeus include *Against Heresies* and *On Apostolic Preaching*. Thirty-one works of Tertullian have survived, including a book on apologetic method (*On the Prescription of Heretics*) and theological writings directed toward the Gnostics (*Against the Valentinians*), the Modalists (*Against Praxeas*), and the Marcionite heresy (*Against Marcion*).

of "the theology of the ever-living word," which he contrasted with the "theology" of pagan philosophers and myth-makers.[13]

The adjective *theological* can also describe individual and cultural beliefs about God or gods. Everyone, whether deeply religious, apathetic toward religion, or adamantly opposed to religion, has some belief about God, their origins, and their final destiny. Consequently, everyone is a "theologian" in this extremely broad sense of the word, though most people never stop to think critically about their religious beliefs.[14] While everyone has what Arthur Holmes called a "world-viewish theology," few stop to analyze their underlying beliefs about God. Even fewer take up the task of studying Christian theology critically.[15]

One common use of the term *theology* is everything taught and affirmed within a local Christian church or denomination. In this sense, *theology* is synonymous with *doctrine*. This is what people mean when they say, "That church has good theology," or "That televangelist has a bad theology." While this usage of *theology* is common, I want to make a more careful distinction between theology and doctrine, which I will explore in the next chapter.

The adjective *theological* can also describe any academic discipline taught in a Bible college, seminary, or divinity school.[16] I regularly tell my students my systematic theology classes are the most important classes they will take in seminary because the word *theological* is in the name of our institution. (I'm not sure my colleagues at the seminary are as amused as I am.) But of course, this broader, academic sense of *theological* also applies to a wide range of disciplines outside of doctrinal studies, including but not limited to biblical studies, church history, philosophy of religion, pastoral ministries, discipleship ministries, counseling ministries, church leadership courses, and worship studies.

---

[13] Clement of Alexandria, *Stromata* 1.13; 5.4.

[14] Stanley J. Grenz and Roger E. Olson, *Who Needs Theology? An Invitation to the Study of God* (Downers Grove, IL: InterVarsity Press, 1996), 12–21.

[15] Arthur F. Holmes, *Contours of a World View* (Grand Rapids: Eerdmans, 1983), 35.

[16] Michael Kibbe, *From Topic to Thesis: A Guide to Theological Research* (Downers Grove, IL: InterVarsity Press, 2016), 32–33.

Finally, most scholars associate "theology" with the scholarly and critical study of doctrine, what Christians believe and teach. The four traditional branches of doctrinal studies are *systematic theology*, *biblical theology*, *historical theology*, and *philosophical theology*. Biblical theology is often divided into *Old Testament theology* and *New Testament theology*. To these common categories we could add *practical theology* (or *pastoral theology*), *Christian ethics*, and *Christian apologetics*. For the purposes of this book, *theology* or *Christian theology* is shorthand for **systematic theology** (sometimes called *dogmatics*).

What Is Systematic Theology?

A superficial survey of systematic theology textbooks would show how much they have in common, especially among evangelical theologians. They are orderly accounts of Christian doctrine usually arranged by headings like "Revelation," "God," "Humanity," "Christ," and the like. Yet theologians vary widely in their respective definitions of systematic theology, largely because they understand the central tasks of theology in various ways. Consider the following examples from evangelical theologians:

- Focusing on the primacy of biblical doctrine, Wayne Grudem defined systematic theology as "any study that answers the question, 'What does the whole Bible teach us today?' about any given topic."[17]

---

[17] Wayne Grudem, *Systematic Theology* (Grand Rapids: Zondervan, 2000), 21.

- Millard Erickson's definition highlights the role of theology in shaping a Christian worldview: "Theology . . . is a discipline of study that seeks to understand the God revealed in the Bible and to provide a Christian understanding of reality."[18]
- Beth Felker Jones stressed that theology is "about discipleship: we learn to speak and think well about God so that we can be more faithful followers of Jesus."[19]
- John Franke focused on mission and witness: "The purpose of theology is to cooperate with the Spirit to form witnessing communities that participate in the divine mission by living God's love in the way of Jesus Christ for the sake of the world."[20]
- John Frame's definition underscores the practical dimension of Christian theology: "Theology is *the application of Scripture, by persons, to every area of life.*"[21]
- Stressing the role of theology in Christian worship, Alister McGrath characterized theology as "reflection upon the God whom Christians worship and adore."[22]

Some of these definitions focus on cognitive content: what we can *know*. Others focus on a *practical* end, like worldview formation, discipleship, obedience, or mission. The final definition focuses on the *heartfelt* dimension of theology in Christian worship. Yet all these definitions speak to essential aspects of Christian theology or its tasks. Before I offer my own definition, I want to explore ten features of systematic theology that set it apart from other forms of doctrinal study.

---

[18] Millard J. Erickson, *Christian Theology*, 3rd ed. (Grand Rapids: Baker, 2013), 3.

[19] Beth Felker Jones, *Practicing Christian Doctrine: An Introduction to Thinking and Living Theologically* (Grand Rapids: Zondervan, 2014), 13.

[20] John R. Franke, "Missional Theology," in *Evangelical Theological Method: Five Views*, ed. Stanley E. Porter and Steven M. Studebaker (Downers Grove, IL: InterVarsity Press, 2018), 60.

[21] John Frame, *Systematic Theology: An Introduction to Christian Belief* (Philipsburg, NJ: P&R, 2013), 8, italics in original.

[22] Alister E. McGrath, *Christian Theology*, 5th ed. (Malden, MA: Wiley-Blackwell, 2011), 102.

First, systematic theology is a distinctively Christian discipline. No other faith tradition has a clear parallel to the Christian study of systematic theology. While non-Christian religions have scholars who study their beliefs, they do not ordinarily work to organize those beliefs into a coherent system for their adherents.[23] Non-Christian scholars of religion often attempt to address belief systems as neutral observers, not trying to shape a belief system as much as they are trying to describe it. By contrast, Christian theologians aim "to build up the body of Christ," to help believers reach "unity in the faith and in the knowledge of God's Son" (Eph 4:12, 13). Christian theologians believe we are being renewed in the image of our Creator through the knowledge of God (Col 3:10). Systematic theology begins and ends with the good news of Jesus Christ.

Second, systematic theology involves critical reflection. "Critical" here does not mean being negative or argumentative, but giving serious thought to ideas. In an age when we have access to the sum of human knowledge on the little devices in our pockets, we need critical reflection more than ever. We must train our senses "to distinguish between good and evil" (Heb 5:14). We must have our minds renewed so that we may "discern what is the good, pleasing, and perfect will of God" (Rom 12:2).

Applied to theology, critical reflection means testing the things believed, said, or taught about God and his Word. Believers firmly footed in Christian truth are not "tossed by the waves and blown around by every wind of teaching" (Eph 4:14). So, Paul encouraged believers to "test all things" (1 Thess 5:21). Likewise, John warned about false teachers and instructed the church to "test the spirits to see if they are from

---

[23] There are historical exceptions to this rule. Medieval Islamic schools like the Muʿtazila dedicated themselves to the study of ʿIlm al-Kalām (the "science of speech") or rational Islamic theology, but few contemporary Muslims believe this to be an important endeavor. See Richard C. Martin, Mark R. Woodward, and Dwi S. Atmaja, *Defenders of Reason in Islam: Muʿtazilism from Medieval School to Modern Symbol* (London: Oneworld, 1997). Under the influence of these Islamic rationalist traditions, the Arabic rabbi Saadia Gaon (c. 892–942) later developed a Jewish Kalam theology titled *The Book of Doctrines and Beliefs* (*Emunoth ve-Deoth*). See Saadia Gaon, *The Book of Doctrines and Beliefs*, trans. Alexander Altmann (Indianapolis: Hackett, 2002).

God, because many false prophets have gone out into the world" (1 John 4:1). We should be like the Berean converts who, after hearing Paul and Silas preach, "examined the Scriptures daily to see if these things were so" (Acts 17:11). The God-given gift of **reason** enables us to reflect on the truth of God as we **experience** his presence, his goodness, and his power through the indwelling of the Holy Spirit.

Third, Christian theology is based on God's self-disclosure in general revelation and in special revelation. Through what theologians call **general revelation**, God has made his existence, power, and eternal nature known to all people everywhere (Rom 1:19–20; cf. Ps 19:1–6). General revelation includes God's self-revelation through nature, the human conscience, and history. But this general revelation is limited in its ability to describe God, his mighty acts, and his salvific plan.

God has given a more complete revelation of himself as Father, Son, and Holy Spirit in **special revelation**. Before Christ, God spoke to patriarchs, prophets, and kings. But in the fullness of time, he gave a superior revelation of himself in his Son, Jesus Christ, who is the "radiance of God's glory and the exact expression of his nature" (Heb 1:3; cf. Gal 4:4–5). Jesus, who is God incarnate, put the invisible God on display for all to see (Col 1:15). Jesus explained the kingdom of God, demonstrated God's character, and made a way for us to have a restored relationship with God through his sacrificial death. "No one has ever seen God. The one and only Son, who is himself God and is at the Father's side—he has revealed him" (John 1:18). The special revelation of God in history is preserved for believers today in Scripture—the written Word of God.

Scripture is the chief *authority* over Christian belief and practice. Some accuse conservative and evangelical Christians of "bibliolatry"—the worship of the Bible—or of serving a "paper pope." But this is a misunderstanding of what we mean by the "authority of Scripture." The authority of the Bible is God's authority expressed through Scripture. When we say we want to submit to God's Word, we mean that we want God himself to govern our beliefs and practices.

Fourth, the primary subject of systematic theology is the triune God of the Bible—his nature, his attributes, and his activity. Christian theology is not the study of a generic deity but the intellectual pursuit of the biblical

God who is Father, Son, and Holy Spirit. We study his *nature* when we study his existence, his being, and the doctrine of the Trinity. We study his *attributes* when we study those characteristics or qualities that make God who he is (e.g., he is holy, all-knowing, all-powerful, etc.). We also examine the *activity* of God in history and in the world and church today. God's past activities include his initial creative act, his rescue of Israel from the Egyptians, and gospel concerning the life, death, and resurrection of Jesus Christ. His ongoing activities include his providential care of the universe, his saving of sinners, and his rule over the church. His future activities are the substance of biblical promises: the return of Jesus, the judgment of sin, the consummation of the kingdom, and the restoration of creation.

Fifth, systematic theology organizes the teaching of the whole Bible into categories or topics, answering critical questions about the content of its teaching. Sometimes the work of systematic theology is derided by those who assert it is foreign to the Bible itself. The Bible does not present its theological content in an organized, categorical way. The reason for this is understandable. Scripture is not a single book written for the academy but a diverse library of books written in many genres by different authors to different audiences at different moments in the history of Israel and the church. Moses, David, Isaiah, Paul, Peter, James, and John wrote "applied theology" to their respective settings, knowing the specific needs of their immediate audiences. They were distinct personalities with their own agendas. Yet God used these human authors to produce the exact words he intended us to have.

Evangelical systematic theologians committed to the full truthfulness of all Scripture want to draw their understanding of God and his world from the whole Bible, not just selected parts.[24] If one, unchanging God inspired every word of Scripture, then all the doctrinal claims of Scripture will cohere without contradiction. So, we diligently work to understand all of Scripture and to resolve any apparent contradictions or

---

[24] Scott R. Swain, "Dogmatics as Systematic Theology," in *The Task of Dogmatics: Explorations in Theological Method*, ed. Oliver D. Crisp and Fred Sanders (Grand Rapids: Zondervan, 2017), 50.

tensions within the text. These tensions will be resolved when Scripture is interpreted properly and all the available data is known.[25] Furthermore, all the truths of Scripture will harmonize with other truths gleaned from other sources of knowledge. The Bible will not contradict scientific or historical truths when they are properly known and understood.

Theologians summarize the doctrinal content of the Bible much the same way any Christian would when asked to answer questions like these:

- How can we know the Bible is true?
- Who is the Holy Spirit?
- Can a truly saved person lose their salvation?
- Does the Bible tell us how a church should be organized?
- What do Christians believe about the end of the world?

Pastors, teachers, and disciple-makers formulate answers to these types of questions that summarize the gist of the biblical message. They relate multiple passages (because they assume the Bible speaks a unified truth to these matters) and organize their thoughts accordingly. Systematic theologians, too, take the distinctive statements of biblical authors on a given topic and work to arrange them in an orderly manner.

The standard categories of systematic theology include *prolegomena* (theological method), *the doctrine of revelation*, *theology proper* (the doctrine of God), *theological anthropology* (the doctrine of humanity), *hamartiology* (the doctrine of sin), *Christology* (the study of the person and work of Christ), *soteriology* (the doctrine of salvation), *pneumatology* (the doctrine of the Holy Spirit), *ecclesiology* (the doctrine of the church), and *eschatology* (the doctrine of last things). These categories are usually arranged in a logical order that resembles the narrative structure of Scripture and the gospel message: creation, fall, redemption, and the future consummation of the kingdom of God.[26]

---

[25] Erickson, *Christian Theology*, 206.
[26] Ashford and Whitfield, "Theological Method," 7–10. See also Christopher W. Morgan and Robert A. Peterson, *Christian Theology: The Biblical Story and Our Faith* (Nashville: B&H Academic, 2020).

Sixth, in addition to Scripture, systematic theology employs the resources of the Christian tradition, reason, and experience to help formulate its doctrinal expressions. Scripture alone is the standard for Christian belief, but theologians often employ other resources to assist in their interpretation of its doctrinal contents. **Tradition**, or how the Scripture has been interpreted and applied throughout the history of the church, can be a helpful guide for theology and biblical interpretation. *Reason* is a gift from God that can help us think through the logic of our interpretation or help clarify concepts not directly addressed by Scripture. *Experience* can confirm the truthfulness of Christian doctrine and spark important questions for contemporary theology.

Seventh, systematic theology should always offer a contemporary and contextually relevant presentation of Christian truth to its intended audience. No one can write the "perfect" systematic theology textbook and call the task forever done. (This means job security for theologians!) Though eternal truths of God passed from one generation to another do not change, the audiences and cultures in which those truths are espoused do change. The church in every era has faced challenges that called for a theological response. In the first century, it was embattled with controversies over Jewish legalism (Gal 1:6–7; 2:11–14; 4:8–20) and teaching that denied the true humanity of Jesus (1 John 4:1–6). In the fourth and fifth centuries, the church needed to articulate what Scripture said about Jesus in the face of heresies that denied his true divinity and humanity. In the nineteenth century, it needed to respond to a new intellectual fad called Darwinism. Now Christians face an uphill battle with the sexual revolution in Western culture. Because the setting in which theology is researched, taught, and practiced is always changing, there is an ongoing need for new and contemporary expressions of Christian teaching that are faithful to Scripture and fitting to the contextual need.

Eighth, systematic theology shapes the worship, behavior, and ministry of the Christian church. We do not teach doctrine simply to win games of biblical Trivial Pursuit. Biblical writers wrote with the expectation that the people of Israel and the church would respond in obedience to what God was saying through them. Following Jesus's instruction, we teach doctrine to make disciples, "teaching them to observe everything [he] . . .

commanded" us (Matt 28:20). Right thinking about God's self-revelation should result in true worship and obedience.

Ninth, systematic theologians articulate a distinctly Christian worldview for their readers. Systematic theology not only aims to organize the doctrinal content of the Bible; it also aims to make disciples by reframing the architecture of our minds around the gospel. In the words of Anselm of Canterbury (1033–1109), "I do not seek to understand in order that I may believe, but I believe in order that I may understand."[27] The aim of the Christian theologian is to help people think about the world the way the divinely inspired authors of Scripture did, to think God's thoughts after him. We want to see people grow in their knowledge and understanding of God, which, in turn, results in wise living (Prov 1:7).

Finally, because systematic theology seeks to understand God and his relationship to the world, it must engage with other academic disciplines that study God's world. Theologians may attempt to relate doctrine to other disciplines outside of theology (e.g., philosophy, history, science, psychology, literary theory, etc.). But whereas all other human disciplines are fallible and prone to error, Scripture is not. Scripture alone provides the key by which other truths are assessed.[28] The theologian can also offer a distinctly Christian point of view on theories or questions derived from other disciplines. What are human emotions and where do they come from? What economic system best addresses human needs? The Bible does not directly address these questions, but a thoughtful Christian with a worldview informed by Scripture can offer creative and biblically faithful solutions to these matters.

Theology involves gleaning *head knowledge* of God as he has revealed himself; *heart knowledge,* which leads to praise and adoration; and *practical knowledge,* which regulates everyday life as a disciple of Jesus.[29] With these ten characteristics in mind, I am now ready to offer a succinct

---

[27] Anselm, *Proslogion* 1; cf. Augustine, *Tractates on the Gospel of John* 29.6.

[28] Spykman, *Reformational Theology,* 76–90 (see intro., n.1).

[29] See John Webster, "What Makes Theology Theological?" *Journal of Analytic Theology* 3 (May 2015): 17–28. These three categories reflect the "scientific," "contemplative," and "practical" dimensions of theology described in John Webster's definition of theology.

definition of systematic theology that I will use going forward in the book. *Systematic theology is critical and organized reflection on God's self-revelation for the purposes of growing in Christ and making disciples.* Systematic theology is (1) critical, (2) organized, (3) Christian, (4) holistic, and (5) focused on disciple-making through worldview formation.

Systematic theology involves critical, organized thinking about God as he is revealed in Scripture and in general revelation. But theology cannot be reduced to an academic discipline designed to satisfy our intellectual curiosities. To be faithful to the Great Commission, theology must be resolved to making and shaping followers of Jesus through the proclamation of Christian doctrine. Over the next two chapters, we will explore the nature of doctrine, religious language, and its impact on Christian discipleship.

KEY TERMS

experience

general revelation

reason

special revelation

systematic theology

theology

theology proper

tradition

2

Doctrine and Truth

Now the goal of our instruction is love that comes from
a pure heart, a good conscience, and a sincere faith.

—1 TIMOTHY 1:5

We encounter Christian doctrine before we ever begin the formal, critical study of theology. Doctrine is taught every week in the life of the local church, in sermons, in in-home Bible studies, and in one-on-one disciple-making. We sing it in the songs of the faith. It is the foundation of wise counsel and much-needed nourishment during times of depression and anxiety. Gospel doctrine is proclaimed in our evangelism and defended in our apologetics. In the same way food and water are necessary for the body, sound, biblically faithful doctrine is a necessary, life-giving staple for the follower of Jesus. But not everyone takes the time to stop and assess what they are hearing or reading.

In the last chapter, I noted some Christians use the words *theology* and *doctrine* interchangeably, especially when talking about the "theology" or "doctrine" of a preacher, a teacher, or a denomination. But I want to make a clearer distinction between the terms here. Though often used interchangeably, I like to think of theology as the *process* of critically reflecting on God's self-revelation in Scripture and doctrine as the product or *fruit* of that study. The study of Christian theology is a way of keeping our doctrine in check, making sure what we are teaching and preaching in a local church is faithful to God's Word and fitting for our ministry context. We study theology critically in an academic setting like a college or seminary so we can learn to teach doctrine properly in the church.

This definition of **doctrine** is consistent with the biblical use of the term. In Scripture, doctrine refers to the authoritative "teaching" or "instruction" of a religious figure or group.[1] Paul warned his readers about false doctrines from false teachers (Eph 4:14; Col 2:2; 1 Tim 4:1) and challenged them to maintain "good" or "sound" doctrine for themselves and their churches (1 Tim 1:10; 4:16; 2 Tim 3:10; 4:3; Titus 1:9; 2:1). Doctrines, whether true or false, are the expressions of beliefs communicated in an authoritative teaching setting. These doctrines in turn shape the beliefs and practices of Christian believers in every vocation and walk of life (e.g., ministers, businessmen, blue-collar workers, homemakers, doctors, lawyers, teachers, etc.).

Yes, the critical study of theology and the teaching of Christian doctrine are closely related, but they are not identical in definition or in practice. I may ask students in my upper-level theology courses who are well-grounded in their faith to read heresy-spouting theologians so they can learn to critique their ideas, but I would never encourage immature believers to read the same sources or advocate those teachings in an authoritative manner in a local church. Theology puts the teaching, preaching, worship, and activity of a church, tradition, or culture under the microscope and asks questions like: Is this doctrine faithful to the intent of biblical authors and Scripture? Does it aid or hinder faithful Christian disciple-making? Doctrine, by contrast, is a bold declaration of biblical truth to the people of God.

---

[1] The English term *doctrine* comes from the Latin *doctrina*, a translation of the Greek term *didaskalia*.

While theologians frequently offer this distinction, there is substantial disagreement among them about the nature and intent of doctrinal expressions. Just what is the *function of doctrine* in the church? What do we expect our hearers to take away from our doctrinal instruction? Do we expect them to gain factual knowledge, have an emotional response, or act in a certain way? Can doctrines speak truthfully about God and his world, or are they merely human responses to religious sentiment? In the intellectual and cultural climate of postmodernity in which we find ourselves today, "truth" is often presumed to be person-relative or something merely constructed by society.

In this chapter, I will discuss the nature of Christian doctrine. I begin by presenting and critiquing three models of doctrine first described by George Lindbeck (1923–2018).[2] Much of the discussion here centers around the nature of truth. In what sense can Christian doctrine be called "true"? Theologians are not uniform in their answer to this question. After exploring these alternative models, I offer what I believe to be a more biblically and theologically robust model for understanding Christian doctrine—one that I believe preserves the strengths of each of Lindbeck's three models without succumbing to their problems. I conclude the chapter with some final observations about doctrinal reassessment and development.

Doctrines as Mere Statements of Fact

The first model for understanding Christian doctrine, which Lindbeck labeled the **cognitive-propositional theory of doctrine**, is the idea that doctrines are *merely* statements that seek to explain God. Doctrines are *cognitive* because they communicate information to the mind, our

---

[2] George A. Lindbeck, *The Nature of Doctrine* (Louisville: Westminster John Knox, 1984). For key critical reactions to Lindbeck's work, see Kevin J. Vanhoozer, *The Drama of Doctrine* (Louisville: Westminster John Knox, 2006); Alister E. McGrath, *A Passion for Truth: The Intellectual Coherence of Evangelicalism* (Downers Grove, IL: InterVarsity Press, 1996), 119–62; McGrath, *The Genesis of Doctrine: A Study in the Foundation of Doctrinal Criticism* (Grand Rapids: Eerdmans, 1997).

cognition. Doctrines are *propositional* because they are statements of fact that are either true or false. In this model, all biblical truth can be reduced to statements of fact.

This model of doctrine presumes a **correspondence theory of truth**, meaning a proposition is true only when it corresponds to the way things really are. A proposition is false when it does not correspond to reality. Most people intuitively think this way. Consider the following statement:

> The New Orleans Saints won Super Bowl XLIV in Miami, Florida, on February 7, 2010.

This statement is true because it corresponds to what happened on that great day when Indianapolis Colts quarterback Peyton Manning lost to his hometown team. On the other hand, look at this proposition:

> The Atlanta Falcons won Super Bowl LI in Houston, Texas, on February 5, 2017.

This statement is false, because in God's gracious providence, the Falcons blew a 28–3 lead in the third quarter to Tom Brady and the New England Patriots. Statements that correspond to reality are true, and those that do not correspond to reality are false.[3]

In the same way, the cognitive-propositional model states doctrines are true only when they correspond to reality. The statement "God is three persons" is true only if God is really three persons.[4] Conversely, the statement "There are three gods" is false because it does not correspond to

---

[3] For an overview of the different versions of the correspondence theory, see Richard L. Kirkham, *Theories of Truth: A Critical Introduction* (Cambridge, MA: MIT Press, 1995), 119–40.

[4] Critics of the correspondence theory might point out that we do not learn this belief by observation, so we can never know (at least on this side of eternity) whether a statement is a true statement. However, the correspondence theory does not necessarily mean we learn a truth by observation. In fact, it says nothing about the process by which we learn something. All it tells us is something about the nature of truth claims. The statement "God is triune" may be learned by the interpretation of Scripture, but regardless of whether it is learned or known, the statement remains true or false.

reality. For adherents of the cognitive-propositional model of Christian doctrine, the primary role of doctrine is to *explain God to the mind*. Doctrine provides propositional information about God that is either true or false.

As a conservative evangelical theologian, I see many obvious strengths in this model. First, the correspondence theory of truth presupposed by its adherents is consistent with the views of truth employed by biblical authors and most of church tradition. Biblical authors frequently use the vocabulary of truth (the Hebrew word *'ĕ-met* and the Greek word *alēthēs*) to describe "conformity to fact" (Gen 42:16; Deut 13:14; 17:4; 22:20; 2 Sam 7:28; Prov 8:7; Jer 9:5; Zech 8:16; John 7:17; 1 John 2:21, 27; 4:6).[5] Biblical admonitions against lying and bearing false testimony make no sense if statements cannot be true (Gen 42:16; Exod 20:16; Acts 5:1–4; 24:11).[6] It is also hard to say in what sense a doctrine can be "false" if it is incapable of communicating divine truth (1 Tim 6:20–21; 2 Pet 2:1–3; 1 John 4:1–3).

Second, proponents of this model affirm doctrine can convey truth about God and reality. We can have confidence in our theological claims. If Christians did not believe they had some ability to capture the "facts," it would be unclear why they would believe Scripture is uniquely authoritative or Jesus Christ is the center of our faith.[7] However, our claim that doctrines can convey truth does not guarantee perfect or complete knowledge, nor does it mean we who are interpreters of the Bible cannot err in deciphering its meaning. The affirmation that language *can* convey truth about the world is not a guarantee that all doctrinal statements *do* convey truth, nor does it mean doctrinal statements cannot be amended or revised. Furthermore, just as a factual statement can be

---

[5] Roger Nicole, "The Biblical Concept of Truth," in *Scripture and Truth*, ed. D. A. Carson and John D. Woodbridge (Grand Rapids: Baker, 1983), 290–92, 293–95.

[6] Norman Geisler, *Systematic Theology* (Minneapolis: Bethany House, 2002), 1:115–16.

[7] McGrath, *A Passion for Truth*, 155–60.

expressed through language in many ways, doctrines can be restated in new ways for diverse contexts.

Some versions of propositional theology are less helpful than others. Evangelical theologians like me find much to appreciate in the emphasis on propositional truth, but we cannot reduce doctrine to abstract statements of fact "like mathematical axioms."[8] While the Bible gives us truth that can be expressed in propositions, it is not a collection of bare propositions isolated from historical or narrative contexts. Propositionalists can fall into a trap I call "Brainiac Theology." Brainiac, one of Superman's most formidable foes, is a cold, calculating alien artificial intelligence who moves from planet to planet collecting all the knowledge of a given world right before destroying it. The ideas of a world are worth preserving, but not their original forms or personalities. The Brainiac-like tendency in *some* forms of propositionalist theology is reducing the Bible to a collection of facts and the task of Christian theology to discovering and relaying information. Some "brainiac" theologians have ignored the beauty and literary complexity of the Bible in their attempt to mine it for doctrinal propositions.[9]

Though the Bible is the ultimate source of truth, it contains more than—not less than—statements of fact. The Bible contains true propositions, but it also contains stories, promises, commands, questions, and practical wisdom. The canon of Scripture contains many different voices and genres, all of which invite the readers to respond to what God is saying and doing through the biblical text. We hear and obey his "living and effective" Word (Heb 4:12).

Doctrine should be both *descriptive*, telling us what God is like, and *prescriptive*, directing us in how God wants us to obey him.[10] Versions

---

[8] See Vanhoozer, *Drama of Doctrine*, 86–88. Vanhoozer observes this overemphasis on the proposition in much of nineteenth- and twentieth-century evangelical theology.

[9] For a less geeky analysis of this problem, see Vanhoozer, *The Drama of Doctrine*, 85–88; Michael Horton, *The Christian Faith: A Systematic Theology for Pilgrims on the Way* (Grand Rapids: Zondervan, 2011), 21. Horton wrote, "Separated from its dramatic narrative, doctrine becomes abstract, like mathematical axioms."

[10] Vanhoozer, *The Drama of Doctrine*, 272–78.

of propositional theology that overemphasize the informational aspects of doctrine are deficient for disciple-making. While theology involves the study of truth and reality, it should not be reduced to a list of facts. This is a valid criticism of some propositional theologies, but it can be overstated, and it does not speak for most propositionalist theologians.[11]

Doctrines as Symbolic Expressions of Religious Feelings

Theologians from the **experiential-expressive theory of doctrine** reduce Christian doctrines to symbolic ways of expressing their religious feelings, attitudes, or orientations.[12] Since the nineteenth century, liberal theologians have reinterpreted the historic creeds and doctrines of Christian orthodoxy to be culturally conditioned expressions of the universal "religious experience" to which all faith traditions attest.[13] For many of these theologians, Jesus is not literally God incarnate but a metaphorical embodiment of God's attitudes toward the downtrodden and disenfranchised.[14] Postmodernity has taken this reinterpretation of religion to its logical end: everyone does what is right in their own eyes (Judg 21:25).

Experiential-expressive theologians affirm the **pragmatic theory of truth**, which states something is "true" if it "works" for the individual

---

[11] McGrath, *A Passion for Truth*, 142. Fairly or unfairly, the most cited example of "hard propositionalism" in theology is the nineteenth-century Princeton theologian Charles Hodge (1797–1878). Hodge referred to the Bible as a "storehouse of facts" and defined the theological task as the scientific harmonization of those facts. See Hodge, *Systematic Theology*, vol. 1 (Peabody, MA: Hendrickson, 2003), 9–12.

[12] Lindbeck, *The Nature of Doctrine*, 16. This view of doctrine resembles *emotivism*, a theory of ethics that states moral language is merely an expression of a person's emotions about a moral point of view. See Scott B. Rae, *Moral Choices: An Introduction to Ethics* (Grand Rapids: Zondervan, 2018), 38–39.

[13] McGrath, *A Passion for Truth*, 73.

[14] Rejections of the classical doctrine of the incarnation can be found in John Hick, *The Metaphor of God Incarnate: Christology in a Pluralistic Age*, 2nd ed. (Louisville: Westminster John Knox, 2006); David Ray Griffin, *The Christian Gospel for Americans: A Systematic Theology* (Anoka, MN: Process Century, 2019).

who believes it. When people make the comment "pray to whomever you call 'God,'" they insinuate that *all religious or theological language is merely an expression of personal religious sentiments.* Because doctrine isn't true or false, your belief is just as valid as mine, so long as it gives expression to *my own personal experience of God.*

Experiential-expressive theologians believe religious doctrines from every religious perspective are *mere symbolic representations of the same universal religious experience.* Christians, Muslims, Buddhists, and atheists share common spiritual experiences but have different ways of expressing them. This modern, liberal take on doctrine would seem quite foreign to the church fathers, medieval churchmen, and Protestant Reformers who called out heresy and false teaching when they saw it, fully believing they were in the possession of true statements about Christ and his kingdom.

This account of doctrine also has difficulties explaining changes in belief or conversion. If doctrine is only an expression of a universal religious feeling, then how does one account for the change in doctrinal beliefs? Why does an atheist or a Muslim become a Christian?[15] Doctrine that is merely the expression of religious platitudes is incapable of changing lives, of making disciples.

Doctrines as Grammatical Rules

Unsatisfied with these two models, Lindbeck proposed an alternative, postmodern model he called the **cultural-linguistic theory of doctrine**. According to this theory, doctrine does not refer to the reality of God or express sentiments. Instead, doctrine is more like a *set of rules or guidelines* that govern the way people in a religious community think about God and behave.[16] A confession of faith does not describe God as much as it prescribes the boundaries for teaching and practice within a tradition.

The cultural-linguistic theory is a little difficult to grasp without some background of Lindbeck's influences. Following the work of cultural

---

[15] McGrath, *A Passion for Truth*, 76–77.
[16] Lindbeck, *The Nature of Doctrine*, 69.

anthropologist Clifford Geertz (1926–2006), Lindbeck described *religion as a type of culture*. In cultural anthropology, religions are viewed as "cultures" that provide beliefs that help us navigate through life and its most complex questions.[17] According to sociologists, religion provides us with a "plausibility structure" that guards us from the harsh realities of life.[18] These shared plausibility structures help us give meaning to life.

Lindbeck gets his idea of *religion as a type of language* from Ludwig Wittgenstein (1889–1951). After observing various sports played around the University of Cambridge, Wittgenstein concluded that every game or sport has its own language, and the rules of the game determine how that language is used. For example, in American sports, a "strike" means something quite different in a game of baseball than it does in bowling. Wittgenstein said this observation of game rules is also true of all human languages and systems of meaning. Without understanding the context of the "language game" at work, one cannot make sense of how to "play" in it.

Building on these concepts, Lindbeck suggested doctrinal statements are like grammatical rules that direct the "culture" and "language" of a religion. Becoming a Christian is like learning a language. After all, Christians do speak a language with strange words, such as *sin*, *salvation*, and *resurrection*. The Christian language may be foreign to outsiders, but understanding this language is crucial for engaging in the beliefs and practices of the faith. For Lindbeck, doctrine does not describe God as much as it provides the basic grammar for understanding "Christian language." Theological disagreements between Christian traditions are simply differences in how we translate concepts such as "baptism" or "salvation." For instance, Baptists and Roman Catholics both practice "baptism," but their respective systems of "grammar" teach them to use that word in contradictory ways.

---

[17] Clifford Geertz, *The Interpretation of Cultures* (New York: Basic Books, 1973), 89; Ronald T. Michener, *Postliberal Theology: A Guide for the Perplexed* (New York: Bloomsbury, 2013), 33.

[18] See Peter L. Berger, *The Sacred Canopy: Elements of a Sociological Theory of Religion* (New York: Anchor, 1990).

Are doctrines *true* in Lindbeck's model? Grammar teachers who teach the rules of a language show little concern for whether the example sentences they use are true. In a grammar class, you might be asked to diagram a simple sentence like this one: "See Jane run." No one in the room is concerned with whether Jane is a real person or whether she really runs. They are simply assigned with describing the parts of speech and their relationships in the sentence. In Lindbeck's understanding, the same is true of Christian doctrine: "Just as grammar by itself affirms nothing either true or false regarding the world in which language is used, but only about language, so theology and doctrine, to the extent that they are second-order activities, assert nothing true or false about God and his relation to creatures, but only speak about such assertions."[19]

Lindbeck is critical of the correspondence theory presupposed by cognitive-propositionalists and conservative theologians.[20] His cultural-linguistic model presupposes what philosophers call a **coherence theory of truth,** which states a proposition or belief is true only when it coheres with a system of true beliefs. A doctrine is true only when it is internally consistent with all other doctrines. Lindbeck asserts that Christians should be less concerned with proving the truthfulness of their beliefs and more concerned about consistently living them out. He gives the example of a medieval crusader cutting off the head of a Muslim enemy while shouting, "Christ is Lord" as an example of an incoherent belief because, for Lindbeck, no one truly living under Jesus's teachings would ever do such a thing.[21]

For Lindbeck, doctrine may direct the way we read the Bible but tells us nothing about whether our beliefs correspond to the real world. Instead, it teaches us how to read the story of the Bible and how it all

---

[19] Lindbeck, *The Nature of Doctrine,* 64–65, 69.

[20] He does not deny a doctrine could be true in the sense that it refers to reality but claims we have no way of definitively proving it does. See Lindbeck, 68–69; Michener, *Postliberal Theology,* 98; cf. Bruce D. Marshall, "Introduction: *The Nature of Doctrine* After 25 Years," in Lindbeck, *The Nature of Doctrine,* xii–xviii.

[21] Lindbeck, 64.

fits together in a coherent way. He compares this to the way we read other narratives, whether they be fiction or nonfiction. When we read a Spider-Man comic, we get that our hero lives in New York City—a place we know really exists—but we do not sit down and try to prove the details of the comic book are historically and geographically accurate. (There is no *Daily Bugle* building in New York, nor is there a feisty publisher named J. Jonah Jameson who works there.) Comic-book readers are only concerned with whether the story is coherent and compelling.[22] A Spider-Man story may have great internal continuity and characterization, but that does not correspond to reality if there are no superheroes with radioactive spider powers.

Lindbeck is correct to say doctrine regulates and governs the belief and behaviors of a faith community. Doctrine can also guide us into the proper use of the language of Christian belief. The early creeds clearly served the function of defining who was in and who was out of the Christian faith.[23] We also see these qualities of doctrine whenever a missionary or a teacher signs the confession of faith held by a school or denomination. It is a pledge on the part of the signee to teach or preach in accordance with that confession. We see the same characteristic whenever someone is excommunicated from a church for teaching false doctrine.

Yet Lindbeck makes three key errors. The first is in his presumption that doctrine can only be one kind of communication. It must be truth, an expression of feelings, *or* community-governing rules. This is a false trichotomy—a dubious set of three choices. Doctrines can and do achieve multiple purposes. Doctrine can govern the belief of a church, express worshipful adoration, *and* refer to the reality of God. When I make the statement "Jesus is Lord!" I state a fact, express my joy in that belief, *and* draw a boundary for Christian fellowship. I also declare Jesus is sovereign, not Caesar or the state.

Second, the cultural-linguistic theory weakens the truthfulness of Christian doctrine. Why should a community of faith give preference

---

[22] See Lindbeck, *The Nature of Doctrine*, 65. Lindbeck uses Denmark in *Hamlet* as his example of a real place in a fictional story.

[23] Lindbeck, 94–95.

to Jesus as Savior and Lord if we are not making claims about a figure rooted in history and fact? An internally coherent fiction about Jesus is still just fiction.[24] As David Clark has illustrated, the legendarium of *The Lord of the Rings*—all the stories, poems, and works related to J. R. R. Tolkien's mythic Middle-earth—is remarkably coherent. But internal coherence alone does not make this high fantasy true![25]

Worst of all, the cultural-linguistic theory undermines the authority of Scripture. Consistent with postmodern scholarship that makes the reader or reading community the final authority on the meaning of the text, Lindbeck's own approach puts the church in charge of its meaning. In contrast to this postliberal position, evangelicals want to assert the ability of authors (especially biblical authors) to convey or communicate their intended meaning to readers and faith traditions. Doctrine regulates the beliefs and practices of the church, yes, but it is only authoritative to the degree that it conforms to Scripture. We want to yield to the authority of the Bible, not make its divinely inspired authors conform to our "grammar."

The Nature of Doctrine

A biblically and theologically informed model of Christian doctrine incorporates all the strengths of these models but evades their weaknesses. With the cognitive-propositional model, we can agree doctrine is capable of truthfully describing God and his world, but we must be careful not to reduce the teaching of Scripture to cerebral information. With the experiential-expressive model, we recognize doctrine can express affections, attitudes, and Christian experience. We are not emotionally or experientially neutral to the truths of the Christian faith, but we must reject any attempt to reduce doctrine to empty sentiments and platitudes. With the cultural-linguistic model, we recognize that doctrine orders and directs our beliefs and practices but deny that doctrine cannot truly describe God or take its direction from the authorial intentions of Scripture.

---

[24] McGrath, *A Passion for Truth*, 157–61.
[25] Clark, *To Know and Love God*, 366 (see chap. 1, n. 8).

As an alternative to these three models of doctrine, I want to make seven statements about doctrine that I believe are most consistent with Scripture and its proper application in the church. *First, Christian doctrines are authoritative teachings used in the ministry of the church.* Doctrine (from the Latin *doctrina*) relates to the Greek term *didaskalia* found in the New Testament and the Hebrew term *leqach* found in the Old Testament. Both terms mean "teaching" or "instruction." The prophets taught with the expectation that Israel would listen to and obey the Lord (Deut 4:1–14; 1 Kgs 8:36). Instruction was also seen as a source of wisdom that aided in decision making (Prov 3:1; 4:2). Teaching was a major part of Jesus's earthly ministry (Matt 4:23; 9:35), and people marveled at the power and authority in his teaching (Matt 7:28–29; Mark 1:22, 27; Luke 4:32).

Paul has much to say about doctrine and the teaching ministry of the church in his letters to Timothy and Titus, providing them with instruction for faithful teaching (e.g., 1 Tim 4:6, 11, 13; 2 Tim 2:2, 24; Titus 1:9; 2:1, 7, 10) and combating false teaching (e.g., 1 Tim 1:10; 4:1; 6:3; 2 Tim 2:17; 4:3; Titus 1:9). Paul understood the burden placed on the teacher because of the authority and influence he wields, for good or for evil, in the local church. James expressed this same concern when he warned his readers that "not many should become teachers . . . because you know that we will receive a stricter judgment" (Jas 3:1).

Second, Christian doctrines are authoritative interpretations of the biblical message.[26] Evangelicals affirm the unrivaled authority of Scripture in the formation of Christian doctrine (*sola Scriptura*). The affirmation of *sola Scriptura* is not a rejection of other sources like tradition, philosophy, or experience, but an acknowledgment that Scripture is a vastly superior source of the knowledge of God. Scripture is the only inspired, infallible, and inerrant resource in theology. Scripture is also the only measure or standard by which these other sources can be tested. Scripture is "the norming norm which cannot be normed" (*norma normans non normata*).

---

[26] McGrath, *The Genesis of Doctrine*, 52–66.

In other words, it is the measure of Christian truth and it is measured by no other source.

Only Scripture is "able to give you wisdom for salvation through faith in Christ Jesus" (2 Tim 3:15), and Scripture alone is "inspired by God" (2 Tim 3:16a). Scripture is the primary authority of Christian belief and practice, and doctrine can only be called an authority in the derivative sense when it presents a correct interpretation of Scripture. Doctrines can be restatements of the *Bible's grand narrative*—the creation, fall, redemption, and new creation pictured in Genesis through Revelation—and the *theological content of Scripture*, but they can also give expression to the *wisdom* and *ethical instruction* of the Bible.

Third, Christian doctrines can speak about God and his world as they really are.[27] Evangelical theologians generally hold to some version of the correspondence theory of truth. Truth may work pragmatically, and truth will always cohere with other truths, but the final criterion for truth is correspondence to the way things really are.[28] For this reason, evangelical theologians emphasize the importance of "sound doctrine" (2 Tim 4:3; cf. 1 Tim 6:3). Sound doctrine speaks truly about God, but it is more than a series of "propositional statements . . . gathered into a system of truths."[29] The Greek word for *sound* (*hygiainō*), from which we get our English word *hygiene*, is a word that means "health." Sound doctrine is propositionally true doctrine accompanied by the spiritual health of mature Christian living and obedience (Titus 2:1–8).

Fourth, Christian doctrines speak truthfully about God in different ways.[30] How can we who are finite creatures describe an infinite God with our language? Theologians have long debated the nature of religious language. Do the descriptors we use to describe God (e.g., "loving," "good," "all-knowing") have the *same, literal straightforward meaning* we give

---

[27] McGrath, *The Genesis of Doctrine*, 72–80.

[28] Coherence is a necessary condition for truth—truth must cohere with other truths—but it is insufficient. The only necessary and sufficient condition for truth is correspondence.

[29] Kevin J. Vanhoozer, *Faith Speaking Understanding: Performing the Drama of Doctrine* (Louisville: Westminster John Knox, 2014), 25–26.

[30] McGrath, *The Genesis of Doctrine*, 79–80.

them in everyday language, as taught by the **univocal** view of religious language? Or do our descriptors of God *mean something entirely different than the way we normally use our words*, as advocated by the **equivocal language** view? Or are these descriptors simply metaphors or **analogical language** that can help our little minds make sense of God by relating some sense of shared meaning, as Thomas Aquinas suggested?[31]

Advocates of the equivocal language position are skeptical about the prospect of human words describing God. For equivocal language proponents, descriptions of God are like homonyms (i.e., words with the same spelling and pronunciation but which have totally unrelated meanings). Human concepts like "goodness" and "love" bear no real correlation with God's nature. The equivocal language position undermines our ability to know anything about God. If we have no way to conceptualize God with our language, of what value is God's written revelation? Why study theology in the first place if we cannot say anything about God?

Some descriptions of God in Scripture seem to be univocal (i.e., they share the same meaning with human language). When we say God "knows" a truth, we mean he literally knows something to be true or false, just like we use that word to describe us knowing something to be true or false, even if God doesn't have to acquire knowledge the same way non-omniscient beings do. The verb "will" in the sentence "Rhyne *wills* to eat an apple" shares the same meaning with the verb "will" in the sentence "God *willed* to create apples," even if an infinite and eternal God does not process decisions the way we do.[32]

Most biblical descriptions of God are analogical or metaphorical, but, this observation does not take away from their truthfulness. The reality-depicting language of Scripture can speak truthfully of God through various literary devices and figures of speech.[33] God is not literally a rock,

---

[31] Thomas Aquinas, *Summa Theologica* 1.13.5.

[32] See William P. Alston, "Functionalism and Theological Language," *American Philosophical Quarterly* 22, no. 3 (July 1985): 221–30.

[33] Kevin J. Vanhoozer, "Augustinian Inerrancy: Literary Meaning, Literal Truth, and Literate Interpretation in the Economy of Biblical Discourse," in *Five Views on Biblical Inerrancy*, ed. J. Merrick and Stephen M. Garrett (Grand Rapids: Zondervan, 2013), 210.

but we call him a "rock" because that descriptor truly conveys his strength to us (Gen 49:24; 1 Sam 2:2; Ps 18:2, 31). God is our "Father" (Isa 63:16; 1 Cor 8:6; 1 Pet 1:3) but not in the human, biological sense of the word. He is our Father in the sense that he created us (Acts 17:28–29), adopted us in Christ (John 1:12–13), and loves us with perfect fatherly love (Ps 103:13). Though the love human beings share with one another pales in comparison to God's love for us, human love can help us understand his love by analogy.

Fifth, doctrine is a vital part of Christian maturity and obedience. While it is possible to have an intellectual grasp on good doctrine and live in disobedience, it is impossible to live in obedience without good doctrine. Because Scripture is inspired, it is "profitable for *teaching*, for rebuking, for *correcting*, for *training* in righteousness, so that the man of God may be complete, *equipped for every good work*" (2 Tim 3:16–17, emphasis added). Several aspects of Christian doctrine stand out in this statement: (1) Scripture is profitable for authoritative teaching or doctrine; (2) true doctrine derived from Scripture is used to correct false doctrine found elsewhere; (3) biblical teaching matures us as it trains us in righteousness; and (4) biblical doctrine fully equips us for good works and obedience.

Sixth, Christian doctrine provides boundaries for the community of faith.[34] We use some essential doctrines to gauge whether a person can rightly be called a Christian. If someone denies the divinity of the Lord Jesus or argues that he was a being created by God, we deny that person fellowship as a believer and work to persuade him of the truth of the gospel message. We use other doctrines to form close communities of common conviction. Teachers in confessional school settings are often required to sign a common confession of faith and assure the trustees of those schools that they will not teach in ways that are contrary to the confession of their institution.

Finally, Christian doctrine provides worldview formation for generations to come. As the psalmist made plain, we are to declare God's Word "so that a future generation—children yet to be born—might know. . . . so that

---

[34] McGrath, *The Genesis of Doctrine*, 37–52.

they might put their confidence in God, and not forget God's works, but keep his commands" (Ps 78:6–7). We who belong to the people of God are charged with contending for and maintaining "the faith that was delivered to the saints once for all" (Jude v. 3). We are all called to be links in the great tradition of the Christian faith.

If the purpose of theology is to reflect critically on God's self-revelation to make disciples and doctrine is the fruit of that study, then the purpose of doctrine is to grow those disciples in the truth of Scripture. I want to highlight the truthfulness of doctrinal statements (or at least their ability to speak truth), the rooting of doctrine in Scripture, and the use of doctrine to make Christ-followers. In sum, *Christian doctrines are faithful and true teachings derived from Scripture and used to grow God's people in knowledge, spiritual maturity, and obedience.*

What Else Should We Know about Doctrine?

Theology is the critical study of doctrine because the teaching of the church needs checks and balances. It must be tested for *fidelity to the Bible*. It must be tested for *logical consistency*. It must be assessed for its *practical value*. And it must offer a *relevant word* for the culture or context into which it is given. The message of Scripture must be properly understood and applied to every age.

Doctrine can be corrected. As interpretations of the biblical message, doctrines can be in error just as any interpreter of the Bible can misunderstand a biblical text. Just as a misinterpretation of the biblical text can be corrected, so too can doctrinal statements. Christian theologians should pursue the *truth*, not simply the confirmation of what they already believe. In this pursuit of truth, theologians will sometimes change their minds.[35]

Theologians seek to understand the objective, unchanging truth of Scripture but only know its truth through our interpretations of the Bible

---

[35] See Rhyne R. Putman, *When Doctrine Divides the People of God: An Evangelical Approach to Theological Diversity* (Wheaton, IL: Crossway, 2020), 175–200.

that are tentative and open to revision.[36] In theology, we are dealing with the reality of God as he has revealed himself, but we also acknowledge we are fallible interpreters of the Bible who can misinterpret the text. The more clearly Scripture teaches a doctrine, the less likely that a theologian under the authority of Scripture is going to change his or her view. Disputed doctrines in Scripture that are open to different interpretive possibilities may change more frequently. We hold closely to some doctrines (e.g., the existence of God, the resurrection of Jesus) and more tentatively to others (e.g., the nature of the spiritual gifts, our understanding of election).

At this point I must interject that a doctrine construed in error is not the same thing as a "false doctrine" as defined by Scripture, even if the propositional statement is, strictly speaking, false. Biblically speaking, false doctrine comes from sinful motives, unbelief, and spiritual immaturity.[37] False doctrines are typically rejections of primary doctrines (e.g., the deity of Jesus, the Trinity), not minor disagreements about those doctrines. Two Christians may disagree about *when* the Lord will return and *how*, but they both agree that Jesus will return. One may be correct about the nature of Jesus's return while the other is wrong, or they may both be wrong, but neither are, biblically speaking, "false teachers" holding to "false doctrine."

Doctrine can be developed. Peter Toon (1939–2009) defined doctrine as "a historically conditioned response by the Church to questions put to her at a particular time and place by . . . her members."[38] Doctrine can (and should) grow over time as the church's understanding of biblical truth grows or matures.[39] Think about many of the key theological ideas of Christian orthodoxy, such as the doctrine of the Trinity, biblical inerrancy, and the notion that God created everything from nothing.

---

[36] N. T. Wright, *The New Testament and the People of God* (Minneapolis: Fortress, 1992), 35.

[37] See Putman, *When Doctrine Divides the People of God*, 205–12.

[38] Peter Toon, *The Development of Doctrine in the Church* (Grand Rapids: Eerdmans, 1979), 81.

[39] See Rhyne R. Putman, *In Defense of Doctrine: Evangelicalism, Theology, and Scripture* (Minneapolis: Fortress, 2015).

These ideas are not *explicitly* taught in Scripture, but they are developments of doctrine faithful to the message of Scripture that were needed in the moments in history in which they emerged.

Sometimes doctrinal development is simply a matter of making more explicit what Scripture already communicates. This kind of development was the case with the Christological and Trinitarian creeds of the early church. When confronted with false teachings like Arianism (which denied the true divinity of Jesus) and Apollinarianism (which denied the full humanity of Jesus), the church had to articulate clearly what they believed about the deity and humanity of Jesus. In the early creeds, the church explained their beliefs about Christ succinctly with the philosophical tools at their disposal.

Other times, doctrinal development entails offering a new application of a permanent biblical truth to a contemporary issue. The truth of Scripture does not change, but the contexts in which it is applied are always changing. Theologians today are forced to define marriage and gender in ways previous generations took for granted. The ubiquity of artificial intelligence technology has prompted questions about what it means to be truly human. Now that artificial intelligence plays a big role in our homes with Siri, Alexa, and Google Assistant, we need to think critically about how this ever-evolving technology relates to human beings, their vocations, their sexual practices, and their knowledge of the world.[40]

Doctrine can find new expressions when taught in new settings or situations. Biblical truth can be expressed in many ways. The Old Testament prophets used many different names and word pictures to describe the same characteristics of God.[41] The New Testament writers described Jesus's sacrificial work on the cross with distinct imagery appropriate for their ministry settings. As we will discover in the coming

---

[40] Jason Thacker, *The Age of AI: Artificial Intelligence and the Future of Humanity* (Grand Rapids: Zondervan, 2020).

[41] For example, the prophets used imagery like the "right hand" (Exod 15:12) and "outstretched arm" (Jer 32:17) to talk about God's power.

chapters, the specific way we teach a Christian truth is largely dependent on the setting or audience we have in mind.

KEY TERMS

analogical language
doctrine
doctrine, cognitive propositional
theory of
doctrine, cultural-linguistic
theory of
doctrine, experiential-expressive
theory of

equivocal language
truth, coherence theory of
truth, correspondence theory of
truth, pragmatic theory of
univocal language

GO DEEPER

Heyduck, Richard. *The Recovery of Doctrine in the Contemporary Church: An Essay in Philosophical Ecclesiology.* Waco, TX: Baylor University Press, 2001.

Lindbeck, George. *The Nature of Doctrine.* Louisville: Westminster John Knox, 1984.

McGrath, Alister E. *The Genesis of Doctrine: A Study in the Foundation of Doctrinal Criticism.* Grand Rapids: Eerdmans, 1997.

McGrath, Alister E. *A Passion for Truth: The Intellectual Coherence of Evangelicalism.* Downers Grove, IL: InterVarsity Press, 1996.

Putman, Rhyne R. *In Defense of Doctrine: Evangelicalism, Theology, and Scripture.* Minneapolis: Fortress, 2015.

Vanhoozer, Kevin J. *The Drama of Doctrine.* Louisville: Westminster John Knox, 2006.

3

Doctrine, Worldview, and Disciple-Making

Do not be conformed to this age, but be transformed
by the renewing of your mind, so that you may discern
what is the good, pleasing, and perfect will of God.
—ROMANS 12:2

For many in the church, theology has a reputation of being a stuffy, pretentious academic discipline disconnected from the practical realities of everyday life. Many believers picture theologians as heady geeks in tweed jackets, sitting comfortably in their ivory towers, surrounded by their books while other Christians are out in the world doing "real ministry." I will admit, some parts of this caricature are spot-on. I own two tweed jackets, and one of them even has the leather patches on the elbows. The surface of my office desk is usually covered with books—a few completely read, some partially read, some only perused for footnotes and research purposes, and others I tell myself I will get around to reading someday soon.

It is also true that we who are "professional" theologians regularly write technical volumes that will only be read by other theologians and their students. We often gather at academic conferences to present formal papers, speaking to one another in strange, scholarly tongues that would be undecipherable to the average believer. While these scholarly endeavors do, in fact, serve a crucial purpose, they are not the main objective of theology. The aim of faithful academic theology is not simply to sustain academic theology. We don't study theology for the sake of seminaries, divinity schools, or Bible colleges. That would be like building medical schools that only exist to teach medicine and never train the doctors who put it into practice with their patients. We should study theology for the glory of God and the edification of his people. Scholars of faith read and write theology to better serve the people who more than likely will never read an upper-level theology textbook by serving the men and women who serve the local church.

The end goal of critical theological study is not building an academic program impenetrable to people in the pews but building the kingdom of God through seeing transformed lives, churches, and cultures through Christian disciple-making. Remember:

> *Systematic theology is critical and organized reflection on God's self-revelation for the purposes of growing in Christ and making disciples.*

and

> *Christian doctrines are faithful and true teachings derived from Scripture and used to grow God's people in knowledge, spiritual maturity, and obedience.*

The critical study of systematic theology you take up as a student can result in life-giving doctrine for the local church and its disciple-making ministries. Doctrine provides not only *cognitive content* (i.e., what people should believe about God and his world); it also provides *practical* and *effective content* that guides what they do and how they are to feel. Well-crafted doctrine faithful to the message of Scripture changes the whole disciple.

In this chapter, I address the relationship between Christian doctrine and discipleship. I begin by introducing readers to the concept of a "worldview," which I argue is central to understanding a person and their transformation into a Christ-follower, then proceed to show specific ways in which Christian doctrine plays a formative role in worldview transformation.

What Are Worldviews?

Every human person, no matter their age, sex, ethnicity, education, or economic background, has something called a **worldview**.[1] As its name implies, a worldview is the way a person views or understands the world, but a worldview is more than a theory or an abstract set of beliefs. As one scholar put it, "Worldviews are . . . the basic stuff of human existence, the lens through which the world is seen, the blueprint for how one should live in it, and above all the sense of identity and place which enables human beings to be what they are."[2] Our worldview colors everything we believe and do.

Despite their importance for every facet of our lives, people rarely stop to reflect on their worldviews. As my doctoral mentor Robert Stewart is prone to say, "Worldviews are like navels. We all have one. We just don't think of it very often." Before we give any serious thought to our worldview, we are already intuitively working from one. We are *involved in*

---

[1] Philosophers, anthropologists, sociologists, and theologians often use other terms closely related to but not necessarily identical to *worldview*, such as "life system," "plausibility structure," "form of life," and "social imaginary." Kevin Vanhoozer adopted Charles Taylor's phrase "social imaginary" in his excellent book on the role of doctrine in discipleship: Kevin J. Vanhoozer, *Hearers and Doers: A Pastor's Guide to Making Disciples through Scripture and Doctrine* (Bellingham, WA: Lexham, 2019). For the sake of clarity, I have opted to keep the term *worldview*, despite the nuances some of these alternative terms offer. See James W. Sire, *Naming the Elephant: Worldview as a Concept*, 2nd ed. (Downers Grove, IL: InterVarsity Press, 2015), 23–69.

[2] Wright, *The New Testament and the People of God*, 124 (see chap. 2, n. 36).

the world before we ever give it any theoretical or critical thought.[3] For this reason, theologians and philosophers stress the *presuppositional* or *pre-theoretical* nature of worldview thinking. We normally look *through* worldviews, not at them.[4]

We are born with faculties that help us perceive the world. As our cognitive abilities and emotional faculties develop, so too does our worldview. It grows and matures as it is shaped by our families, our education, our culture, and our time and place in history. While we never approach the world from outside a worldview, having a worldview does not necessarily lock us into one way of thinking for the rest of our lives. Our worldviews can be challenged or even changed, which is good news for Christian disciple-makers who want to see people converted to faith in Christ.[5]

Though worldviews are often defined as a set of foundational beliefs, they are more than mental assertions, just as human beings are more than thinking things.[6] The Bible does not use the word *worldview* but does describe something like a worldview when it refers to the human heart.[7] For biblical authors, the "heart" does not describe the physical organ that pumps blood through the circulatory system but the "center of intellectual and spiritual life," "the center of personality," and the place where conversion of the whole person takes place.[8] Paul tells us that belief originates in the heart: "One believes with the heart, resulting in righteousness, and one confesses with the mouth, resulting in salvation" (Rom 10:10).

---

[3] James K. A. Smith, *Desiring the Kingdom: Worship, Worldview, and Cultural Formation*, Cultural Liturgies, vol. 1 (Grand Rapids: Baker, 2009), 50.

[4] Wright, *The New Testament and the People of God*, 125.

[5] Wright, 125. The dramatic conversion stories of Scripture, such as the conversion of Saul or Paul, illustrate this possibility (Acts 7:57–8:1a; 9:1–31; 22:1–21).

[6] Smith, *Desiring the Kingdom*, 40–46.

[7] The German philosopher Immanuel Kant (1724–1804) coined the term *Weltanschauung*, which we translate as "worldview." See David Naugle, *Worldview: The History of a Concept* (Grand Rapids: Eerdmans, 2002).

[8] *NIDNTTE*, 2:625–26, s.v. "Καρδία."

Like the heart, worldviews are innately spiritual and involve a religious commitment. James Sire defined a worldview as "a *commitment, a fundamental orientation of the heart*, that can be expressed as a story or in a set of propositions (assumptions which may be true, partially true or entirely false) which we hold (consciously or subconsciously, consistently or inconsistently) about the basic constitution of reality, and that provides *the foundation on which we live and move and have our being*."[9] This basic orientation of the heart is directed in one of two ways: toward God or away from him.[10]

How Do Worldviews Work?

Worldview specialists in cultural anthropology, biblical studies, philosophy, and theology nuance their respective definitions of worldview in different ways, but their definitions often share common elements. While there are other elements that could be included, I have selected four here that are essential to Christian disciple-making: *grand narrative, truth, practices*, and *affections*.[11]

*First, every worldview contains a **grand narrative** that controls all the other aspects of the worldview.* Every worldview has what cultural anthropologists call a "myth"[12] or grand narrative that shapes the lives of its

---

[9] Sire, *Naming the Elephant*, 141, emphasis mine.

[10] Sire, 35.

[11] I am indebted to N. T. Wright for the four elements selected here. See Wright, *The New Testament and the People of God*, 122–26. Wright offers four categories: *story, questions, praxis*, and *symbols*. My use of *story* (or *grand narrative*), *truth*, and *practices* closely relates to those first three. While I do affirm what Wright is saying about the significance of cultural symbols in our worldview, I have opted to emphasize *affections* instead to address the noncognitive dimension of our worldviews.

[12] See Paul G. Hiebert, *Transforming Worldviews: An Anthropological Understanding of How People Change* (Grand Rapids: Baker, 2008), 27. On the anthropological use of "myths" Hiebert (1932–2007) wrote, "Unfortunately, the word 'myth' in popular use has come to mean fiction or fantasy. In its technical, scientific sense, it means the grand narrative in which history is embedded, the narrative by which the history and the stories of human lives are interpreted. . . .

adherents. Ancient and modern myths feature stories about how the world came into existence, who human beings are, and where they are going in the future. These myths direct the beliefs, behaviors, and personal identities of their adherents.

By contrast, Christians tell a "myth" or controlling story about a God who created human beings, who made a way to redeem them through Jesus, and who will ultimately set all the wrongs of this world right, once and for all. Yet, as C. S. Lewis (1898–1963) remarked, "the story of Christ is simply a *true myth*: a myth working on us in the same way as the others, but with this tremendous difference that it *really happened*: and one must be content to accept it the same way."[13] Every worldview has a controlling story, but the Christian one actually happened in history.

*Second, worldviews seek out **truth**—answers to the "big questions" all human beings have about their lives, regardless of their cultural or religious perspectives.* People wrestle with these ultimate concerns before they can even give them conscious expression. Brian Walsh and Richard Middleton summed up these ultimate concerns in four basic worldview questions: (1) Who am I?; (2) Where am I?; (3) What's wrong with the world?; and (4) What's the solution? These important questions address (1) the basic human condition and our sense of identity in the world, (2) our beliefs about the world in which we live and where we come from, (3) our beliefs about the problems that create suffering and discomfort in this world, and (4) our ultimate hope for what will remedy the world's problems.[14] To these four questions, N. T. Wright added a fifth question meant to help us understand the present moment in which we live: (5) What time is it?[15] This fifth question means understanding how the first

---

Myths are transcendent stories believed to be true that bring cosmic order, coherence, and sense to seemingly senseless experiences, emotions, and ideas in the everyday world by telling people what is real, eternal, and enduring."

[13] Walter Hooper, ed., *The Collected Letters of C. S. Lewis*, vol. 1 (San Francisco: Harper, 2005), 977, emphasis mine.

[14] Brian J. Walsh and J. Richard Middleton, *The Transforming Vision: Shaping a Christian Worldview* (Downers Grove, IL: InterVarsity Press, 1984), 35.

[15] N. T. Wright, *Jesus and the Victory of God* (Minneapolis: Fortress, 1996), 138, 467–72.

four questions are applied in real-world situations in the time and space we occupy.[16]

*Third, our worldviews relate to our **practices** or habits.* What we do says more about what we really believe than what we say. Our aims, intentions, and motivations reveal our worldview.[17] The ways we worship, vote, dress, eat, and raise our families are shaped by our worldviews. But this is a two-way street: our worldviews are also shaped by our behaviors and habits.[18] Though we may use arguments to *justify* our beliefs, we do not normally arrive at our worldviews through argumentation alone. Our cultural practices and habits can have a greater effect on what we believe about the world than rigorously logical arguments.

*Finally, our worldviews are shaped by our **affections**.* Josh Moody and Robin Weekes defined affections as *"the movement of our thoughts, feelings and will towards a desired object, person or event. An affection is what inclines us to something. . . . Affections are what move us towards action."*[19] Our affections, more than our rational beliefs, ultimately control the way we see the world and move around in it.

As James K. A. Smith has observed, our ultimate "love" shapes our identity and makes us who we are. This identity-shaping love does not include more trivial loves like my love for Mississippi State athletics or charbroiled oysters, nor does it include my more significant loves like those I have for my wife or my children. Worldviews are shaped by *ultimate loves* "to which we are fundamentally oriented, what ultimately governs our vision of the good life, what shapes and molds our being-in-the-world." Ultimate loves are *objects of worship*, "what we desire above all else, the ultimate desire that shapes and positions and makes sense of all our penultimate desires and actions."[20]

---

[16] Trevin K. Wax, *Eschatological Discipleship: Leading Christians to Understand Their Historical and Cultural Context* (Nashville: B&H Academic, 2018), 32–35.

[17] Wright, *The New Testament and the People of God*, 124, 126.

[18] Walsh and Middleton, *The Transforming Vision*, 32–33.

[19] Josh Moody and Robin Weekes, *Burning Hearts: Preaching to the Affections* (Ross-shire, UK: Christian Focus, 2014), 14.

[20] Smith, *Desiring the Kingdom*, 51.

In a secular culture, ultimate love may be the love of personal autonomy or the pursuit of pleasure (both forms of self-love). By contrast, a Christian worldview truly rooted in the instruction of Scripture puts the love of God and others first (Matt 22:36–40). Doctrine that does not direct our hearts to the love of God and others is of little value for disciples.

How Does Doctrine Shape the Worldviews of Disciples?

When Jesus gave us the Great Commission, he told us to go and make disciples of people from all nations, baptizing them and teaching them how to observe all that he commanded us (Matt 28:19–20). Unfortunately, some evangelistic methods can come off like a sales pitch, as though if people would just sign on the dotted line, then Jesus would be contractually obligated to give them a "Get Out of Hell Free" card and let them go about their lives unaffected. But when we are obeying the Great Commission as Jesus gave it, we are doing more than a one-off witnessing encounter. The Christian life begins with repentance and confessing Christ (Rom 10:9, 13), but we are not called simply to get people to "repeat these words" or echo a prayer. We are called to help people change the way they see and move through the world!

Discipleship is not merely about dispensing information.[21] As James K. A. Smith put it, "Discipleship and formation are less about erecting an edifice of Christian knowledge than they are a matter of developing a Christian know-how that intuitively 'understands' the world in the light of the fullness of the gospel."[22] Gospel-centered discipleship changes the way people understand every single aspect of their lives. Biblical, Christian discipleship rewrites our inner lives and our sense of identity

---

[21] Eric Geiger, Michael Kelley, and Philip Nation, *Transformational Discipleship: How People Really Grow* (Nashville: B&H Academic, 2012), 18–20.

[22] Smith, *Desiring the Kingdom*, 68.

and purpose. It is, as Trevin Wax observed, holistic "spiritual formation" that leads to "contextual obedience."[23]

The Bible itself provides the *grand narrative*. The biblical story of the triune God is our story too. The most common genre in Scripture is narrative, but even those books of the Bible that are not composed of stories play a role in the grand story of redemption.[24] The authors of Scripture also wrestle with *ultimate truths*—our worldview questions about human origins, identity, and purpose. God gives clear, normative directions for *practice* in both ancient Israel and in the life of the early church. Scripture also has much to say about our *affections*. We were created to worship God, to ascribe glory to him in our hearts, and to sing his praise.

Under the apprenticeship of God's Word and the leadership of the Holy Spirit, disciples learn how to *think* God's thoughts after him, to *obey* God's direction in their lives, and to *value* God with our whole hearts. Christian teaching rooted in the authority of Scripture reorients the beliefs, practices, and affections of those who follow Jesus. Using the elements of worldview addressed above, we can extract four clear ways doctrine speaks into the transformation of disciples. As an interpretation of Scripture directed toward Christian disciple-making,

1. Doctrine rehearses the *story* of Scripture and helps the disciple find her place in it.
2. Doctrine answers life's biggest questions with *truth* derived from Scripture.
3. Doctrine provides wisdom for how we *practice* our faith.
4. Doctrine stirs our *affections* to give us a deeper love for God and others.

---

[23] Wax, *Eschatological Discipleship*, 41.

[24] For example, psalms, proverbs, and prophetic literature can only really be understood against the background of the stories of Israel, her kings, and her prophets. As part of Israel's story, these genres contribute to the larger story of God's mission in Christ.

Story: Doctrine Rehearses the Grand Narrative of Scripture

Christian disciple-making always begins by telling a story—the gospel story. No one can ever trust in Christ unless they have heard his story properly told: "Faith comes from what is heard, and what is heard comes through the message about Christ" (Rom 10:17; cf. Acts 14:21; 15:7). The methods we use in evangelism may vary, but the basic plot and essential characters of the gospel do not change. Whenever we share the good news about the death, burial, and resurrection of Jesus Christ articulated in 1 Cor 15:1–8, we frame it in the Bible's overarching story of creation, fall, redemption, and new creation.[25] The proclamation of the story then calls for a response of faith and repentance (Acts 3:19–20; Rom 10:9–13).[26]

We may not automatically think about personal evangelism as "teaching doctrine," but it fits the bill perfectly when doctrine is understood as *authoritative teaching derived from Scripture and employed to make disciples of Jesus.* Whenever we tell the gospel story, we assert doctrinal statements about the nature of God, the creation and plight of humanity, the identity of Jesus, his death in our place, his resurrection, and our hope for the future. Most approaches to systematic theology follow the logical order of the gospel and the narrative structure of the biblical canon, beginning with God and moving through the doctrines of creation, humanity, Christ, salvation, the Spirit, the church, and the study of last things. As I like to remind my students, gospel tracts are often the first systematic theology textbooks people read, even if they are much smaller in scale.

Yet training in the Christian worldview is more than *telling* the gospel story; it is about helping the disciple *find his or her place* in it. But before someone can fully realize their place in God's story, they must grow in their basic biblical literacy. They must become familiar with the stories of

---

[25] Ashford and Whitfield, "Theological Method," 7–10 (see chap. 1, n. 2).

[26] See Bruce Riley Ashford and Heath A. Thomas, *The Gospel of Our King: Bible, Worldview, and the Mission of Every Christian* (Grand Rapids: Baker, 2019), 11–96.

the Bible—stories about Adam, Noah, Abraham, Moses, David, Elijah, Elisha, Peter, James, John, and Paul—and learn how they relate to create one grand story about God's saving plan through Jesus. Every narrative of Scripture relates to one another on one of three levels:[27]

3 Levels of Biblical Narrative	**Level 3:** The Grand Narrative (i.e., the Bible's storyline from Genesis to Revelation)
	Level 2: Covenant narratives (e.g., Abrahamic, Noahic, Mosaic, and Davidic covenant in Israel; the new covenant with the church)
	Level 1: Individual Narratives (e.g., the call of Abraham; the anointing of David; Paul before Felix)

The first-level stories are scenes from the lives of individuals in the Old and New Testaments. But mature Christ-followers must do more than learn stories about the heroes of the Bible. They must learn to appreciate the connections between these stories and the covenant promises God made with Israel throughout the Old Testament (the second-level narratives). Together, both the covenants made with Israel and the church make up the third level: the grand narrative of the Bible beginning with creation and ending with new creation. Think of individual Bible stories as pieces in a mosaic. Up close, they look like smaller and broken fragments of glass and stone, but walk farther back and you see that they make up a larger image. If all the biblical scenes in Scripture were put together, the composite image would be God's redemptive plan for humanity in Christ Jesus.

Doctrine in story form rehearses this grand narrative across Scripture.[28] Pastors, teachers, and leaders need to teach individual biblical stories, but

---

[27] These three levels originate in Gordon D. Fee and Douglas Stuart, *How to Read the Bible for All Its Worth*, 4th ed. (Grand Rapids: Zondervan, 2014), 95–96.
[28] Wright, *The New Testament and the People of God*, 127.

they also need to make the logical and narrative connections of these units to the whole canon of Scripture. Every level-one local narrative (and every non-narrative passage of Scripture) connects to the second- and third-tier levels of the narrative. We need to train Christians to think canonically about God's work in every stage of biblical history. By rein- forcing the grand narrative frequently in our preaching and teaching— showing ways in which individual passages of Scripture play into creation, the fall, redemption, and new creation—we help reinforce the architec- ture through which they read Scripture daily.

Doctrine teaches us that we are all part of the same ongoing story found in Scripture. Like the scenes from the lives of Abraham, Moses, David, and Paul, the scenes from our lives are also part of the same divine mosaic! The God who created Adam created every other member of the human race. The same God who rescued Noah and his family made a way for us to be rescued from our sin (1 Pet 3:20b–22). The promises made to Abraham apply to all who are blessed through his seed, Jesus Christ (Gal 3:16). Like many of us, David knew great failure and great redemption, but David's eternal heir is both his Lord and ours (Ps 110:1; Matt 22:44). New covenant believers in Jesus Christ take part in the same mission with the apostles and every other first-century believer. The same Holy Spirit who was at work in the early church is still at work today in the twenty-first-century church.

Doctrine teaches us how to "perform" or live out the story well. How are we supposed to "live out" the biblical story when we are so far removed from it chronologically? Scholars such as N. T. Wright, Kevin Vanhoozer, and Samuel Wells use a creative analogy from the theater to explain how we are to do this.[29] They compare reading the Bible to discovering a previously unknown play by William Shakespeare in which one of the

---

[29] Wright, *The New Testament and the People of God*, 139–43; Wright, "How Can the Bible Be Authoritative?" *Vox Evangelica* 21 (1991): 7–32; Vanhoozer, *The Drama of Doctrine*, 2 (see chap. 2, n. 2); Samuel Wells, *Improvisation: The Drama of Christian Ethics* (Grand Rapids: Brazos, 2004); Craig G. Bartholomew and Michael W. Goheen, *The Drama of Scripture: Finding Our Place in the Biblical Story* (Grand Rapids: Baker, 2004), 202–6.

five acts is missing. Were such a play discovered, Shakespeare scholars, playwrights, actors, and directors would need to come along and "fill in" the missing part of the story in such a way that it was consistent with the plot and characters established in the other four acts. With the Bible, we have discovered four completed acts in God's cosmic drama: creation and the fall of humanity (Act 1), the story of Israel (Act 2), the life of Christ (Act 3), and the future consummation of God's kingdom (Act 5). Yet one part of the story is incomplete: the church age that began on the day of Pentecost (Act 4).[30]

The biblical story begins with creation and the "inciting incident" of human rebellion in the garden of Eden (Act 1). The world is broken, and chaos ensues. The story of Israel is part of the "rising action" of the Bible (Act 2) building up to the climactic moment when God would carry out his rescue mission in Christ (Act 3). Jesus's resurrection is the great "moment of reversal" in which sin and death are defeated. The church age is a work in progress, and the Bible only accounts for the details of its beginning (Act 4). As God's new covenant people living in the church age, we are part of the fourth act still being written. Act 5 brings what J. R. R. Tolkien (1892–1973) called the "eucatastrophe"—the sudden and unexpected happy ending in which great sorrow is turned into great joy.[31] The following diagram inspired by German playwright Gustav Freytag (1816–1895) shows how these elements work together in the grand narrative of Scripture:

---

[30] This order of the "acts" of the biblical drama comes from Wells, *Improvisation*, 53. Unlike Wright, who says the church is living in the fifth act, Wells asserts we are living in the fourth act before the end of the drama portrayed in biblical eschatology.

[31] J. R. R. Tolkien, "On Fairy-Stories," in *Essays Presented to Charles Williams*, ed. C. S. Lewis (Grand Rapids: Eerdmans, 1966), 81; Vanhoozer, *The Drama of Doctrine*, 38, 410.

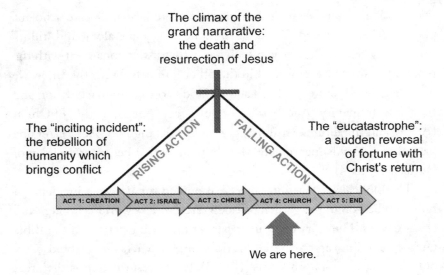

The climax of the
grand narrarative:
the death and
resurrection of Jesus

The "inciting incident":
the rebellion of
humanity which
brings conflict

RISING ACTION

FALLING ACTION

The "eucatastrophe":
a sudden reversal
of fortune with
Christ's return

ACT 1: CREATION   ACT 2: ISRAEL   ACT 3: CHRIST   ACT 4: CHURCH   ACT 5: END

We are here.

Wright, Vanhoozer, and Wells assert that while we live in this "missing act," we must learn to *improvise* the biblical story in a way that is faithful and consistent with the story that has gone before us. As this former drama club geek can tell you, improvisation does not mean "just making stuff up." Improv requires the actor to play out the scene given to her. The actor must *accept* the storyline set up for her—what is called the *offer*—and advance the narrative in a way that is consistent with the scene that has been staged. To *over-accept* the offer means to accept the story given to us and advance the narrative in such a way that it builds and expands on the original offer. Whatever we do, we must not *block* the story offered to us by ignoring the setup of the scene. The best improv artists reincorporate details of the whole story into their performance.[32]

In a second-season episode of *The Office*, Michael Scott, the regional manager of Dunder Mifflin Scranton and an aspiring actor-screenwriter, modeled for us how *not* to improvise. In this episode, Michael takes an improv class, with disastrous results. Much to the chagrin of his fellow improvisers, every time Michael is thrown into a scene, whether it is a

---

[32] Vanhoozer, *The Drama of Doctrine*, 338–39; cf. Wells, *Improvisation*, 103–13.

funny, romantic, or dramatic moment, he "blocks" the offer of the scene setup by turning it into an action movie where he is transformed into a secret agent with a gun. Michael's complete lack of self-awareness and incompetence as an actor turns everyone in the improv class against him.[33]

This cringe-worthy sequence also illustrates the frivolity of human beings who "block" the story God is writing in our lives. We live in his story, and we are his privileged bit players. In his sovereignty, he has determined the time and place in the story we would enter stage right (Acts 17:26). Disciples must learn *the roles they were meant to play* in the unfolding drama of Scripture and *respond to new scenes in ways that are fitting with the characters they were assigned to play*. Discipleship involves envisioning ourselves as part of God's story told in Scripture, not rewriting God's role to fit the story we want to tell or live out.

We improvise our part in the divine drama by becoming well acquainted with the character study laid out for us in the canonical script of the Bible. In more concrete terms, this means we are not freed to redefine obedience to God. We have the same Great Commission first-century believers had. We are called to the same standards of personal holiness as the early church. We are not free to "reinvent" the story by changing the gospel message or shifting its focus.

Truth: Doctrine Answers Life's Big Questions

Everyone eventually must come face-to-face with life's biggest questions. Theologians can help disciples who are seeking to grow in the knowledge of the faith, but they can also help answer the questions of unbelievers who are trying to make sense of the beliefs Christians confess. I may be asked by a Jehovah's Witness why I affirm the deity of Jesus, or I may need to answer a question my child has about what happens to us when we die. I need clear, shorthand ways of answering complex questions like these. Doctrines and doctrinal statements make the grand narrative

---

[33] Paul Feig, dir., *The Office*, season 2, episode 9, "E-Mail Surveillance," aired November 22, 2005, on NBC.

"portable," providing summary answers to these big questions.[34] Doctrine in its creedal, confessional, and propositional forms addresses these questions with biblically informed answers derived from Scripture.

Systematic theologians work to present cogent and coherent answers to these questions. They give critical thought to these questions and help train pastors and other disciple-makers how to best answer the big questions posed to them in their ministry contexts. Systematic theologies aim for coherent and detailed answers that harmonize the theological content of Scripture. The topical organization of systematic theology is designed to help answer the big questions people have about God and his world. Major doctrines or first-tier theological issues usually relate to the larger worldview questions, while minor or secondary doctrines, though important, do not directly answer these larger questions.

The first big question—Who am I?—is a question about human identity, origins, and purpose. *Theological anthropology*, the doctrine of humanity, gives concise answers to these questions consistent with the grand narrative of Scripture. We are special and distinct creatures created by God in his image to accomplish his purposes in the world (Gen 1:27–28). We are loved by God and are valuable to him (Ps 8:1–8; John 3:16–17; Rom 5:8). The doctrine of humanity teaches us about the human constitution: the relationship between our physical bodies and our spiritual natures. *Ecclesiology*, the doctrine of the church, also helps answer this question. Our new identity in Christ gives us a new family and a new sense of purpose and mission. We are now brothers and sisters in Christ. We are "citizens of heaven" (Phil 1:27; 3:20) tasked with the ministry of reconciliation, called as "ambassadors for Christ" (2 Cor 5:20).[35]

The second big question—Where am I?—is about the world we live in, the setting of the story. The Bible plainly states the world God made was inherently good (Gen 1:3, 9, 12, 18, 21, 24, 31). And while all Christians agree that God is the creator and sustainer of this world,

[34] N. T. Wright, "Reading Paul, Thinking Scripture," in *Scripture's Doctrine and Theology's Bible: How the New Testament Shapes Christian Dogmatics*, ed. Markus Bockmuehl and Alan J. Torrance (Grand Rapids: Baker, 2008), 64.

[35] Hiebert, *Transforming Worldviews*, 280–90.

they disagree about *how* God created it and continues to govern it. Did God create the world instantaneously or through a long process? Does he govern the world with a hands-off approach that provides genuine creaturely freedom, or does he meticulously plot every decision human beings make?

The Christian doctrine of sin, *hamartiology*, addresses the third big question we all must face: What's wrong with the world? Though everything God made was good, the world as we know it is in disrepair. We struggle to find meaning and significance. We all endure pain, suffering, and death. But why? The Christian doctrine of sin gives answers to these questions, summarizing the Bible's message about human rebellion and its disastrous consequences. The doctrine of sin also unravels the mystery of why we who desire to do good cannot seem to carry it out (Rom 7:18–24).

The gospel provides the answer to the penultimate question: What's the solution? What will bring resolution to the story? The doctrines of Christ (*Christology*), salvation (*soteriology*), and last things (*eschatology*) explicate how God's redemptive work in Christ frees us from the power and effects of sin. Christology explains how Jesus is capable of being the solution. He is the incarnate deity who has both the power to save us and the ability to represent us in our humanity. It also explains the revealing, reigning, and reconciling activities of Christ that make our redemption possible. Soteriology explores the biblical concepts related to salvation. It shows how the solution of Christ's redemption applies to us in both changing our status before God and freeing us from sin's power over us. Finally, eschatology gives us a picture of the future in which the problems of sin and suffering are vanquished forever.

The final question—What time is it?—helps us understand (1) our own historical and cultural context, as well as (2) our place in the divine drama of Scripture. As Trevin Wax has noted, with a better understanding of our own place in God's timeline and our cultural moment, we are better equipped as disciples and disciple-makers.[36]

---

[36] Wax, *Eschatological Discipleship*, 41.

Practice: Doctrine Can Produce the Fruit of Obedience

Doctrine does more than change our thoughts or outward actions; it is capable of growing virtue in us. In other words, it can change our character, our habits, and our disposition. When Jesus gave the Great Commission, he tasked his disciples to make disciples by teaching obedience (Matt 28:19). Doctrine and Christian ethics have always been interlocked because we cannot know **orthopraxy**, or right practice, apart from **orthodoxy**, right belief. Orthodoxy without orthopraxy is dead, as faith without works is also dead (Jas 2:14–26). Because what we do is such a big part of our worldview, we need the instruction of doctrine to inform our practice and behavior. Paul stressed the relationship between reflection on truth and the transformation of our *character* when he told us to "be transformed by the renewing of your mind, so that you may discern what is the good, pleasing, and perfect will of God" (Rom 12:2).

The early church engaged in theological debates about doctrine for very practical reasons. The debate held at the Nicene Council in AD 325 over the teaching of an Alexandrian elder named Arius was not a mere academic discussion. Arius denied the divinity of Jesus and went around preaching that "there was a time when the Son was not." The practical concerns of the Nicene Council were clear. If Jesus were not truly God made flesh, how could he save us from our sins? Worse, if Jesus is not God, then we have worshipped him in error and are guilty of idolatry! Many of the debates in modern theology have been over real-world concerns like the trustworthiness of the Bible and the exclusivity of Christian truth claims. All these matters eventually trickle down to the preaching and teaching ministries of local churches.

Doctrine provides not only the reason for why we do ministry in the first place but also the substance for our public discourse on the faith. Why would we go to the hard places to do missions if we were not convinced of the theological truths of God's Word, the inherent dignity and value of peoples created in the image of God, and the exclusivity of the gospel message? Why would we do evangelism if we were not convinced that sinful men and women need to repent? And if we are not talking about doctrine in ministry, what then is the content of our preaching and disciple-making?

Doctrine teaches us how to live together as a community of saints. While the Bible does not explicitly prescribe a model of church government or detail how its business should be conducted, we can infer good practices from the early church described in Scripture that we can emulate in our own churches. We order our church governments around theological beliefs rooted in biblical interpretation. The way we exercise ordinances like baptism and communion reflects doctrinal understanding of the practices. The distinctive practices of believer's baptism and infant baptism stem from different theological frameworks.

Doctrine can direct holy living. It is one thing to say God is holy in an abstract sense and quite another to live holy lives as he himself is holy (Lev 11:44–45; 19:2; 20:7, 26; 1 Pet 1:16). We can give lip service to the idea that every human is made in the image of God (Gen 1:26–28), but this doctrine means nothing to us if we are violent toward fellow image-bearers (Gen 9:6) or slanderous toward them with our speech (Jas 3:9–10). When we train our minds to see fellow men and women as image-bearers, pornography, which displays them as sex objects, will become abhorrent to us. We must train ourselves to believe these truths and to develop holy habits and behaviors and seek to practice what we preach and teach about them.

Doctrine gives us plain guidance on ethical matters directly addressed in Scripture. When Yahweh gave the law to Israel, he gave them clear parameters for how they should order their individual and institutional lives. Obedience to the law set them apart from their pagan neighbors and brought God's blessing into their lives. With the New Testament, God gave clear principles for Christian living to the early church through Jesus and later, his disciples. As Christians we are under obligation to follow what the New Testament says about our conduct, our speech, our marriages, our parenting, our money, and our interaction with the non-believing world.

Doctrine also gives us wisdom for discerning what to do in matters Scripture does not address directly. Scripture does not address every contemporary ethical issue Western Christians face today. Our world of surgical sex changes and human stem-cell research would have been quite foreign to first-century Jewish authors. Our cultural moment is quite different from theirs, as will be the cultural moments of our descendants if the Lord tarries. However, doctrine, as an interpretation of Scripture, can help give us wisdom to navigate whatever crises we face. These issues require "improvisation" faithful to Scripture and the leadership of the Holy Spirit.

Doctrine can guide us in our worship and liturgy, and our worship and liturgy can instruct us in doctrine. The worship of the church teaches doctrine in its hymnody and liturgy, and theology provides a needed critical examination of the church's worship. The Bible does not prescribe a musical style but describes the spirit with which we should teach and admonish one another through song (Col 3:16). We must test and examine the hymnody and liturgy of the church to see if they cohere with God's self-revelation in Scripture. Some songs in the history of church music reflect the culture of their day more than the Bible. Some have taught problematic and unbiblical ideas. In the same manner, some songs sound more like erotically charged pop songs than songs that facilitate prayer and worship. Many of these songs also neglect trinitarian doctrine and the nature and mission of the church. Theologians should be involved in writing the hymnody of the church and driving it back to a gospel-centered focus.[37]

Affections: Doctrine Stirs Our Hearts and Feelings

We are more than thinking things who reason our way through the world. God wired human beings with feeling. Because God loved us, he created us to love him. "We love because he first loved us" (1 John 4:19). Yet because of human sin and rebellion, the hearts created to love God have been directed toward other things. We can let our hearts dictate our beliefs, but we must remember that the human "heart is more

---

[37] See Robert Woods and Brian Walrath, eds., *The Message in the Music: Studying Contemporary Praise and Worship* (Nashville: Abingdon, 2007).

deceitful than anything else" (Jer 17:9). Thoughtful meditation on God's self-revelation is an act of obedience that changes not only our minds but also our hearts and affections. If faithful doctrine produces in us right thinking (orthodoxy) and right practices (orthopraxy), it can also help us grow in right feelings (**orthopathy**).

When we read the psalms, we get a window into the worship of ancient Israel. The psalms are also profoundly theological, praising God for who he is and what he has done. The psalter directed the worship of Israel, but it was also meant to train the people of Israel in what they should believe. The psalmists made no distinction between the cognitive dimension of their worldview (i.e., the facts about God's nature and acts) and the affective dimension (i.e., the response of their hearts). They used song and art to express truth and direct our emotions. Their reflection on God's acts in history stirred their hearts to worship.

Meditation on theological truth results in praise and adoration. Romans 9–11 constitutes the heart of Paul's entire theological thought-world. In this section, he explains God's sovereign and gracious selection of Israel (9:6–29); he laments Israel's present condition apart from Christ (9:1–5, 30–33; 10:14–21); he proclaims the centrality of faith in the gospel (10:1–13); and he promises the eventual restoration of Israel through Christ (11:1–32). But what I love most about this unit is how it ends, when a passionate Paul breaks out in written song in 11:33–36:

> Oh, the depth of the riches
> and the wisdom and the knowledge of God!
> How unsearchable his judgments
> and untraceable his ways!
> *For who has known the mind of the Lord?*
> *Or who has been his counselor?*
> *And who has ever given to God,*
> *that he should be repaid?*
> For from him and through him
> and to him are all things.
> To him be the glory forever. Amen. (emphasis added)

The truth of God found in the wisdom and knowledge of God is rich and beyond human comprehension (Job 41:11; Isa 40:13; Jer 23:18). Extended meditation on this truth led Paul to worship the One for whom all things exist, to sing of his greatness and magnify him with his pen. Contemplation on the nature and activity of God in Christian doctrine sanctifies our imaginations and brings us into the presence of God. There, we are invited to join in the song of praise and adoration the Father, the Son, and the Spirit have been singing to one another for all eternity.

Doctrine can also retrain our sinful and unhealthy passions and emotions. Our doctrine tells us that human feelings—while created to be a good and beautiful thing—were corrupted by sin and human depravity after the fall. As a result, we are emotionally broken creatures who wrestle with idolatry, lustful appetites, bitterness, anxiety, insecurity, and people pleasing. Doctrine explains these realities with biblical truth but also provides the cognitive content for retraining our minds and our habits. Our minds—as well as our practice, worship, and affections—are renewed through God's truth (Rom 12:1–2).

Paul instructed those overcome with worry and anxiety to reflect on the truth they have learned from God's Word: "Whatever is true, whatever is honorable, whatever is just, whatever is pure, whatever is lovely, whatever is commendable—if there is any moral excellence and if there is anything praiseworthy—dwell on these things" (Phil 4:8). He told them to listen to the doctrine and tradition they have received from him—to dwell on it—so that they can experience God's presence and peace (Phil 4:9).

Doctrine faithful to God's Word will stir our affections and move us to love of God and others. As Jesus observed, all of Scripture ultimately drives us to the double-love expressed in the Great Commandments: "*Love the Lord your God with all your heart, with all your soul, and with all your mind. This is the greatest and most important command. The second is like it: Love your neighbor as yourself.* All the Law and the Prophets depend on these two commands" (Matt 22:37–40, emphasis added). Critical reflection on God's nature and activity should stir us to *adore* the Lord with our affections and to *love* fellow image-bearers as we love ourselves.

Biblical doctrine reshapes our worldview and colors the way we see every person we encounter. Our family members, our friends, our neighbors, our coworkers, our acquaintances, those we meet in our comings and goings, and even our enemies are made in God's image and are valuable to him. For that reason alone, they should be valuable to us.

KEY TERMS

affections

discipleship

grand narrative

orthodoxy

orthopathy

orthopraxy

practices

truth

worldview

GO DEEPER

Naugle, David. *Worldview: The History of a Concept.* Grand Rapids: Eerdmans, 2002.

Ryken, Philip Graham. *Christian Worldview: A Student's Guide.* Wheaton, IL: Crossway, 2013.

Sire, James W. *Naming the Elephant: Worldview as a Concept.* 2nd ed. Downers Grove, IL: InterVarsity Press, 2015.

Smith, James K. A. *Desiring the Kingdom: Worship, Worldview, and Cultural Formation.* Cultural Liturgies, vol. 1. Grand Rapids: Baker, 2009.

Vanhoozer, Kevin J. *Hearers and Doers: A Pastor's Guide to Making Disciples Through Scripture and Doctrine.* Bellingham, WA: Lexham, 2019.

Wax, Trevin K. *Eschatological Discipleship: Leading Christians to Understand Their Historical and Cultural Context.* Nashville: B&H Academic, 2018.

Wright, N. T. *The New Testament and the People of God.* Minneapolis: Fortress, 1992.

4

The Theological Disciplines

The relationship between theology and philosophy [as well as
other theological disciplines] is akin to the relationship between
siblings; they are either the best of friends or the worst of enemies,
depending on the situation and who else is in the room.

—JAMES K. BEILBY[1]

B iblical, historical, philosophical, practical, and systematic theologies,
as well as Christian ethics and apologetics, all belong to the same
family tree: specialized academic studies focused on the various aspects
of teaching God's Word. While they occupy different spaces in university and seminary settings, most theologians throughout church history
would have considered all these categories to be different aspects of the

---

[1] James K. Beilby, "Introduction: The Contribution of Philosophy to
Theology," in *For Faith and Clarity: Philosophical Contributions to Christian
Theology*, ed. James K. Beilby (Grand Rapids: Baker, 2006), 13. I have broadened
Beilby's original quote that compares "theology and philosophy" to include all
the other theological disciplines, which, I believe, is an equally fitting description.

same discipline, part of the same "encyclopedia" of knowledge.[2] Medieval theologians called the academic study of God's special revelation in Scripture *theologia*, and they declared this science or form of knowledge "the queen of the sciences"—the discipline that rules over all others in the university. Though they are now more segregated, all these theological disciplines involve critical reflection on God's self-revelation for the purposes of growing in Christ and making disciples, but they all go about this task in extremely different ways.

For centuries, the job description of a theologian involved mastery of the biblical languages, knowledge of the historical tradition, philosophical prowess, oratory skills, and the ability to shepherd the flock. Following trends in other disciplines, such as the natural sciences and the humanities, theology eventually fragmented into the distinct subdisciplines we know today, including biblical scholarship, theology, philosophy of religion, and church history.[3] Yet this fragmentation of theological disciplines would have been foreign to Augustine, Anselm, Thomas Aquinas, Luther, and Calvin.

Following the Enlightenment, theological disciplines began to operate in distinct "intellectual traditions."[4] While they often occupy the same schools or departments and work with the same datum in Scripture, biblical scholars and systematic theologians have such distinct methods and specialized interests that they are often incapable of communicating effectively with one another. Go to a professional meeting where Christian scholars have gathered, and you will have the choice of going to sessions led by Bible scholars and sessions led by theologians or Christian

---

[2] For a discussion of this type of "theological encyclopedia," see Abraham Kuyper, *Principles of Sacred Theology*, trans. J. Hendrik DeVries (New York: C. Scribner's Sons, 1898), 1–55.

[3] A brief overview of this history can be found in Clark, *Know and Love God*, 166–78 (see chap. 1, n. 8). See also Edward Farley, *Theologia: The Fragmentation and Unity of Theological Education* (Philadelphia: Fortress, 1983), 49–124.

[4] Alasdair MacIntyre, *Whose Justice? Which Rationality?* (Notre Dame: University of Notre Dame Press, 1988), 12; cf. Oliver D. Crisp, *Analyzing Doctrine: Toward a Systematic Theology* (Waco, TX: Baylor University Press, 2019), 28.

philosophers. If you sit in the study group of one discipline and move over to another group led by the other, you may feel as though you have heard vastly different versions of the English language. Each of the theological disciplines has its own scholarly language.

Students of the various theological disciplines can sometimes feel like the children of a nasty divorce, pressed to choose which parent they will live with and forced to listen to their parents talk ill of one another. But when one says, "I am of biblical studies," or another, "I am of theology," are we even acting like Christian scholars? What Paul says of the numerous spiritual gifts in the church is also true of the theological family tree: "There are different ministries, but the same Lord. And there are different activities, but the same God works all of them" (1 Cor 12:5–6).

This chapter introduces students to the theological family tree, highlighting the primary activities and contributions of each member. As *"critical and organized reflection on God's self-revelation for the purposes of growing in Christ and making disciples,"* systematic theology integrates the tools and findings of all these other theological disciplines to present a cogent vision for Christian belief and practice. This frequently dysfunctional academic family may have been torn asunder by bickering and divorce, but we are going to stage an intervention for theological disciplines because we believe they are better together than apart.

Biblical Theology

The academic study of **biblical theology** dates back to the late eighteenth century when biblical scholars first distinguished their work from the project of systematic theologians.[5] "Biblical theology" is notoriously difficult to define because sometimes it seems as if there are as many definitions

---

[5] See Johann Philipp Gabler (1753–1826), "An Oration on the Proper Distinction between Biblical and Dogmatic Theology and the Specific Objectives of Each," in *The Flowering of Old Testament Theology: A Reader in Twentieth-Century Old Testament Theology, 1930–1990*, ed. Ben C. Ollenburger, E. A. Martens, and Gerhard F. Hasel (Winona Lake, IN: Eisenbrauns, 1992), 493–502.

for biblical theology as there are scholars who practice it.[6] In one sense, the term refers to any theology "based on and faithful to the teachings of the Bible."[7] But the term usually refers to an academic specialization within the larger field of *biblical studies* (e.g., Old Testament studies, New Testament studies, etc.). "Professional" biblical theologians usually have advanced degrees in Old Testament, New Testament, or a related field like biblical hermeneutics. Instead of arranging the doctrines of Scripture by topic, the biblical theologian normally strives to understand the doctrinal content of the Bible on its own terms. The noble goal of biblical theology, then, is to ensure what we are teaching and preaching matches what biblical authors were trying to communicate through their texts.

Biblical scholars differ greatly in the way they practice biblical theology, but they do share some common tendencies. Within the field of biblical theology, there are two broad camps: (1) those who see the task of biblical theology as a purely *descriptive* historical task, and (2) those who see it as *prescriptive*.[8]

Advocates of the descriptive approach (usually non-evangelical scholars) want to describe the doctrines and beliefs of ancient biblical authors, not prescribe what people of faith today should believe or practice.[9] It is a field of study primarily about literature and history that, to quote Indiana Jones, "belongs in a museum!" Descriptive biblical theologians usually

---

[6] A most helpful summary of major views of biblical theology can be found in Edward W. Klink III and Darian R. Lockett, *Understanding Biblical Theology: A Comparison of Theory and Practice* (Grand Rapids: Zondervan, 2012). Klink and Lockett identify five major models: BT1: biblical theology as historical description; BT2: biblical theology as history of redemption; BT3: biblical theology as worldview-story; BT4: biblical theology as canonical approach; and BT5: biblical theology as theological interpretation. The approach to biblical theology I take up in this book most closely resembles what Klink and Lockett label BT3.

[7] Erickson, *Christian Theology*, 11 (see chap. 1, n. 18).

[8] These categories come from the best introduction to biblical theological method available today: Klink and Lockett, *Understanding Biblical Theology*.

[9] See Krister Stendahl, "Biblical Theology, Contemporary," in *The Interpreter's Dictionary of the Bible, A–D*, ed. George Buttrick (New York: Abingdon, 1962), 418–32; James Barr, *The Concept of Biblical Theology: An Old Testament Perspective* (Minneapolis: Fortress, 1999).

treat the theologies of the Old and New Testaments separately, but they will also focus on the theologies of individual books or authors. Given their descriptive emphasis, they understand biblical theology to be a task for the historian or biblical scholar, not the preacher or pastor.[10]

By contrast, biblical theologians in the prescriptive group want not only to understand what biblical authors believed in their historical contexts but also to apply their message to the contemporary context of the church. These scholars put more emphasis on the unity of the biblical message than their descriptive counterparts, but they disagree among themselves about how the parts of Scripture relate to one another. The so-called canonical approach to biblical theology pays attention both to the original historical contexts of Scripture, the formation of the canon itself, and the various ways the church has read the Bible throughout history.[11] Another whole-Bible approach organizes theology around a central theme or motif found in Scripture, such as *the covenants, the kingdom of God*, or *the glory of God*.[12] Other biblical theologies take their shape from the overarching story of Scripture rather than its individual ideas or concepts.[13]

Biblical theology can focus on the theological content of (1) an individual book, (2) the theology of a single biblical author across his corpus of writings, (3) the theology of an individual Testament, (4) the exploration of a theological theme throughout the Bible, or (5) the theology of

---

[10] For a critical assessment of this tendency in Barr's writing, see Klink and Lockett, *Understanding Biblical Theology*, 43–56.

[11] See Brevard S. Childs, *Introduction to the Old Testament as Scripture* (Philadelphia: Fortress, 1979); Childs, *Old Testament Theology in a Canonical Context* (Minneapolis: Fortress, 1990); Childs, *Biblical Theology of OT and NT: Theological Reflection of the Christian Bible* (Minneapolis: Fortress, 1993).

[12] See Thomas R. Schreiner, *The King in His Beauty: A Biblical Theology of the Old and New Testaments* (Grand Rapids: Baker, 2013); James M. Hamilton, *God's Glory in Salvation through Judgment: A Biblical Theology* (Wheaton, IL: Crossway, 2010).

[13] See Wright, *The New Testament and the People of God* (see chap. 2, n. 36); Wright, *Jesus and the Victory of God*; Wright, *Paul and the Faithfulness of God*, 2 vols. (Minneapolis: Fortress, 2013); Christopher J. H. Wright, *The Mission of God: Unlocking the Bible's Grand Narrative* (Downers Grove, IL: InterVarsity Press, 2006).

the whole Bible. Following Andrew David Naselli, I take biblical theology to be "a way of analyzing and synthesizing the Bible that makes organic, salvation-historical connections with the whole canon on its own terms, especially regarding how the Old and New Testaments integrate and climax in Christ."[14] *Biblical theology faithfully retells the grand narrative of Scripture in a way that coheres with the intentions of its divine-human authorship.*

Biblical and systematic theologies are in a mutually beneficial symbiotic relationship. Biblical theology rooted in solid exegesis and historical data can do a lot of the heavy lifting for systematic theologians. On the other hand, systematic theology forms the worldviews and assumptions of biblical scholarship, as well as providing an important check to its logical coherence and its orthodoxy. Theologians need solid biblical exegesis, and biblical scholars need systematic theology.

Historical Theology

As Gregg Allison has defined it, **historical theology** is "the study of the interpretation of Scripture and the formulation of doctrine by the church of the past."[15] Aspects of social or cultural history may play a crucial background role in historical theology, but they are not the primary concern of the historical theologian. Historical theology is closely related to the study of church history but more narrowly focused on the historical development of doctrine and the ideas of Christian theologians of the past. Works in historical theology can describe (1) an overview of all the teachings of a theologian, (2) a more narrow treatment of an individual doctrine held by a theologian (e.g., Augustine's doctrine of sin, Luther's doctrine of justification), (3) the teachings of a distinct period in church history, or (4) the study of an individual doctrine throughout history.

---

[14] Andrew David Naselli, *How to Understand and Apply the New Testament: Twelve Steps from Exegesis to Theology* (Phillipsburg, NJ: P&R, 2017), 231.

[15] Gregg R. Allison, *Historical Theology: An Introduction to Christian Doctrine* (Grand Rapids: Zondervan, 2011), 23.

While Scripture is the only divinely inspired source of revelation theologians need, theologians *must* engage with the tradition of the church as the shapers of the church's growing tradition. Tradition, "the Spirit-enabled reception of Scripture, is the divinely appointed *goal* of theology."[16] In other words, theology longs to see people interpret the Word of God and apply it to their lives under the leadership of the Spirit. After this happens, it becomes part of the tradition. The systematic theologies written today will be the subject matter studied by the historical theologians of the future. Studying the theology of the past with our departed brothers and sisters in Christ helps systematic theologians in the present better articulate their own understandings of biblical doctrine, see the various ways context can shape theology, and catch a glimpse of the practical consequences of our ideas.

Philosophical Theology

Philosophical theology, closely related to the philosophy of religion, is the branch of theology that employs the resources of philosophy to speak about Christian doctrine. I will detail this discipline more in chapter 9, but for the moment, understand philosophy has always played a role in the history of Christian doctrine. The second-century Christian theologians and apologists interacted with pagan philosophers to build a case for the gospel. The fourth- and fifth-century creeds about Christ and the Trinity relied heavily on philosophical language and concepts from that day. Medieval theologians like Anselm, Thomas Aquinas (1225–1274), and William of Ockham (c. 1287–1347) had distinctive philosophical influences and systems but nevertheless practiced theology intertwined with philosophical concepts, reasoning, and arguments. Twentieth-century theology saw a resurgence of philosophical influence with the development of analytical theology.

---

[16] Michael Allen and Scott R. Swain, *Reformed Catholicity: The Promise of Retrieval for Theology and Biblical Interpretation* (Grand Rapids: Baker, 2015), 36.

Theologians are often skeptical about whether philosophy can provide any substantial content for theology, but most theologians recognize the value of philosophy in clarifying and defending the doctrinal concepts revealed in the Bible. Philosophical theologians use reason to address questions that Scripture incites but does not answer directly. If God is all-good, all-powerful, and all-knowing, why does he allow evil and suffering in the world? What is free will and do all humans have it? How does God relate to time and what does that mean for eternity?

Philosophical theology has a crucial role to play in theological method. After all, we are asking philosophical questions about the nature of theology (prolegomena), how we can know anything about God (epistemology), how we argue our theological convictions (logic), the way our doctrinal language works (philosophy of language), how we interpret biblical texts (hermeneutics), and how we decide what is right and wrong (ethics).

Apologetics

Christian apologetics (from the Greek work *apologia*, meaning "defense") is a discipline devoted to providing rational defenses of the Christian faith. People often associate apologetics with making arguments, but there is more to this discipline than "winning" Facebook discussion threads. Apologists can use the tools of philosophy, biblical studies, or theology to make a case for the reasonableness of Christian truth claims like the existence of God, the reliability of the Bible, or the resurrection of Jesus. Apologetics is an indispensable complement to (but not a replacement of) personal evangelism because it can help clear away intellectual obstacles that prevent a person from believing the gospel and trusting in Christ.

Apologetics also serves the church by strengthening the faith of believers. Apologists may disagree about what method is most helpful or effective in apologetics but agree about its importance in ministry and Christian practice.[17] One salient distinction to know about: apologetic

---

[17] See Steven B. Cowan, ed., *Five Views on Apologetics* (Grand Rapids: Zondervan, 2000).

arguments are crafted in response to objections to Christianity from outside the church (e.g., atheism, Islam, etc.), while *polemics* or polemic arguments usually are directed toward false teaching within the church or operating under the guise of the Christian faith (e.g., Word-Faith theology). Many apologists collapse the work of polemics into their larger task.

Like systematic theology, apologetics is an interdisciplinary exercise that draws from biblical studies, philosophy, history, and the natural sciences. The work of apologists and systematic theologians often overlaps, as both are concerned with defending the tenets of the faith and making reasonable cases for them.

Christian Ethics

Christian ethics is the distinctively Christian "process of determining right and wrong."[18] The critical study of ethics addresses the moral choices made in hot-button issues like abortion, cloning, gun control, immigration policy, same-sex marriage, or sex-change therapy. Unlike secular, philosophical approaches to ethics, Christian ethics is rooted in biblical teaching and theological truth. A Christian ethical framework takes its shape from (1) explicit commands in Scripture, (2) a desire to glorify God, and (3) the desire to develop Christlike character.[19] Some theologians believe Christian ethics to be one of the tasks of the systematic theologian.[20] While Christian ethics can be logically distinguished from systematic theology, ethics is built on the foundations of theology. Christian ethics is the application of systematic theology to our lives and moral choices.

Christian ethicists normally speak of three basic approaches to moral instruction employed in the Bible. The first category is **divine command ethics**, direct instructions given by the Lord. The key question of divine

---

[18] Rae, *Moral Choices*, 15 (see chap. 2, n. 12).

[19] Wayne Grudem, *Christian Ethics: An Introduction to Biblical Moral Reasoning* (Wheaton, IL: Crossway, 2018), 40–43.

[20] See James Wm. McClendon, Jr., *Ethics: Systematic Theology*, vol. 1, 2nd ed. (Nashville: Abingdon, 2002).

command ethics is, *What is God telling me to do in this passage?* The commands of the Law and many of the direct statements of Jesus and the epistles fit in this category.[21]

- "Do not misuse the name of the LORD your God, because the LORD will not leave anyone unpunished who misuses his name" (Exod 20:7).
- "You have heard that it was said, 'Love your neighbor and hate your enemy.' But I tell you, love your enemies and pray for those who persecute you, so that you may be children of your Father in heaven" (Matt 5:43–45a).
- "And we have this command from him: The one who loves God must also love his brother and sister" (1 John 4:21).

Divine commands are also associated with a wider category of ethical instruction known as **deontological ethics** (from the Greek word *deontos*, meaning "duty") because we have an obligation or a duty to do what God commands us.

The second category, **consequentialist ethics**, is a type of moral instruction based on the consequences of our actions, whether they are good or bad.[22] The main question of the consequentialist ethic is, *What will result from this action?* Some non-Christian ethicists who take up this approach may justify any behavior that does not hurt another individual (in their own estimation anyway). Some may justify hedonistic behaviors like theft or adultery if they do not get caught. Disciples of Jesus are concerned with different ends than pleasure or self-satisfaction. In the Corinthian debate over meat offered to idols (1 Cor 10:23–33), Paul offered liberty to those whose consciences would allow them to eat it (10:25–27) but also encouraged sensitivity to those whose consciences would not (10:28). The moral instruction at the heart of Paul's advice is consequential: "Whether you eat or drink, or whatever you do, do everything for the glory of God" (10:31). The Christian is concerned about

---

[21] Rae, *Moral Choices*, 91–99.
[22] Rae, 70.

whether her actions glorify God and the impact moral decision making has on her witness (10:27–28).

The final aspect of Christian ethics is **virtue ethics**.[23] The key question in virtue ethics is not What should I do? but *Who should I be?* Character is not something we do but something we are, that shapes the way we respond to the situations we face in this life. The Old Testament speaks of men with impeccable character: people who are "blameless" (Gen 6:9; Job 9:21; 2 Sam 22:24) and "righteous" (Gen 6:9) before the Lord. Because God is righteous and blameless, his people must pursue that characteristic as well.

In the New Testament, this virtue ethic is associated with disciples of Christ being made remade in his likeness (Rom 8:29–30). Jesus—the perfectly virtuous one—becomes the exemplar for everyone who follows him. This transformation of character comes through the Spirit's sanctifying work: "We all, with unveiled faces, are looking as in a mirror at the glory of the Lord and are being transformed into the same image from glory to glory; this is from the Lord who is the Spirit" (2 Cor 3:18). Through the fruit of the Spirit (Gal 5:22–23), the character of God's people begins to reflect the character of Christ.

Pastoral Theology

Pastoral theology is the area of study that brings together the theoretical discussion of Christian teaching with its practical application in the ministry and leadership of local churches. It is theological because it is grounded in the study of divine revelation, but pastoral or practical because "it seeks to give clear definition to the tasks of ministry and enable its improved practice."[24]

In dialogue with the content of systematic theology, pastoral theology can provide a substantive foundation for the offices and ministries

---

[23] Rae, 68–70.

[24] Thomas C. Oden, *Pastoral Theology: Essentials of Ministry* (San Francisco: Harper & Row, 1983), x.

of the church.[25] Pastoral theology might help answer tough questions for a local church like whether it should be one or many campuses, whether it should have one pastor or multiple elders, or how often a church performs the Lord's Supper and who should participate in it. For this reason, pastoral theology often overlaps with the study of ecclesiology (i.e., the doctrine of the church) in systematic theology.

Systematic theology is also an essential element in the training of pastors. Pastors preach sermons informed by a theological framework. Many of the questions raised in pastoral ministry must be answered systematically: What happens to children who die in infancy? Does suicide send a person to hell? Are we living in the end times? Pastors will be expected to offer cogent answers to these questions that are defensible from Scripture (either directly or indirectly).

Getting the Theological Family Back Together

Despite the unfortunate (and sometimes sinful) fragmentation in the larger theological guild, biblical scholars, theologians, philosophers, apologists, ethicists, and pastoral theologians need one another. All have something beneficial to contribute. How does this academic colabor work in practice? *First, biblical scholars, systematic theologians, church historians, philosophers, ethicists, and pastoral theologians within the evangelical academy work with a shared task: to grow in our relationship to God and to build God's kingdom through disciple-making.* We share the same Great Commandments (Matt 22:36–40) and the same Great Commission (Matt 28:18–20)! In the Great Commission, no one discipline is needed more than another. The biblical scholar cannot say to the systematic theologian, "I don't need you!" Nor can the systematic theologian say, "I don't need you!" to the historian. Just as the body of Christ "is one and has many parts" (1 Cor 12:12), with each member gifted by the Spirit to

---

[25] See Daniel L. Akin and R. Scott Pace, *Pastoral Theology: Theological Foundations for Who a Pastor Is and What He Does* (Nashville: B&H Academic, 2017).

serve a distinct role, Christian scholars are uniquely suited to serve the church in different ways.

Second, theological disciplines can be unified by a common conviction that God has revealed himself in a truthful and coherent way. Every truth belongs to God. So, our goal as biblical scholars, systematic theologians, philosophers, ethicists, apologists, and pastoral theologians is to use all our respective insights to talk about the whole of reality. As David Clark has noted, each discipline has unique advantages and insights, but each discipline can become distorted by their area of focus and the neglect of other studies.[26]

Third, the complex nature of the world God created requires different approaches to studying it. Reality is complex and multilayered. Each aspect of reality requires its own method of study.[27] Alister McGrath applies this insight to theology by observing God at work in every stratum of creation. The natural sciences, the social sciences, philosophy, biblical studies, history, and theology all are ways of studying God's world. Truths in chemistry do not contradict truths in systematic theology because they address different aspects of reality. For our present discussion, this means the truths discovered by the biblical theologian overlap with the truths maintained by the systematic theologian. The work of the historical theologian coincides with the work of the philosopher and the apologist. No one theological discipline trumps the others as each speaks with its own voice to testify to the world made by God.

Consider how many ways we could answer the question, Why did Jesus die? A theologian will usually answer this question with something about Jesus dying in the place of sinners, though theologians often debate how exactly his death remedied sin (i.e., debates about atonement theories). But others could answer the same question with *correct* answers that address the same real event in its various layers. A medical doctor could say Jesus died because of asphyxiation caused by crucifixion. A

---

[26] Clark, *To Know and Love God*, 182–83.

[27] Alister E. McGrath, *A Scientific Theology*, vol. 2, *Reality* (Grand Rapids: Eerdmans, 2002), 209–44.

historian could say Jesus died because he was perceived to be a threat to Caesar's regional authority and the religious establishment of Israel. All these answers can be true if reality is complex and each aspect of reality demands its own method of study. A biblical theologian may explore the distinctive descriptions of the crucifixion in the Gospel accounts or ways in which it was interpreted in the various letters of the New Testament. A systematic theologian may seek to understand God's plan behind the manifold biblical witness to it. These various approaches are complementary, not contradictory.

Finally, all theological disciplines interrelate by the way in which they contribute to one another in an ongoing process of biblical interpretation and theological engagement. The systematic theologian builds on the exegetical and historical work of biblical scholarship. The biblical scholar has preconceived ideas that he draws from the work of the systematic theologian. No scholar works with a "blank slate," and Christian scholars who have been discipled in the life of the church bring a host of theological assumptions to the table. For example, an evangelical biblical theologian who acknowledges the inspiration and inerrancy of the entire Bible begins her work of interpretation with a systematic doctrine that colors her whole process. As David Buschart and Kent Eilers have remarked, "Theology always begins already in the middle."[28]

As D. A. Carson carefully explained, the complex relationship between theological disciplines is not a simple linear process. Interpretation of the Bible is never "done in a vacuum."[29] Carson also rejects the idea that these disciplines are locked into a flat, circular pattern like this one:

---

[28] W. David Buschart and Kent D. Eilers, *Theology as Retrieval: Receiving the Past, Renewing the Church* (Downers Grove, IL: InterVarsity Press, 2015), 11.

[29] D. A. Carson, "Unity and Diversity in the New Testament," in *Scripture and Truth*, ed. D. A. Carson and John D. Woodbridge (Grand Rapids: Baker, 1983), 91.

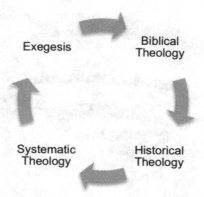

Carson presumably rejects this "hermeneutical circle" because of the endless circularity of its thought.[30] Instead, he proposes theological disciplines work together in a series of feedback lines like this:

Carson recognizes exegesis is informed by systematic theology but rejects the idea that it is bound or shackled by theology.[31]

Some get discouraged at the thought that we are in a never-ending loop between exegesis, biblical theology, and systematic theology. Yet rather than thinking about this move between worldview and doctrine as a flat circle or a linear process, I embrace the notion of a three-dimensional spiral put forward by Grant Osborne (1942–2018).[32]

---

[30] Since Schleiermacher, many have depicted the process of reading and interpreting Scripture as a circle that begins with "pre-understanding" (*Vorverständis*) and that moves toward "understanding" (*Verständis*). See Friedrich D. E. Schleiermacher, *Hermeneutics: The Handwritten Manuscripts*, trans. and ed. James Duke and Jack Forstman (Atlanta: Scholars Press, 1977).

[31] Carson, "Unity and Diversity in the New Testament," 92.

[32] Grant R. Osborne, *The Hermeneutical Spiral: A Comprehensive Introduction to Biblical Interpretation* (Downers Grove, IL: InterVarsity Press, 2006).

Systematic   Devotional
Theology   reading

Historical   Biblical
Theology   Theology

Philosophical   Biblical
Theology   Exegesis

We never do the work of biblical exegesis or biblical theology without a systematic-theological framework, but we always seek to correct our theological framework by engaging with the supreme authority of our faith in Scripture. Biblical exegesis can also be informed by philosophical theology, historical theology, Christian ethics, and apologetics. For disciples of Jesus, this is a lifelong process in which we go "further up and further in" in our understanding and maturity as biblical interpreters and theologians.[33] Protestants have long recognized that the people of God "must always be reformed" (*semper reformanda*) by Scripture, meaning we continually check our beliefs and our practices against the authority of the Bible. "All Scripture . . . is profitable . . . for correcting" (2 Tim 3:16). Humble interpreters of Scripture are teachable and willing to be corrected by its precepts when needed.

All our academic specializations can benefit the theological guild and the church. The academy benefits from expertise in biblical languages, textual criticism, archeology, apologetics, ethics, historical theology, philosophy, and systematic theology. The church benefits from having faithful academics whose expertise trickles down by the men and women they train to serve in local churches. All this expertise helps us better grasp the meaning of the Bible, defend the truths of the faith from its opponents, and apply these truths to the Christian life and the ministry of the church. However, an overly specialized theological academy that operates in disciplinary ghettos is powerless to serve the church.

---

[33] See C. S. Lewis, *The Last Battle*, The Chronicles of Narnia 7 (New York: HarperCollins, 2000), chap. 15.

KEY TERMS

apologetics, Christian

biblical theology

ethics, Christian

ethics, consequentialist

ethics, deontological

ethics, divine command

ethics, virtue

historical theology

pastoral theology

philosophical theology

GO DEEPER

Bockmuehl, Markus, and Alan J. Torrance, eds. *Scripture's Doctrine and Theology's Bible: How the New Testament Shapes Christian Dogmatics.* Grand Rapids: Baker, 2008.

Carson, D. A. "Unity and Diversity in the New Testament: The Possibility of Systematic Theology." In *Scripture and Truth*, edited by D. A. Carson and John D. Woodbridge, 65–95. Grand Rapids: Baker, 1983.

Clark, David K. "Unity in the Theological Disciplines." In *To Know and Love God: Method for Theology*, 165–93. Wheaton, IL: Crossway, 2002.

Green, Joel B., and Max Turner. *Between Two Horizons: Spanning New Testament Studies and Systematic Theology*, 165–93. Grand Rapids: Eerdmans, 1999.

Klink, Edward W., III, and Darian R. Lockett. *Understanding Biblical Theology: A Comparison of Theory and Practice.* Grand Rapids: Zondervan, 2012.

Kuyper, Abraham. *Principles of Sacred Theology.* Translated by J. Hendrik DeVries. New York, 1898.

Muller, Richard A. *The Study of Theology: From Biblical Interpretation to Contemporary Formation.* Grand Rapids: Zondervan, 1990.

Naselli, Andrew David. *How to Understand and Apply the New Testament: Twelve Steps from Exegesis to Theology.* Phillipsburg, NJ: P&R, 2017.

PART TWO

Preparations

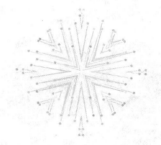

*Developing the character and the
intellect of the Christian theologian*

5

A Heart Prepared for Christian Theology

> There can be no spiritual health without doctrinal knowledge; but
> it is equally true that there can be no spiritual health *with* it, if it is
> sought for the wrong purpose and valued by the wrong standard.
>
> —J. I. PACKER[1]

The apostle Paul was not pleased with the church at Galatia.

In his letter to the Galatians, Paul left out the customary "thanksgiving" section in which he normally praises God for all the good things going on in a church.[2] Even with all the snobs, jerks, backbiters, perverts, and chaotic personalities one could find in the church in

---

[1] J. I. Packer, *Knowing God* (Downers Grove, IL: InterVarsity Press, 1993), 22.

[2] See E. Randolph Richards, *Paul and First-Century Letter Writing: Secretaries, Composition, and Collection* (Downers Grove, IL: InterVarsity Press, 2004), 130–33. Richards illustrates the shocking way Paul opens his letter to the Galatians with a modern letter that opens like this: "Dear Randy, What were you thinking?" (132).

Corinth, Paul still found enough good to say about them to write a word of thanksgiving for them (1 Cor 1:4–9). But with the Galatians, Paul cut straight to the tough love: "I am amazed that you are so quickly turning away from him who called you by the grace of Christ and are turning to a different gospel" (Gal 1:6).

Paul marveled in astonishment at how quickly this church seems to have forgotten the core of the gospel. He declared anyone among them preaching a false gospel to be under a curse and in danger of hellfire (Gal 1:8). He even called them "foolish" or "mindless" for their behavior (Gal 3:1).

Yikes. One does not want to be on the other end of an apostolic callout.

The occasion for this rebuke? Troublemakers from within the church distorted the gospel of grace Paul had preached to them. They were requiring Gentiles to be circumcised, to change their diets, and to "live like Jews" (Gal 2:14) before they could be saved and join the church (5:1–15). Though many in the church at Galatia put on the hats of religious and theological expertise, even their religious acts were sinful and dishonoring to God. They had lost their way with culture-bound theological reasoning, exchanging their spiritual life for a religion in the flesh.

Paul contrasted this religion carried out in the "flesh" (*sarx*) with a "walk" or "lifestyle" (from the verb *peripateō*) "by the Spirit" (5:16). While the word *sarx* can refer literally to flesh or physical bodies, Paul used it "as shorthand for the present evil world and for human existence apart from God, both of which have a drive that is opposed to God."[3] According to Paul, "the flesh desires what is against the Spirit, and the Spirit desires what is against the flesh; these are opposed to each other" (5:17). What we learn from Paul's overarching argument throughout the book is that religious belief can be exercised in one of two ways: a freedom-producing faith in Christ or a burdensome, ritualistic religion according to the present evil age in opposition to the gospel and the grace of God.

One can be an interested observer of the faith without being an active participant in it. Just because a person can talk about God properly

---

[3] *NIDNTTE*, 4:258, s.v. "σάρξ."

does not mean he or she knows him personally. People can speak about God as a subject without ever making themselves subject to God. Pastors can prep well-crafted sermons without preparing themselves for spiritual attack. I have known more than a few Bible college and seminary students, as well as professional theologians and Bible scholars, who "abandoned the love [they] had at first" (Rev 2:4) for something else.

The same is true of the study of theology. We have the choice between studying doctrine in the Spirit or in the flesh. We can practice a kind of God-honoring theology led by the Spirit that results in our sanctification, or we can practice a theology in the flesh with "the form of godliness" (2 Tim 3:5) but hellbent on vainglory and divisiveness. The Bible warns against false teachers who teach doctrine not out of a love for truth but out of ungodly ambition, desiring to be known as teachers rather than living in obedience (1 Tim 1:6–7). False teachers are "conceited," lacking in understanding, and have an "unhealthy interest in disputes and arguments over words" (1 Tim 6:3–4). False teachers insincerely study and teach doctrine out of an interest in material gain rather than making genuine Christ-followers (2 Cor 2:17; cf. 1 Tim 6:4b–5, 10; 2 Pet 2:3). False teachers teach, preach, and study doctrine in the flesh. By contrast, men and women of God who walk in the Spirit study and teach doctrine with worshipful and contrite hearts. They "equip the saints for the work of ministry, to build up the body of Christ" (Eph 4:12).

Theology in the Flesh

Before Paul described the fruit of the Spirit, he expanded on what he meant by the "works" of the flesh with a list of vices: "sexual immorality, moral impurity, promiscuity, idolatry, sorcery, hatreds, strife, jealousy, outbursts of anger, selfish ambitions, dissensions, factions, envy, drunkenness, carousing, and anything similar. I am warning you about these things—as I warned you before—that those who practice such things will not inherit the kingdom of God" (Gal 5:19–21). These works are focused on the self and opposed to the things of God. Again, Paul wasn't warning pagans outside the church of these manifestations of the flesh, but those within the church. Even with all the trappings of spirituality, theology still must yield to works of the flesh.

Theology in the flesh can promote "sexual immorality, moral impurity, promiscuity, . . . drunkenness, carousing, and anything similar." These immoral acts are manifestations of the flesh, so it should not surprise us when theology in the flesh results in this kind of licentiousness. How might the study of theology or religion result in sexual sin and wild, pagan partying? Two ways come to mind. First, theology can be used to *justify* sinful deeds. Some reject or reinterpret the commands and teachings of Scripture to suit "their own desires . . . because they have an itch to hear what they want to hear" (2 Tim 4:3). Of such teachers the prophet Isaiah lamented, "Woe to those who call evil good and good evil, who substitute darkness for light and light for darkness, who substitute bitter for sweet and sweet for bitter" (Isa 5:20).

Second, another group of theologians may give mental assent to biblical teaching on moral issues but fail to live it out in their own lives because they have disconnected their theological knowledge from a vibrant walk with God. This is often what happens in the lives of pastors who are caught up in pornography, adultery, or sexual abuse. Unfortunately, church history records sad stories of Christian intellectuals who had sinister secret lives in which pride blinded them to their blatant and gross sin. Some of the most influential theologians of the twentieth century were later discovered to have affairs, mistresses, and sexually abusive relationships.[4]

A Christian battling perpetual sexual sin may profess belief in the holiness of God, the dignity of fellow human beings made in his image, and the sanctity of marriage, but the patterns of his behavior and thought life prove he is "double-minded" (Jas 1:8) and has not let his intellectual assertions become deeply rooted convictions. We may learn the cognitive

---

[4] The use of theology to rationalize sexual sin recently came to light in the life of the Swiss Reformed theologian Karl Barth (1886–1968). See Mark Galli, "What to Make of Karl Barth's Steadfast Adultery?," *Christianity Today*, October 20, 2017, https://www.christianitytoday.com/ct/2017/october-web-only/what-to-make-of-karl-barths-steadfast-adultery.html; Christiane Tietz, "Karl Barth and Charlotte von Kirschbaum," *Theology Today* 74 (July 2017): 86–111.

content of the Bible through the hard work of exegesis and interpretation without ever applying it to our lives. Theology in the flesh never allows the "living and effective" Word of God "to judge the thoughts and intentions of the heart" (Heb 4:12). Theology in the flesh denies the Spirit his illuminating activity whereby he convicts us of our sin (John 16:8) and frees us from it (Rom 8:2).

Theology in the flesh can be idolatrous in nature. Rather than stirring our minds and hearts to the worship of God, theology studied for the sake of theology makes the acclaim of others or intellectual curiosity its pursuit. A few common traits characterize the theologians, pastors, and seminary students I know who have walked away from their faith. They "loved human praise more than praise from God" (John 12:43). They often seemed more concerned about being open-minded than having their minds renewed (Rom 12:2). They often flexed their scholarly muscles in study but were lethargic in ministering to the church or the needs of others. Their lifestyles showed patterns of sinful decadence rather than the pursuit of holiness, and their love for God grew cold (Matt 24:12). Worst of all, they seemed bored by the gospel. The cross of Christ no longer seemed to stir their affections. The academic pursuit of biblical and theological knowledge, while noble if pursued with the right motives, is no substitute for a personal and intimate knowledge of God achieved through prayer, devotion to his Word, and obedience.

We can pervert the wonderful thing God has given us in theology when we worship a field of study instead of the One about whom it speaks. For this reason, the apostle Paul warned about people who are zealous for God without knowledge (Rom 10:2). He likewise told his disciple Timothy, "Watch your life and doctrine closely" (1 Tim 4:16 NIV). Apart from knowledge of God's revealed character and will in Scripture, people will live in unbelief and disobedience (Rom 10:3).

Theology in the flesh often produces "hatreds, strife, jealousy, outbursts of anger, selfish ambitions, dissensions, factions, [and] envy." Disagreements are part and parcel of any intellectual pursuit, so we should not be surprised when faithful Christians disagree about doctrine. However, when theological disagreements turn into "strife" or "dissension" in which people are separated for all the wrong reasons, God is not honored or glorified. God is not glorified by mean-spirited debates over nuance. He is not honored by those theologians who, in the words of Batman's butler, Alfred Pennyworth, "just want to watch the world burn."

I grow frustrated with professing Christians who don't seem content unless they have something to be angry about. With their own "outbursts of anger," they police the thoughts and behaviors of others but seem blind to their own quarrelsome and bullyish ways (cf. 1 Tim 3:3). They do not practice love for neighbors when they are always suspicious of their motives. They are impulsive and more concerned with the public appearance of being right on a hot-button issue than taking time to work patiently through their disagreements with others. Theologians who are only concerned with correcting others often do theology from selfish ambition and envy rather than God-honoring motives.

Even "professional" Christians with seminary degrees can grow cold in their own faith, especially if they are not faithful in spending time with God in his Word and in prayer. Our academic endeavors should be motivated by the love of God and a desire to bring him glory, not by notoriety, prestige, or a strong social media following (Gal 1:10).

Theology in the Spirit

In contrast to the works of the flesh, Paul described the Spirit's fruit as "love, joy, peace, patience, kindness, goodness, faithfulness, gentleness, and self-control" (Gal 5:22–23). Note that he didn't talk about the "fruits of the Spirit" but the singular "fruit" (5:22). In contrast with the list of plural vices partaken in by some and not by others, Paul described a single fruit that should be manifested in people of the Spirit. Not every sinner has every work of the flesh in his life, but the church should be united by believers who all bear this same fruit.[5] As Ben Witherington III spelled out, this fruit is in sharp antithesis to the works of the flesh:

---

[5] Ben Witherington III, *Grace in Galatia: A Commentary on Paul's Letter to the Galatians* (Grand Rapids: Eerdmans, 1998), 408.

Acts of hatred *versus* Love (and joy)
Discord *versus* Peace
Anger (quick temper) *versus* Patience
Fits of rage *versus* Acts of kindness
Acts of selfish ambition *versus* Acts of generosity
Dissensions leading to factions *versus* Faithfulness to others
Acts of envy *versus* Acts of considerateness.[6]

The attributes of this fruit provide a "character sketch" of Christ, and we are called here through the Spirit to be conformed to his image.[7] These Christlike characteristics could be applied to any ministry or calling within the church: pastoral ministry in the Spirit, teaching in the Spirit, evangelism in the Spirit, service in the Spirit, and so forth. However, here I want to apply them directly to the task of Christian theology as we have described it: *critical and organized reflection on God's self-revelation for the purposes of growing in Christ and making disciples.*

A loving theology. Love should be the defining characteristic of all followers of Jesus: love for God (Matt 22:37), love for others (Matt 22:39), and love for truth (2 Thess 2:10). The Spirit-filled theologian is driven by the Greatest Commandment in everything he does. He loves the Lord with all his heart, all his soul, all his mind, and all his strength (Mark 12:30). Put another way, he gives undivided love to God from his whole worldview: loving God with his affections, his beliefs, and his practices. The theological task should always be approached prayerfully, and there is wisdom in opening every study or paper-writing session with a request for the Spirit's help. *God, by your grace, help us know you better and love you more as we reflect on your Word to us.*

Theologians naturally love truth (or at least the idea of truth) and express love for God, but does a genuine love for others manifest itself in our theological research and conversations? How do we display a love for our neighbor like the love we have for ourselves? It matters little whether

---

[6] Witherington, *Grace in Galatia*, 402.
[7] James D. G. Dunn, *The Epistle to the Galatians*, Black's New Testament Commentary (Peabody, MA: Hendrickson, 1993), 310.

we as Christian scholars "understand all mysteries and all knowledge" (1 Cor 13:2) if we do not love. Consider Paul's description of love in 1 Cor 13:4–7: "Love is patient, love is kind. Love does not envy, is not boastful, is not arrogant, is not rude, is not self-seeking, is not irritable, and does not keep a record of wrongs. Love finds no joy in unrighteousness but rejoices in the truth. It bears all things, believes all things, hopes all things, endures all things."

Uche Anizor applies this text to theological reading, showing the need for theologians who are patient and kind with their sources, reading charitably any way they can.[8] Loving theological engagement is not boastful or proud. It does not presume to know all the answers before reading commences.[9] Moreover, charitable theology "does not keep a record of wrongs" and "believes all things, hopes all things." For Anizor, this means replacing prejudicial suspicion with loving discernment. Instead of jumping to conclusions about the salvation of those who disagree with us on every single issue, loving theology recognizes fallen human nature and seeks to find "goodness, sincerity, or truth in the proposal."[10]

A joyful theology. Those whose lives evidence true joy do not give the impression that they are constantly rattled or bothered by every challenge or difficulty they face. Instead, they express joy and contentment in every situation (see Phil 4:11–12).[11] The theologian in the flesh is combative, reactionary, and prone to outbursts. The theologian living in the Spirit beams with the joy of the Lord in every circumstance, whether good or ill (see Phil 4:4). This theologian rejoices in disciples being made, in churches flourishing, and the people of God being built up "in the knowledge of God's Son" (Eph 4:13).

A peaceful theology. Christians who disagree with one another have two mirroring postures with which they can engage one another: a

---

[8] Uche Anizor, *How to Read Theology: Engaging Doctrine Critically & Charitably* (Grand Rapids: Baker, 2018), 3–23. See also Alan Jacobs, *A Theology of Reading: The Hermeneutics of Love* (New York: Routledge, 2001).

[9] Anizor, *How to Read Theology*, 9–10.

[10] Anizor, 13.

[11] *NIDNTTE* 4:648, s.v. "χαίρω."

polemic reaction or an irenic response. The word *polemic* comes from a Greek term that means "war" or "warlike" (*polemikos*). We engage in polemics when we go to war against dangerous or heretical theological ideas that have the ring of truth. Paul's letter to the Galatians is unquestionably polemic in nature, and justly so. One does not pull the big guns of an apostolic curse lightly, but Paul needs to do this when these agitators are adding burdens that keep men from coming to Jesus (Gal 1:8).

Other times call for the mirror disposition of irenic theology. The word *irenic* traces its origins to the Greek word for "peace" (*eirēnē*) used here in Gal 5:22. The Spirit's fruit of peace is not "inner peace" or "peace of mind" but peace in social relationships. Because we have attained peace with God through Christ's finished work on the cross, we are called to relate to one another peaceably (Rom 14:19).[12] An irenic theologian pursues peace where he can amid disagreement, especially in the life of the church. Scripture repeatedly bears witness to the importance of peacemaking. Jesus called the peacemakers blessed (Matt 5:9). We are told to "pursue peace with everyone" (Heb 12:14; cf. Ps 34: 19). James described the wise as "peace-loving, gentle, compliant" (Jas 3:17). Paul said to "live at peace with everyone" whenever possible (Rom 12:18).

We cannot always control those circumstances. Just as there is "a time for war and a time for peace" (Eccl 3:8), there are times for peaceful theology and polemic theology—peaceful, irenic theology directed toward disagreements of minor consequence and polemic theology toward denials of Christ and the gospel. Yet whether we find ourselves practicing polemic theology or irenic theology, our goal as theologians in the Spirit is to achieve peace through "unity in the faith" (Eph 4:13). The Spirit-filled theologian has nothing to do with "dissensions" or "factions" associated with the flesh.

A patient theology. The word for "patience" or "forbearance" (*makrothymia*) in Gal 5:22 is a word meaning "steadfastness" or "staying power." F. F. Bruce (1910–1990) described it as the opposite of being "short-tempered," which would be equivalent to being "long-tempered" if such

---

[12] Witherington, *Grace in Galatia*, 409.

a phrase were part of our language.[13] Just as God shows patience for his people (Luke 18:7) and patience toward unbelievers (Rom 9:22), those who bear the fruit of the Spirit exude "patience, bearing with one another in love" (Eph 4:2).

Theologians can exercise this aspect of the fruit of the Spirit in several ways. First, they labor patiently through the resources of Christian theology. Biblical interpretation is hard. Most theological books worth reading are tough reads in one way or another. Theology is a most rewarding exercise, but it is not for the faint of heart.

Second, we should exercise patience with our interlocutors—especially when we disagree with them. A word to the wise in the era of social media: not every theological conflict demands your immediate response (or a response at all). Many times, patiently waiting out conflict prevents unnecessary dissension and misunderstanding.

Third, teachers of Christian doctrine (whether academic, pastoral, or in a disciple-making relationship) must be patient with those whom they teach and disciple. Maturation in Christian truth and practice takes time. Just as God shows patience to us who are slow learners, we ought to show patience to those maturing in the faith. Young preachers and teachers often feel the urge to tell congregations and classes *everything* they learned in their preparation, but they should be warned: it's hard to drink the living water if it is coming from a fire hydrant. We must resist the temptation of "information dumping" on the people in our pews and classrooms. Patiently speak to your people where they are and allow the Holy Spirit to do his ongoing work in their hearts and minds.

A gentle theology. I will sometimes hear Christians justify harsh or mean-spirited criticisms of other Christians by qualifying them with the statement "the Bible nowhere calls us to be nice." While it is true there is a kind of "niceness" typified by silence on matters of truth, people-pleasing, and friendship with the world (Jas 4:4), the opposite of this tendency is not being a self-righteous, snarky jerk. When I see this behavior on display in my life or the lives of others, it is usually a good indication

---

[13] F. F. Bruce, *The Epistle to the Galatians* (Grand Rapids: Eerdmans, 1982), 253.

of theology in the flesh—not theology in the Spirit. The Spirit produces the fruit of "kindness" (*chrēstotēs*), "gentleness" (*prautēs*), and "self-control" (*enkrateia*). Though distinguishable, each of these qualities is closely related and each foils the "outbursts of anger" associated with works of the flesh.

In Pauline thinking, "kindness" is an attribute of God contrasted with his severity (Rom 11:22). God has raised us up with Christ Jesus "so that in the coming ages he might display the immeasurable riches of his grace through *his kindness to us* in Christ Jesus" (Eph 2:7, emphasis added; cf. Titus 3:4). As recipients of God's kindness in Christ, we are called to put on "kindness . . . bearing with one another and forgiving one another if anyone has a grievance against another" (Col 3:12–13). Paul distinguished this kindness from "bitterness, anger and wrath, shouting and slander" (Eph 4:31) when he instructed the Ephesians to "be kind and compassionate to one another, forgiving one another, just as God also forgave you in Christ" (4:32).

The term Paul used for "gentleness" also appears in Aristotle's ethics as a golden mean between "excessive anger and the inability to be angry." It describes "a person who is in control of his or her emotions and can choose to act with gentleness and mildness in dealing with others."[14] Paul reflected this happy medium between anger and passivity when he defended his own authority as an apostle: "Now I, Paul, myself, appeal to you by the meekness and gentleness of Christ—I who am humble among you in person but bold toward you when absent" (2 Cor 10:1). A gentle theology is not a people-pleasing theology for pushovers, nor is it an impulsive theology prone to fits of anger and dissension. It strikes the perfect balance in its ability to speak the truth in love (Eph 4:15).

A faithful theology. "Faith" or "faithfulness" (*pistis*) in Gal 5:22 describes the ongoing commitment to Christ in the life of the believer. This adjective in the New Testament relates to the Hebrew adjective *aman*, which means "trustworthy," "faithful," or "reliable."[15] The Spirit produces in us a faithfulness like the faithfulness of God (Deut 7:9; Lam 3:22–23;

---

[14] Witherington, *Grace in Galatia*, 409.
[15] *NIDNTTE* 4:761, s.v. "πιστεύω."

2 Tim 2:13; Heb 10:23b) or Jesus's own faithfulness (*pisteōs Christou*; Gal 2:16). The disciple of Jesus *believes* theological truth about him but, more importantly, continually *places trust in Jesus*. The Spirit-filled believer is also *dependable* and *trustworthy*; he exhibits faithfulness like a true friend.

William Klein, Craig Blomberg, and Robert Hubbard have identified five necessary qualifications for faithful interpretation of Scripture.[16] These five earmarks of faithful biblical interpretation also extend to faithful theologizing. First, a faithful theologian trusts in God, believing he wants to speak to his people through his Word.[17] Second, a faithful theologian places herself "under" the authority of the text, submitting her will to obey the text as it directs and guides her.[18] Third, a faithful theologian prays for the illumination of the Holy Spirit (John 14:26; 16:12–15; 1 Cor 2:10–13; Eph 1:17–18).[19] Fourth, a faithful theologian is a member and active participant in a local church. A theologian who does not live among and minister to the body of Christ is living in disobedience. We cannot grow in obedience or make disciples apart from a local expression of God's church.[20] Finally, a faithful theologian seeks to understand the biblical message on its own terms by reading the Bible correctly.[21] More will be said about this in chapters to come.

The Spirit-filled theologian is faithful to the truth of Scripture and the gospel message, holding "on to the confession of our hope without wavering" (Heb 10:23a). He is a faithful servant of the Lord, who uses the gifts God has given him to further God's kingdom (Matt 25:14–23). He is faithful to the Great Commission, desperately longing to make disciples from all nations (Matt 28:19–20). As a faithful friend, he is

---

[16] William Klein, Craig Blomberg, and Robert Hubbard, *Introduction to Biblical Interpretation*, 3rd ed. (Grand Rapids: Zondervan, 2017), 202–10.

[17] Klein, Blomberg, and Hubbard, 202–5.

[18] Klein, Blomberg, and Hubbard, 205. Elsewhere I have labeled this orientation the *hermeneutic of submission*. See Putman, *When Doctrine Divides the People of God*, 56 (see chap. 2, n. 35).

[19] Klein, Blomberg, and Hubbard, *Introduction to Biblical Interpretation*, 206–8.

[20] Klein, Blomberg, and Hubbard, 208–9.

[21] Klein, Blomberg, and Hubbard, 209–10.

"closer than a brother" (Prov 18:24), and he sharpens other brothers with grace-filled speech (Prov 27:17). He does not cause dissension or lead out in forming factions. Instead, he calls for unity in the truth. Inevitably, any theologian seeking to be faithful to God's Word will face criticism from the unbelieving world (and unfortunately, often within the church). But the Spirit-filled pastor, teacher, or theologian "is the one who endures trials, because when he has stood the test he will receive the crown of life that God has promised to those who love him" (Jas 1:12).

GO DEEPER

Grenz, Stanley J., and Roger E. Olson. *Who Needs Theology? An Invitation to the Study of God.* Downers Grove, IL: InterVarsity Press, 1996.

Kapic, Kelly M. *A Little Book for New Theologians: Why and How to Study Theology.* Downers Grove, IL: InterVarsity Press, 2012.

Kreider, Glenn R., and Swigel, Michael J. *A Practical Primer on Theological Method: Table Manners for Discussing God, His Works, and His Ways.* Grand Rapids: Zondervan, 2019.

Packer, J. I. *Knowing God.* Downers Grove, IL: InterVarsity Press, 1993.

Thielicke, Helmut. *A Little Exercise for Young Theologians.* Translated by Charles L. Taylor. Grand Rapids: Eerdmans, 1962.

6

A Mind Prepared for Christian Theology

If we submit everything to reason, our religion will contain
nothing mysterious or supernatural. If we shock the principles
of reason, our religion will be absurd and ridiculous.
—BLAISE PASCAL, *PENSÉES*

Two mirroring temptations confront every Christian when it comes
to the use of our minds and reason in theology. The first is a refusal
to believe Christian truth without thoroughgoing rational proof that
would convince everyone who hears it. We can use skepticism to reject
the gospel or to justify wicked behavior. The second is a kind of anti-
intellectualism that comes from those who claim to be followers of Jesus
but who scoff at all forms of reason, study, and intellectual pursuits (even
though Scripture encourages these practices). This anti-intellectualism
pits faith and knowledge against one another and casts the study of theology and its sister disciplines in a suspicious light.

The **rationalist** demand for proof and the **fideist** refusal to think about what we believe may seem worlds apart, but both stem from the same error: a failure to love God "with all your heart, with all your soul, with all your mind, and with all your strength" (Mark 12:30). In addition to loving God with our affections and our actions, Jesus told us that God wants us to love him with our mental abilities as well.[1] The hard work of study may not come naturally to us. It may be something we would never desire to pursue on our own, but we do the work because we love our Lord.

Throughout church history, Christian theologians have battled one another over the relationship between faith and reason. Why should we exert mental energy trying to understand our faith? Isn't faith enough? Should we feel obligated to prove our faith by reason? Donald Bloesch (1928–2010) went so far as to call the relationship between faith and reason "the single most important issue in a theological prolegomenon."[2] We will take up this issue in this chapter and conclude with a discussion of intellectual virtues every Christian theologian should practice. Following Augustine and Anselm, most Christian understandings of the relationship between faith and reason can be summed up in one of three basic approaches to the issue: "believing without understanding," "understanding in order to believe," and "faith seeking understanding."[3] All Christian theologians and philosophers use reason to some degree. The question is not whether reason will have a place in Christian theology but whether reason is necessary to validate our belief systems.[4]

---

[1] Craig A. Evans, *Mark 8:27–16:20*, Word Biblical Commentary 34B (Nashville: Thomas Nelson, 2000), 264.

[2] Donald G. Bloesch, *A Theology of Word and Spirit: Authority and Method in Theology* (Downers Grove, IL: InterVarsity Press, 1992), 35.

[3] See Anselm *Proslogion* 1; cf. Augustine *Tractate 29 on John 7.14–18*. Some Christian philosophers offer more nuanced models than this three-tiered approach. See Steve Wilkens, ed., *Faith and Reason: Three Views* (Downers Grove, IL: InterVarsity Press 2014); James K. Dew Jr. and Paul M. Gould, *Philosophy: A Christian Introduction* (Downers Grove, IL: InterVarsity Press, 2019), 57–71; Paul M. Gould and Richard Brian Davis, eds., *Four Views on Christianity and Philosophy* (Grand Rapids: Zondervan, 2016).

[4] Michael Peterson et al., *Reason & Religious Belief: An Introduction to the Philosophy of Religion*, 3rd ed. (New York: Oxford University Press, 2003), 41.

Faith without Understanding

Tertullian once asked, "What has Jerusalem to do with Athens, the Church with the Academy, [or] the Christian with the heretic?"[5] Tertullian opposed giving philosophical systems ("Athens") a place of authority with theology built on divine revelation ("Jerusalem"). He also objected to the idea that the gospel message needed rational proof, calling Christian beliefs like the resurrection rationally "absurd" and "impossible."[6]

Centuries later, the Protestant Reformer Martin Luther (1483–1546), who wasn't exactly known for subtlety or gentle speech, put his distrust of "reason" (or philosophical speculation) in these terms:

> Reason is the Devil's greatest whore; by nature and manner of being she is a noxious whore; she is a prostitute, the Devil's appointed whore; whore eaten by scab and leprosy who ought to be trodden under foot and destroyed, she and her wisdom. . . . Throw dung in her face to make her ugly. She is and she ought to be drowned in baptism. . . . She would deserve, the wretch, to be banished to the filthiest place in the house, to the closets.[7]

Despite the hostility directed at a particular use of reason in theology—namely the medieval practice of building a theology around Aristotelian philosophy—Luther used reason well in theology and biblical interpretation. He was known for brilliant argumentation of his theological positions. Yet for Luther, like Tertullian before him, faith should never be placed under the dominion of reason.

This faith-against-reason position is sometimes called *fideism* (from the Latin *fides*, meaning "faith"). According to one definition, fideists contend that "belief systems are not subject to rational evaluation."[8] For

---

[5] Tertullian, *The Prescriptions against the Heretics* 7; quoted in *Faith and Reason*, Oxford Readers, ed. Paul Helm (New York: Oxford University Press, 1999), 62.

[6] Tertullian, *On the Flesh of Christ* 5; *ANF* 3:525.

[7] Martin Luther, *Dr. Martin Luther's sämmtliche Werke*, Erlangen Ausgabe Erlangen 16 (Enlangen, 1828), 142–48.

[8] Peterson et al., *Reason & Religious Belief*, 45.

the fideist, faith does not require rational proof or justification. Faith involves commitment and trust, not intellectual certainty. Consequently, fideists downplay the need for rational proofs for God's existence, scientific evidence, and historical support for the gospel accounts. The label of fideism can be used pejoratively, and none of the major representatives often associated with fideism in Christian history (including the ones discussed in this section) were completely against the use of reason.

However, the extreme, anti-intellectual form of fideism undermines Christian belief and practice. *First, without any appeal to reason, the fideist has little or no means to establish the truthfulness of his beliefs when confronted with contrary claims.* Does God exist? Is the Bible reliable? Was Jesus raised from the dead? The extreme fideist feels no need to defend these positions against external criticisms. They only demand belief and trust in what Scripture tells us. Fideism gives little focused attention to one's worldview. This kind of anti-intellectualism is more than lazy thinking; it is a rejection of the gift of reason Carl F. H. Henry (1913–2003) called "a divinely fashioned instrument for recognizing truth."[9]

Second, without reason, the fideist opens himself up to holding logically incoherent or contradictory views of God.[10] Fourteenth-century theologian William of Ockham believed the doctrine of the Trinity was a logical contradiction but affirmed it anyway. He also contended the idea God can still be morally upright if he commanded us to commit murder or adultery because the morality of an action is arbitrarily rooted in God's decision to call it good or evil.[11]

Finally, if faith is a blind, irrational decision, how does one decide which faith to believe in?[12] Why should I take a leap of faith to biblical Christianity and not Shintoism or radical Islam? What *reasons* do I have for choosing one faith over another? Without a means to argue

---

[9] Carl F. H. Henry, *God, Revelation, and Authority*, 6 vols. (Wheaton, IL: Crossway, 1999), 1:225.

[10] Peterson et al., *Reason & Religious Belief*, 48.

[11] See Thomas M. Osborne, "Ockham as Divine-Command Theorist," *Religious Studies* 41.1 (March 2005): 1–22.

[12] Peterson et al., *Reason & Religious Belief*, 46.

for religious truth, fideists inadvertently open the back door to religious pluralism, the idea that all religions are equally valid expressions of belief responding to the same divine reality.[13] Furthermore, without reason, we cannot "guard what has been entrusted" to us (1 Tim 6:20).

Understanding in Order to Believe

By contrast, proponents of **rationalism** argue that one should not hold religious beliefs without convincing proofs from evidence or reason. Strong rationalists maintain that *for a religious belief system to be properly and rationally accepted, it must be possible to prove that the belief system is true.* Furthermore, a belief can only be proven when it is shown to be true "*in a way that should be convincing to any reasonable person.*"[14] Faith is "assumed guilty until it proves its innocence by evidence."[15]

Some rationalists use reason to undermine the credibility of the Christian faith, but others believe it makes Christian belief certain. The British philosopher John Locke's (1632–1704) discussion of the relationship between faith and reason came in response to religious enthusiasts of his day who claimed to have private revelation without any evidence or rational support.[16] Locke believed that the ordinary way people learned truth was through reason, which provides certainty or great confidence in its deductions. At the same time, he considered divine revelation another important way human beings discover truth, though people can only receive this revelation through faith.[17] Locke

---

[13] A notable philosophical defense of this position can be found in John Hick, *An Interpretation of Religion: Human Responses to the Transcendent*, 2nd ed. (New Haven, CT: Yale University Press, 2005).

[14] Peterson et al., *Reason & Religious Belief*, 41.

[15] Nicholas Wolterstorff, "The Migration of the Theistic Arguments: From Natural Theology to Evidentialist Apologetics," in *Rationality, Religious Belief, and Moral Commitment: New Essays in the Philosophy of Religion*, ed. Robert Audi and William J. Wainright (Ithaca, NY: Cornell University Press, 1986), 38.

[16] Wolterstorff, "The Migration of the Theistic Arguments," 40. See John Locke, *An Essay Concerning Human Understanding* 4.18.1–19.16.

[17] Locke, 4.18.2.

insisted that something genuinely revealed by God would never contradict "the clear evidence of reason."[18]

Strong rationalism may be attractive to those who want to find certainty in their religious beliefs but is not without its problems. *First, it is unlikely that a strong rationalist will find an argument for theism (or an argument for atheism) that is "convincing to any reasonable person."*[19] Arguments that compel some to religious belief meet with objections in the minds of other reasonable people. Scripture anticipates this conflict of rational perspectives. Paul remarked that the "Greeks seek wisdom" (1 Cor 1:22) or a rational defense of their beliefs, but many still do not believe the message of the cross. Yet for those who do believe the good news about Jesus, "God's foolishness is wiser than human wisdom" (1 Cor 1:25).

Second, strong rationalism naively assumes a neutral starting point in human reason. Many Enlightenment philosophers, like René Descartes (1596–1650), believed all human beings were born with the same **rationality**: a set of rules or reasons for determining what is true and what is false.[20] However, human thinking is always shaped by context. The time, place, and culture into which we were born shapes the way we reason about the world. In debates about the existence of God, this means what may be convincing to one reasonable person shaped by her context will not be convincing to another.

Third, strong rationalism undermines the idea of faith and trust.[21] The Christian faith requires a certain degree of risk and uncertainty. After his resurrection, Jesus told the disciples that they believed because they had a direct encounter with him, but he also called those who had not yet seen and still believe "blessed" because of their trust in him (John 20:29). We "walk by faith, not by sight" (2 Cor 5:7) or rational guarantees.

*Finally, strong rationalism often fails to take into consideration what theologians call the **noetic effects of sin**, or the effects of sin on the mind.* As the proverb tells us, "There is a way that seems right to a person, but its end is

---

[18] Locke, 4.18.5.
[19] Peterson et al., *Reason & Religious Belief*, 43.
[20] René Descartes, *Discourse* 1, AT 6:2.
[21] Peterson et al., *Reason & Religious Belief*, 43.

the way to death" (Prov 14:12). Because of human depravity and idolatry, the thinking of idolatrous people "became worthless, and their senseless hearts were darkened" (Rom 1:21). The apostle Paul added that "the god of this age has blinded the minds of the unbelievers to keep them from seeing the light of the gospel of the glory of Christ, who is the image of God" (2 Cor 4:4).

Faith Seeking Understanding

Another way of reconciling faith and reason is the position Anselm called **"faith seeking understanding"** (*fides quaerens intellectum*). Following Augustine, Anselm explained, "I do not seek to understand in order to believe; I believe in order to understand."[22] Anselm began his *Proslogion* with a worshipful reflection on the greatness of God and the sinfulness of humanity, then proceeded to make his famous **ontological argument** for the existence of God and describe his attributes. Instead of starting with faith and rejecting reason or requiring reason to establish personal faith, it is his reflection on God as the greatest conceivable being that leads him to make a logical argument for God's existence. Faith precedes his reason.

Advocates of "faith seeking understanding" use reason and argumentation to analyze, defend, and assess their faith but also acknowledge the limitations of human reason. In describing faith seeking understanding, Anthony Thiselton wrote:

> Christian faith demands a rational, faithful, and growing understanding of truth. This does not mean that we know the answer to every question, any more than the Bible is meant to be a comprehensive encyclopedia of all arts and sciences, or of all human knowledge. But this does *not* prevent us from asserting many truths with confidence, while we simultaneously suspend judgment on others. Our growth may even include times when we doubt certain claims. . . . We may have assurance of faith, while

---

[22] Anselm, *Proslogion* 1; cf. Augustine, *Tractates on the Gospel of John* 8.6.

regarding Christian faith as a pilgrimage and adventure in which we constantly seek further understanding.[23]

Faith-seeking-understanding philosophers and theologians clash with fideists who believe religious faith is beyond critical evaluation and strong rationalists who assert that faith must be proven with certainty. They seek reasonable confidence in the truthfulness of their beliefs, not absolute certainty.

Christian theologians do not reason themselves to God. As John Webster (1955–2016) summarized this relationship, "God is not summoned into the presence of reason; reason is summoned before the presence of God."[24] We reason about God in the presence of God and under his direction in special revelation. We also reason *from* our belief in God, not *toward* it. Our belief in God colors our entire worldview. In the words of C. S. Lewis, "I believe in Christianity as I believe that the sun has risen: not only because I see it, but because by it I see everything else."[25]

Biblical faith is neither blind faith nor guaranteed conclusions delivered by reason. The New Testament verb *pisteuó* means "to believe," "to trust," or "to entrust." Biblical faith involves both *belief* in revealed truth about God and *trust* in God. Faith is not blind or unwarranted but rooted in God's self-revelation.

The Protestant Reformers made the helpful distinction between three types of belief: *notitia*, *assensus*, and *fiducia*. *Notitia*, from a Latin word meaning "knowledge," describes the understanding a person has of the contents of the Christian faith. Even skeptics and unbelievers can have *notitia*, or a cognitive understanding of the gospel, as can demons. "You believe that God is one. Good! Even the demons believe—and they shudder" (Jas 2:19). *Assensus* takes this one step further and approves of this belief, assenting to

---

[23] Anthony C. Thiselton, *Systematic Theology* (Grand Rapids: Eerdmans, 2015), 5–6.

[24] John Webster, *Holiness* (London: SCM, 2003), 17.

[25] C. S. Lewis, "Is Theology Poetry?" in *The Weight of Glory and Other Addresses* (San Francisco: HarperCollins, 2001), 140.

the truthfulness of a proposition. They may honor God with lip-service but have hearts far from God (Isa 29:13). *Fiducia* is personal trust in a belief. Saving faith involves understanding the gospel (*notitia*), affirming the gospel (*assensus*), and trust in the person and work of Christ (*fiducia*).

A mind prepared for Christian theology needs to avoid the mistakes of extreme fideism and strong rationalism. We can embrace the Christian worldview in *faith* and still seek to *understand* it with our God-given powers of reason. We neither pursue truth from a worldview-neutral position nor blindly follow a set of religious principles. We believe the Word of God but use our reasoning processes to make sense of its meaning, and we reasonably assess theological claims in light of its meaning. We act in faithful obedience but ready ourselves to give a defense at any time to anyone who asks us for a reason for the hope we have (1 Pet 3:15).

Disciples of Jesus are not perfect people but redeemed people who are saved by their faith in him alone (Rom 5:1; Eph 2:8–9). The author of Hebrews included a list of men and women throughout the grand narrative of the Bible who were "approved through their faith" (Heb 11:39). Everyone in this list was born in total depravity, and some were drunkards, liars, scoffers, backstabbers, murderers, and adulterers. Nevertheless, they all belong to a "large cloud of witnesses surrounding us" who were saved through their faith (Heb 12:1).

But the Bible also records numerous instances where men and women of God deal with doubt: Abraham and Sarah (Gen 17:17–22; 18:10–15), Gideon (Judg 6:36–40), Elijah (1 Kgs 19:1–22), John the Baptist (Matt 11:1–3), Peter (Matt 14:30–32), Thomas (John 20:24–29), and other disciples in the presence of the risen Lord (Matt 28:17; Luke 24:37–39). From the stories of these individuals, one important distinction needs to be made in the discussion of biblical faith: *doubt* and *unbelief* are not synonyms. Doubt, biblically speaking, is someone having trouble trusting God through a difficult situation. Jude prayed for "mercy on those who doubt" (Jude v. 22 ESV), indicating believers can wrestle with doubt without committing apostasy. God can even use our doubt to strengthen our faith, as illustrated in the lives of many Christian apologists who moved from doubt to confident belief (e.g., Descartes, C. S. Lewis, etc.).

Unbelief, by contrast, usually means a conscious choice to reject God, the gospel, or other biblical truths.[26] Unbelief stems from hardened hearts. Sin begets more sin (2 Kgs 17:14–15; Neh. 9:16; Ps 78:17–22; Jer 7:26; Acts 7:51). In unbelief, one refuses to believe God's Word and, consequently, stands condemned (John 3:18–19; 12:48; 2 Thess 2:11–12). Whereas doubt is passive—feelings of doubt come over us with no intention of our own—unbelief is more active. It is a decision an individual makes not to trust in Christ or live in obedience to him. Against this kind of unbelief, the author of Hebrews warned, "Watch out, brothers and sisters, so that there won't be in any of you an evil, unbelieving heart that turns away from the living God" (Heb 3:12).

Biblical faith involves belief in the content of the gospel, trust in the person and work of Christ, and a reasonable response to the testimony of God in Scripture. Scripture warns about irrational fear and conspiracy theories (Isa 8:12). Reason is a necessary element of biblical interpretation and application. The apostle Paul made reasonable cases for the faith everywhere he went in his missionary journeys (Acts 17:2, 17; 18:4). Hearing his message, the Berean converts "received the word with eagerness and *examined the Scriptures daily to see if these things were so*" (Acts 17:11, emphasis added). Paul encouraged the Thessalonians to "test all things" according to the Word of God they received (1 Thess 5:21).

Can We Have Confidence Our Beliefs Are True?

If people of faith should use reason and pursue understanding, the question for Christian philosophers and theologians becomes, How can we know what we believe is true? How can we know anything at all?

---

[26] One possible exception to this definition of "unbelief" is from the narrative of a man whose son had an unclean spirit giving him convulsions (Mark 9:14–29). Hearing of this man's situation, Jesus warns the crowd about their unbelief in the sense of actively refusing to trust God's Word (9:19). Hearing these words from Jesus, the man repents, saying, "I do believe; help my unbelief!" (9:24) and his son is healed.

Epistemology (from the Greek word *episteme*, meaning "knowledge") is the branch of philosophy dedicated to studying these types of questions.

Knowledge may be more difficult to define than many people assume, and we use the word very differently depending on the context. Observe three ways I can use the word *know* in everyday conversations:

1. "I know my wife and children."
2. "I know how to fix a broken computer."
3. "I know that Ronald Reagan was the fortieth president of the United States."

The first sentence is an example of **acquaintance knowledge**, or first-hand knowledge of a person or thing. The second example is **competence knowledge**, or know-how. The final example is what philosophers call **propositional knowledge**, or descriptive knowledge. While all three types of knowledge play considerable roles in Christian discipleship and theological formation, most of the questions related to epistemology and theological method are about propositional knowledge.

While Christian philosophers and theologians disagree among themselves over the nature of knowledge and how we come to know things,[27] we can all agree on a few ground rules before proceeding in the study of Christian theology. *First, God is the ultimate source of all knowledge.* As the proverb states, "The fear of the LORD is the beginning of wisdom, and the knowledge of the Holy One is understanding" (Prov 9:10; cf. 1:7). God has given us a threefold "Word": the word of God in creation, the Word of God incarnate in the person of Jesus Christ, and the written Word of God in Scripture. All our knowledge of the world from the natural sciences, social sciences, philosophy, and theology have their origin in God who reveals himself in the world he created, his Son, and his written Word.[28]

---

[27] See James K. Dew Jr. and Mark W. Foreman, *How Do We Know? An Introduction to Epistemology* (Downers Grove, IL: InterVarsity Press, 2014).

[28] Spykman, *Reformational Theology*, 76–136 (see intro., n.1). Glenn R. Kreider and Michael J. Swigel give the clever descriptors "the Word of the World" (Creation), the "Word in the World" (Jesus Christ), and "the Word to

Second, Christian theology involves knowledge in all three senses: acquaintance knowledge, competence knowledge, and propositional knowledge. Christian believers long to know God and make him known to others in the sense of knowledge of personal acquaintance. We want to know God intimately. We also long to grow in our competence knowledge. We want to be better at the practice of Christian theology (why this book was written), and more importantly, we long to know how to follow God more closely in obedience to his Word. As we have seen already, theologians may do more than study propositional knowledge, but they certainly do no less.

Third, propositional knowledge in Christian theology requires having true beliefs about reality: knowledge of God and knowledge of the world he created. Christian philosophers and theologians may disagree about whether we need to be able to justify every belief, but all agree *knowledge requires believing something that is true.* As J. P. Moreland and William Lane Craig observed, "There could be truth without knowledge, but no knowledge without truth."[29] Evangelical theologians and philosophers typically affirm the correspondence theory of truth described in chapter 2. According to this theory of truth, our beliefs about God are true only when they relate to who he is in reality.

Fourth, knowledge of God is not "blind faith" but belief accompanied by good reasons for holding those beliefs. Christian philosophers may define "knowledge" differently, but all agree that we have biblical warrant for using our God-given gift of reason to form our beliefs. Arguments for God's existence and evidence for the reliability of the Bible can give us confidence in our faith. Religious experiences can also be used to support our claims, especially if they come from reliable witnesses or well-functioning mental faculties.

---

the World" (Scripture) to describe this threefold Word of God. See Kreider and Swigel, *A Practical Primer on Theological Method: Table Manners for Discussing God, His Works, and His Ways* (Grand Rapids: Zondervan, 2019), 17–19.

[29] J. P. Moreland and William Lane Craig, *Philosophical Foundations for a Christian Worldview,* 2nd ed. (Downers Grove, IL: InterVarsity Press, 2017), 72.

Finally, knowledge in Christian theology does not require complete certainty. This claim throws some of my students for a loop, especially when talking about theological claims like the existence of God, the deity of Jesus, and the resurrection. But as Moreland observed, we can only be certain about a belief "if it is utterly impossible that one be mistaken about it."[30] The only beliefs that fall into this category include basic principles of math and certainty of our own existence. Not putting the burden of certainty on Christian beliefs for knowledge is important.

Even when I deal with occasional doubt or encounter a plausible argument against the resurrection of Jesus, *I can still know Jesus has been raised from the dead.* Moreland added, "When we seek knowledge of God, specific biblical texts, morality, and a host of other things, we should not assume that our search requires reaching a state with no doubt, no plausible counterarguments, no possibility of being mistaken. When people believe that knowledge *requires* certainty, they will fail to take themselves to have knowledge if they lack certainty. In turn, this will lead to a lack of confidence and courage regarding one's ability to count on the things one knows."[31]

Becoming an Intellectually Virtuous Disciple

In recent decades, Christian philosophers have turned their attention toward **virtue epistemology**, a flourishing new field in the study of knowledge that focuses on developing *the character of the knower.*[32] Whereas the traditional epistemology has a been a *descriptive* discipline, virtue

---

[30] J. P. Moreland, *Kingdom Triangle: Recover the Christian Mind, Renovate the Soul, Restore the Spirit's Power* (Grand Rapids: Zondervan, 2007), 121.

[31] Moreland, 121.

[32] Linda Trinkaus Zagzebski, *Virtues of the Mind: An Inquiry into the Nature of Virtue and the Ethical Foundations of Knowledge* (Cambridge: Cambridge University Press, 1996); W. Jay Wood, *Epistemology: Becoming Intellectually Virtuous* (Downers Grove, IL: InterVarsity Press, 1998); Robert C. Roberts and W. Jay Wood, *Intellectual Virtues: An Essay in Regulative Epistemology* (New York: Oxford University Press, 2007).

epistemology is more *prescriptive* in nature. For virtue epistemologists, how we use our mind is a matter of moral character or virtue.

An intellectually virtuous person pursues truth in much the same way a morally virtuous person pursues righteousness or justice. Christian philosopher W. Jay Wood has identified different intellectual virtues required in four stages of belief: (1) when we *acquire* beliefs, (2) when we *maintain* beliefs, (3) when we *communicate* our beliefs, and (4) when we *apply* our beliefs to specific challenges we face.

Virtues of the Lifelong Theology Student

When we are acquiring beliefs, being *inquisitive*, being *teachable*, and being *attentive* are all valuable characteristics in the pursuit of truth.[33] These virtues have clear parallels to statements found in the wisdom literature of Scripture. Of the virtue of studiousness, the proverb tells us, "The mind of the discerning acquires knowledge, and the ear of the wise seeks it" (Prov 18:15).

By contrast, the intellectual vice of foolishness spurns knowledge and instruction (Prov 1:7). An individual with a teachable spirit loves knowledge and is humble enough to receive correction when needed (Prov 12:1). Ponder this: the desire to be right is quite different from the desire to know truth. Only an insecure person afraid of what the truth will cost him insists he is right no matter what. By contrast, the desire to know truth grows out of humble engagement with reality. The person with a teachable spirit cares more *about knowing* than about being right!

The intellectually virtuous pay attention to their surroundings and observe carefully what they need to learn. The idea of paying careful attention to wise instruction and the instruction of the Lord is a repeated theme throughout the Old Testament (Prov 4:20; 22:17; Jer 6:19; 9:20). The author of Hebrews added, "We must pay attention all the more to what we have heard, so that we will not drift away" (Heb 2:1). Christian theologians need to be characterized by holy curiosity

---

[33] Wood, *Epistemology*, 34–35.

and attention to detail in their reflection on God's self-revelation in nature and in Scripture.

Virtues of a Steadfast Faith

Though teachability is an important virtue of the mind, it should not be confused with a brand of open-mindedness susceptible to any idea. Biblical authors care more about having a renewed mind than an open one (Rom 12:1–2). They warn us about deceptive ideas that can result in our destruction (2 Cor 11:3–4; Gal 1:6–9; 2 Pet 2:1–3). We live our lives under the authority of God's Word, openly receiving what he has for us. We also need to practice intellectual virtue when maintaining our beliefs. In the study of Christian theology, this means going deeper in our understanding of what we already believe (again, faith seeking understanding) and being prepared to defend our beliefs when they come under the scrutiny of others.[34]

As an intellectual virtue, *firmness* speaks to the tenacity of our beliefs—not a closed-mindedness unable to self-correct but rather a healthy and reasonable confidence in what we believe that will not be easily shaken.[35] Biblical authors tell us to "hold fast" to the instruction we have been given (1 Cor 11:2) and "to hold fast to our confession" (Heb 4:14). In developing this kind of mental toughness, we won't be "tossed by the waves and blown around by every wind of teaching" (Eph 4:14).

Virtues of Teachers and Disciple-Makers

If the aim of learning theology is the proclamation of Christian doctrine, then we need the intellectual virtues associated with communication as well. In addition to skills like eloquence and being able to speak articulately, we will better serve disciples and local churches if we embody what Wood calls *pedagogical virtues*. These virtues include clarity, creativity,

---

[34] Wood, 37–38.
[35] Roberts and Wood, *Intellectual Virtues*, 183–214.

humility, and patience.[36] The best teachers of any subject strive to know their students, discern their capabilities, and communicate ideas in ways that make sense to their hearers. They are patient with their learners, more concerned about instilling knowledge than checking boxes or submitting grades. This is especially true of the Christian disciple-maker: he is more interested in seeing people learn to obey Jesus than hearing his own voice.

The Christian theologian must also practice intellectual virtues relevant to application. Theologians must reply to other theologians, to cultural crises, or to situations in the life of the church. This part of the job calls for a lot of thinking on our feet and flexibility. A theologian capable of responding to new challenges has virtues like clarity of thought, foresight, and problem-solving abilities.[37] Scripture has much to say about planning for contingencies (Prov 15:2; 21:25; Luke 14:28) and growing in wisdom for decision-making (Prov 3:5–6).

The pursuit of intellectual virtues goes hand-in-hand with our call as Christian disciples to love God with our whole minds. We become intellectually virtuous by learning habits and patterns of virtue. As a student preparing for ministry, this means, at some point, we need to put down the smartphones and Xbox controllers. We need to read widely. Exchange laziness of thought for a thought life of devotion to Christ, but forging these habits takes time and discipline.

KEY TERMS

epistemology
"faith seeking understanding"
fideist
knowledge, acquaintance
knowledge, competence
knowledge, propositional

noetic effects of sin
ontological argument
rationalism
rationalist
rationality
virtue epistemology

---

[36] Wood, *Epistemology*, 39–40.
[37] Wood, 40–41.

GO DEEPER

Dew, James K., Jr., and Mark W. Foreman. *How Do We Know? An Introduction to Epistemology*. Downers Grove, IL: InterVarsity Press, 2014.

McGrath, Alister E. *The Passionate Intellect: Christian Faith and the Discipleship of the Mind*. Downers Grove, IL: InterVarsity Press, 2014.

Moreland, J. P. *Kingdom Triangle: Recover the Christian Mind, Renovate the Soul, Restore the Spirit's Power*. Grand Rapids: Zondervan, 2007.

Mouw, Richard J. *Called to the Life of the Mind: Some Advice for Evangelical Scholars*. Grand Rapids: Eerdmans, 2014.

Wood, W. Jay. *Epistemology: Becoming Intellectually Virtuous*. Downers Grove, IL: InterVarsity Press, 1998.

PART THREE

Procedures

*Working through the resources
of Christian theology*

Scripture and
Its Interpretation

Sanctify them by the truth; your word is truth.
—JESUS, IN JOHN 17:17

All Scripture is given by inspiration of God,
and is profitable for doctrine.
—2 TIMOTHY 3:16 NKJV

The way we see the Bible will shape the way we read it and approach the whole theological enterprise.[1] A good many unbelieving academics reduce the Bible to an ancient literary artifact, meant to be examined and observed only for what it tells us about long-dead cultures and their religious beliefs. If you peruse the "Christian living" section at your local bookstore, you might find many people seem to think of the Bible

---

[1] While I disagree with many of his conclusions, David Kelsey effectively argued this in his *Proving Doctrine: The Uses of Scripture in Modern Theology* (Harrisburg, PA: Trinity Press International, 1999).

primarily as an instruction manual for better eating, better finances, better marriages, and living your best life now. Still others use the Bible solely for emotional support, as a morning pick-me-up meant to be casually perused with coffee and a five-minute devotional reading.

While the Bible is, in fact, a collection of literary works that tells us of other times and places, it is more than a sourcebook for history or ancient religion. Yes, the Bible gives us practical guidance for daily living and instills in us much-needed wisdom, but it is more than a guidebook to the good life. While no source is richer for nourishing our emotional wounds and guiding us through the dark nights of the soul, the Bible is more than a self-help manual. All these uses of the Bible are woefully insufficient, falling short of its intended purpose.

The people of God see and confess Scripture as the Word of God. The work of biblical scholarship is crucial. We need a solid grasp of biblical languages, the historical settings of these texts, and the cultures that shaped them. But Christian theology is much more than biblical exegesis—and considerably more than a simple description of what biblical writers said in the past. Theologians want more than a mere grasp of the textual medium that conveys God's message. We want to grow in our understanding of the divine subject matter of Scripture himself. We read the Bible as the Word of God in order to know God, to grow in our love for him, and to obey him more fully.

Scripture as Special Revelation

Our notion of divine revelation is always closely tied to our understanding of God's nature.[2] For atheists, no god means no divine revelation. For pantheists who believe everything is god, everything is revelation, albeit impersonal revelation. The eighteenth-century English Deists believed in a god who wound creation up like a clock and let it go without any further involvement. Consequently, they had no concept of or need for

---

[2] John Webster, *Holy Scripture: A Dogmatic Sketch* (New York: Cambridge University Press, 2003), 13–17.

direct revelation. Their absentee father apparently wanted to stay out of sight, unbothered by those pesky human beings who are always asking for miracles, signs, and loving affirmations.

Unlike the gods of atheism, pantheism, and Deism, the God of the Bible is, by nature, a communicative agent who wants to make himself known. As Kevin Vanhoozer described him, "The God of Israel, Jesus, and the church is not an idea to debate or a force to manipulate but an agent who speaks and acts."[3] The activity of the Trinity described in the Bible is all about intentional communication. The Father sends the Son to communicate his grace and truth (John 1:14, 18). The Son conveys the words the Father gave him (John 17:8). The Spirit guides us in all truth, communicating the message he has received from the Son (John 16:13).[4]

As John Webster so eloquently defined it, "revelation is the self-presentation of the triune God, the free work of sovereign mercy in which God wills, establishes, and perfects saving fellowship with himself in which humankind comes to know, love, and fear him above all things."[5] God reveals *who he is* to us by gifting us with *his presence.* He *freely* chooses to reveal himself to us, meaning we cannot discover him on our own. This self-revelation is an act of *mercy* toward sinful creatures whereby he establishes *salvation* for and *fellowship* with those whom he loves.[6]

God reveals himself in both his *world*, through general revelation, and his *Word*, through special revelation. General revelation is God's self-presentation to all individuals everywhere in nature (Ps 19:1–4; Rom 1:19–20), the human conscience (Rom 2:14–16), and providential history (Acts 17:24–27). This general revelation in nature only affords us impressions of his "eternal power and divine nature" (Rom 1:20) and moral obligations (Rom 2:15). General revelation points us to God's

---

[3] Kevin J. Vanhoozer, *Remythologizing Theology: Divine Action, Passion, and Authorship* (New York: Cambridge University Press, 2010).

[4] Kevin J. Vanhoozer, *First Theology: God, Scripture, and Hermeneutics* (Downers Grove, IL: InterVarsity Press, 2002), 168–69.

[5] Webster, *Holy Scripture*, 13, italics in original.

[6] Webster, 13–17.

existence, but it also condemns us. Because we *know* of God's existence through creation and still *suppress that truth*, God is justified in revealing his wrath against us (Rom 1:18–19).

Without special revelation, we would know nothing of God's activity in the church or Israel, his covenants, or his plan of salvation. Special revelation is God's gracious self-disclosure through the patriarchs, prophets, apostles, and most importantly, Jesus Christ (John 1:18; Col 1:15). As the author of Hebrews explained, "Long ago God spoke to our ancestors by the prophets at different times and in different ways. In these last days, he has spoken to us by his Son . . . the radiance of God's glory and the exact expression of his nature" (Heb 1:1–3). Yet God's word in creation, the Word made incarnate in Christ, and the written Word of God all constitute a single message: "I am the Lord, and there is no other; there is no God but me. I will strengthen you, though you do not know me" (Isa 45:5).[7]

All Scripture Is Inspired by God

In what sense does the church today receive God's self-disclosure in Christ if Jesus ascended to the right hand of God two millennia ago (Acts 1:9–11)? As Scripture itself attests, God's self-revelation in Christ is preserved for us in the **inspiration of Scripture**. The sixty-six books of the biblical canon are Scripture through which God covenants with his people, providing a way for them to know of his salvation and paternal care. Scripture is more than a human record of God's past revelation; it continues to act as God's revelation to us now. It is the primary means by which God communicates his nature and will to his people today. God has spoken, and we who are his people will listen carefully (Deut 32:1–2; Luke 11:28; John 8:47; Rom 10:17; Jas 1:22).

When we speak of the inspiration of Scripture, we are calling attention to its divine origin. It is related to a term the apostle Paul coined that means "God-inspired," "God-breathed," or "God-spirited" (*theopneustos*) in 2 Tim 3:16: "All Scripture is *breathed out* by God" (ESV, emphasis

---

[7] Spykman, *Reformational Theology*, 85–87 (see intro., n.1).

added). Just as God gave Adam life by breathing "the breath of life into his nostrils" (Gen 2:7), God gave the words of Scripture life by his Spirit (Heb 4:12).

While Scripture is inspired by the Holy Spirit of God, it is also human in its expression, concepts, and content. Scripture is God's Word written by men who "spoke from God as they were carried along by the Holy Spirit" (2 Pet 1:21). Paul recognized this aspect of God's work in his life when he commended the Thessalonian Christians for receiving "the word of God that you heard from us . . . not as a human message, but as it truly is, the word of God, which also works effectively in you who believe" (1 Thess 2:13). We recognize Scripture has a dual divine-human authorship; it is truly God's word in human words.[8]

Theologians outside of evangelicalism differ greatly on the doctrine of inspiration. On one extreme, theologians in liberal Protestant traditions have reduced the "inspiration" of Scripture to a kind of metaphor, saying the Bible is only "inspired" in the way a great work of art or literature is inspired. God may have been a muse to biblical authors, giving them heightened religious insight, but he was not a direct source of revelation or even a collaborator on their work. But if the Bible is merely a human book, no one reading it can ever say "this is what the LORD says" (Exod 4:22; Josh 24:2; Judg 6:8) with any confidence. If the Bible is merely a human book, it cannot be the final standard of Christian doctrine as human knowledge is subject to growth and change.

On the opposite side of the theological spectrum, a few fundamentalist theologians assert God literally dictated the words of Scripture to its authors, like a manager would dictate a letter to a secretary.[9] This theory, while seeking to preserve God's work in inspiration, neglects the human element of Scripture. While it is true that the biblical authors were occasionally told to write down what they saw and heard (Exod 34:27;

---

[8] David S. Dockery, *Christian Scripture: An Evangelical Perspective on Inspiration, Authority, and Interpretation* (Nashville: B&H, 1995), 38.

[9] The most infamous twentieth-century example of this view of inspiration can be found in John R. Rice, *Our God-Breathed Book—The Bible* (Murfreesboro, TN: Sword of the Lord, 1969).

Jer 30:2; Rev. 1:19), biblical writers also described a process of writing by investigative reporting (Luke 1:1–4, Acts 1:1) and personal letter writing (Gal 6:11; 2 John 12; 3 John 13). The personalities and interests of human authors explain why there are multiple accounts of the same story told from different angles (e.g., stories about David in 1 and 2 Samuel and 1 Chronicles, the Gospels, etc.). Biblical authors talk about the styles of other authors, such as the case of Peter describing "some things that are hard to understand" in Paul's letters (2 Pet 3:16 NIV). While divine in origin, the Bible is still a human book.

Evangelicals seek a way between the impasse of liberal and fundamentalist options. Evangelical theologians apply the phrase **verbal-plenary inspiration** to describe the inspiration of Scripture. Verbal-plenary simply means "every word." This theory states that every word, somehow, someway was inspired by God. By this phrase, we mean that God spoke through human beings in such a way that (1) every word of Scripture is in fact the Word of God but also (2) human words, thoughts, and ideas are still expressed.

The verbal-plenary theory of inspiration does not tell us *how* God inspired the words of Scripture, only *that* God inspired all the words, that he sovereignly worked through human agency to produce exactly what he wanted his people to have preserved in his written Word. Because it does not focus on mechanics, this theory allows for God to inspire human authors in various ways. In some cases, God does directly tell authors what to write down, but in most cases, he is orchestrating the free choices, actions, and personalities of human beings in order to bring about the exact result he wanted in Scripture. Verbal-plenary inspiration means we not only possess the ideas God wanted to convey through human personalities but also have the direct communication of God through words.

The Authority of Scripture

Paul made an important correlation between the inspiration of Scripture and its authority in the lives of God's people: "All Scripture is inspired by God and is profitable *for teaching, for rebuking, for correcting, for training in righteousness*, so that the man of God may be complete, equipped for every good work" (2 Tim 3:16–17, emphasis added). Only Scripture has been divinely inspired in this way, and consequently, only Scripture has authority over what we teach, over how we correct, and over how we train men and women in personal holiness.

When we call the Bible an "authority," we do not mean biblical authors are merely experts on subject matters pertinent to our lives (though they are). We do not call the Bible an "authority" in the democratic sense of the term; we do not authorize the Bible to rule over us by popular consensus. The church does not grant the Bible its divine authority; it merely recognizes God's divine authority through Scripture.[10]

Instead, we are called to walk in submission to the authority of Scripture, or rather, the authority of God expressed through it. The authority of Scripture is not the authority of an independent book, like a law code. As N. T. Wright has remarked, "The 'authority of Scripture' is shorthand for 'God's authority exercised *through* Scripture.'"[11] Through his written Word, God conveys what we need to know to follow him and to train others to follow him. As disciples, we must yield to the authority of God in Scripture; learn what he desires to teach us; and place our complete trust in him as he communes with us through Scripture.

All Scripture Is Trustworthy and True

The affirmation of biblical **inerrancy** is an indispensable characteristic of evangelicalism as a movement and as a theological framework. Though the term *inerrancy* only dates back to the modern period, it was not, as erroneously suggested by some, a fabrication of nineteenth-century conservative scholarship.[12] Faithful Christians have always made

---

[10] Webster, *Holy Scripture*, 56.

[11] N. T. Wright, *Scripture and the Authority of God: How to Read the Bible Today* (New York: HarperCollins, 2013), 21.

[12] This idea was made popular by Jack B. Rogers and Donald K. McKim, *The Authority and Interpretation of the Bible: A Historical Approach* (San Francisco: Harper & Row, 1979).

this judgment about Scripture.[13] For Irenaeus, "the Scriptures are indeed perfect, since they were spoken by the Word of God and his Spirit."[14] Augustine declared biblical authors under the inspiration of the Spirit to be "completely free from error."[15] For Thomas Aquinas, only Scripture could correct the errors of human reason.[16] Martin Luther asserted Scripture "never erred" and "cannot err."[17] This consensus of the church went virtually undisputed until the Enlightenment, which resulted in a distrust of revealed religion and the rise of higher biblical criticism. In the nineteenth and twentieth centuries, Protestant evangelicals, including my own Southern Baptist tradition, fought vigorously over the inerrancy of Scripture.

The evangelical doctrine of biblical inerrancy is a recognition of the total truthfulness and trustworthiness of the biblical text as it was originally inspired. This doctrine is the necessary logical consequent of the beliefs that God is truthful and trustworthy in everything he does and that all Scriptures are inspired by God. God, who cannot lie (Num 23:19; Titus 1:2; Heb 6:18), gives us a completely true and trustworthy expression of himself in his written Word. Without a commitment to the full truthfulness and trustworthiness of Scripture, the notion of biblical authority over our lives is greatly diminished. Those who limit the truthfulness of the Bible to spiritual matters (however they may define them), reduce Scripture to a sounding board useful only where it confirms preconceived ideas.

Inerrancy does not mean every single idea or statement quoted in Scripture is true. The fool, for example, says, "There's no God" (Ps 14:1; cf. 10:4; 53:1). But inerrancy does mean everything the authors of Scripture do affirm to be true is true. In the book of Job, which reads like a poetic play, Job's well-meaning but knuckleheaded friends Eliphaz,

[13] Every historical reference in this paragraph comes from Allison, *Historical Theology*, 99–119 (see chap. 4, n. 15).

[14] Irenaeus, *Against Heresies* 2.28.2.

[15] Augustine, *Letter* 28, to Jerome, in *NPNF*[1], 1:350.

[16] Thomas Aquinas, *Summa Theologica* 1.1.1.

[17] Robert D. Preus, "The View of the Bible Held by the Church: The Early Church through Luther," in *Inerrancy*, ed. Norman L. Geisler (Grand Rapids: Zondervan, 1982), 379.

Bildad, and Zophar counsel their grieving friend with untruths, such as the only cause for suffering is sin (4:1–5:27; 8:1–22; 11:1–20; 15:1–35; 18:1–21; 20:1–29) and assert Job's calamity must be a consequence of his sin (22:1–30; 25:1–6). The author of Job does not affirm these beliefs but truthfully conveys them as alternatives to the worldview of Job and God's dramatic self-disclosure at the end of the book (38:1–41:34).

Critics will often charge the Bible with factual errors, grammatical errors, contradictions, changes in the manuscript tradition, and other inconsistencies. The phenomena of Scripture do present us with difficulties regarding chronologies, numbers, and theological tensions.[18] Many of these difficulties stem from the imposition of modern standards of precision on the Bible. But as Matthew Barrett observed, "Truth and precision are *not* the same thing. Scripture can be completely truthful in what it asserts and affirms, without being totally precise."[19] Barrett then pointed to eight qualifications of inerrancy given by Paul Feinberg (1938–2004) as a helpful guide for distinguishing between truth and scientific or historical precision:

1. Inerrancy does not demand strict adherence to the rules of grammar. . . .
2. Inerrancy does not exclude the use either of figures of speech or of a given literary genre. . . .
3. Inerrancy does not demand historical or semantic precision. . . .
4. Inerrancy does not demand the technical language of modern science. . . .
5. Inerrancy does not require verbal exactness in the citation of the Old Testament by the New. . . .
6. Inerrancy does not demand that the *Logia Jesu* (the sayings of Jesus) contain the *ipsissima verba* (the exact words) of Jesus, only the *ipsissima vox* (the exact voice). . . .

---

[18] See Erickson, *Christian Theology*, 198–99 (see chap. 1, n. 18).

[19] Matthew Barrett, *God's Word Alone: The Authority of Scripture: What the Reformers Taught . . . and Why It Still Matters* (Grand Rapids: Zondervan, 2016), 269.

7. Inerrancy does not guarantee the exhaustive comprehensiveness of any single account or of combined accounts where those are involved. . . .

8. Inerrancy does not demand the infallibility or inerrancy of the noninspired sources used by biblical writers.[20]

We cannot expect the human authors of Scripture to use all literal language, journalism-standard quotations, and mathematical accuracy if such precision was beyond their authorial intent and irrelevant to the literary and historical contexts in which they wrote.

Recognizing these challenges, contemporary evangelical definitions of inerrancy seek "to be faithful to the phenomena of Scripture as well as theological affirmations in Scripture about the veracity of God."[21] David Dockery achieved this balance in his own definition of inerrancy: "When all the facts are known, the Bible (in its original writings) properly interpreted in light of which culture and communication means had developed by the time of its composition will be shown to be completely true (and therefore not false) in all that it affirms, to the degree of precision intended by the author, in all matters relating to God and his creation."[22]

Vanhoozer streamlined this definition, noting that faith in biblical inerrancy means the biblical "authors speak the truth in all things they affirm (when they make affirmations), and will eventually be seen to have spoken truly (when right readers read rightly)."[23] Scripture guarantees us that what the Bible says is true, but it does not guarantee our interpretations of its truth will be. The pursuit of true doctrine rooted in God's true and trustworthy Word requires close attention to "the language and

---

[20] Paul Feinberg, "The Meaning of Inerrancy," in *Inerrancy*, ed. Norman L. Geisler (Grand Rapids: Zondervan, 1980), 299–302; Barrett, *God's Word Alone*, 268.

[21] Dockery, *Christian Scripture*, 64.

[22] Dockery, 64.

[23] Vanhoozer, "Augustinian Inerrancy," 207 (see chap. 2, n. 33).

the literary form" of biblical books.[24] Faithful theological interpretation requires "right-hearted and right-minded readers."[25]

Perhaps the most important implication of the doctrine of inerrancy for theological method is the unified message of the Bible. If all Scripture is true, and no Scripture disagrees with any other passage of Scripture, then the Bible presents a unified, coherent vision of God and his world. Biblical authors take diverse approaches to biblical truth to be sure, but they never contradict one another. Because the same truthful God is the ultimate source of all biblical revelation, it is quite possible for interpreters and theologians to arrive at *the* biblical perspective on theological and practical issues.

All Scripture Is Capable of Being Understood

The church has historically recognized the **clarity of Scripture**—the idea that the Bible plainly teaches truths everyone must believe.[26] But this recognition does not mean all portions of Scripture are equally easy to understand or that the meaning of biblical texts cannot be distorted by lousy interpretations (2 Pet 3:15–16). The doctrine of Scripture's clarity only means God has made his message intelligible by the inspiration of Scripture and the **illumination of the Holy Spirit**. As Wayne Grudem explained it, the clarity of Scripture means "*the Bible is written in such a way that its teachings are able to be understood by all who read it, seeking God's help and being willing to follow it.*"[27] Gregg Allison contended that the Bible is "comprehensible to all believers who possess the normal acquired ability to understand oral communication and/or written discourse, regardless of their gender, age, education, language, or cultural background."[28]

---

[24] Vanhoozer, 211–12.

[25] Vanhoozer, 207n24.

[26] See Allison, *Historical Theology*, 120–41.

[27] Grudem, *Systematic Theology*, 108, italics in original.

[28] Gregg R. Allison, "The Protestant Doctrine of the Perspicuity of Scripture: A Reformulation on the Basis of Biblical Teaching," (PhD diss., Trinity Divinity School, 1995), 516.

Through the illumination of the Holy Spirit, believers can believe God's Word, grasp its most basic truths, and respond in obedience to its direction (John 14:26; 16:13; 1 Cor 2:14–16).[29] However, the meaning of the Bible is not gleaned automatically or by osmosis. The Bible must be read and interpreted. As imperfect interpreters of Scripture who eagerly await the day in which the things that hinder our complete knowledge of God are removed (1 Cor 13:12; 1 John 3:2b), we are capable of misunderstanding Scripture.[30] For this reason, we must continually seek to grow in our understanding of God's Word. The canon of Scripture may be closed, but Christians must continue to grow in their understanding of its meaning and application.[31]

Scripture Is Sufficient

The slogan *sola Scriptura* ("Scripture alone") became a common catchphrase to describe the Protestant understanding of the **sufficiency of Scripture**. *Sola Scriptura* is *not* a denial of other sources of knowledge but rather an affirmation of the adequacy of Scripture in things that pertain to salvation, faith, and Christian obedience. For evangelicals, theology may have many sources, but it only has one norm, one measuring rod to which these theological sources must be subjected. James Leo Garrett (1925–2020) coined the phrase *suprema Scriptura* as a helpful complement to the Reformation phrase *sola Scriptura*.[32] Scripture, the only inerrant and infallible resource of Christian theology, is the supreme source of theological knowledge and only standard for Christian belief and practice.

---

[29] John Calvin, *Institutes of the Christian Religion*, 1.9.3.

[30] Putman, *When Doctrine Divides the People of God*, 37–66 (see chap. 2, n. 35).

[31] Daniel J. Treier, "The Freedom of God's Word: Toward an 'Evangelical' Dogmatics of Scripture," in *The Voice of God in the Text of Scripture*, ed. Oliver D. Crisp and Fred Sanders (Grand Rapids: Zondervan, 2016), 31.

[32] James Leo Garrett, *Systematic Theology*, vol. 1, 3rd ed. (North Richland Hills, TX: B.I.B.A.L., 2007), 206–9.

First, it is a declaration that the knowledge of God gleaned from general revelation is insufficient to save.[33] Second, the sufficiency of Scripture also means we who are God's people need no additional signs or revelations from God to know him and obey him. Third, sufficiency is also a statement about the clarity of Scripture. With the help of the Holy Spirit, the basic meaning of Scripture can be understood by an ordinary believer. She does not need a "magisterium" or an official church teaching office to tell her what the Bible means.[34]

The Protestant and evangelical devotion to scriptural sufficiency does not mean Scripture is the only resource for studying theology or learning about God's world, but it does mean every other resource (e.g., creeds, confessions, philosophy, science, psychology) must be subjected to Scripture. Because Scripture alone is inerrant and infallible, Scripture is the only measuring rod by which these other sources based in human reason, experience, and general revelation can be assessed. The integration of other resources like tradition, reason, and experience into the theological method of John Wesley (1703–1791) has been called the **quadrilateral method**. This quadrilateral refers to a four-sided fortress used for defense in battle. Wesley did not regard tradition, reason, and experience as equals to Scripture but as other sources that can support or defend biblical truth.[35]

Matthew Barrett lists two helpful measures that must be acknowledged whenever we employ extrabiblical resources like tradition, philosophy, experience, or any other academic discipline from the humanities, the natural sciences, and the social sciences. First, we must acknowledge

---

[33] As the authors of *The Second London Baptist Confession* (1689) contrast the sufficiency of Scripture with the insufficiency of general revelation, "The Holy Scripture is the only sufficient, certain, and infallible rule of all saving knowledge, faith, and obedience, although the light of nature, and the works of creation and providence do so far manifest the goodness, wisdom, and power of God, as to leave men inexcusable; yet are they not sufficient to give that knowledge of God and his will which is necessary unto salvation" (1.1).

[34] See Mark D. Thompson, *A Clear and Present Word: The Clarity of Scripture* (Downers Grove, IL: InterVarsity Press, 2006), 21–24.

[35] Thomas C. Oden, *John Wesley's Teaching*, vol. 1, *God and Providence* (Grand Rapids: Zondervan, 2012), 83–84.

all extrabiblical resources in theology are fallible and capable of error. Protestant evangelicals do not acknowledge an inerrant church council or an infallible pope. Second, "our use of extrabiblical sources can never be done *independently* of Scripture."[36] These resources *aid* us in our interpretation of Scripture by providing clarification, additional support, or supplemental knowledge of the world God created. Where "the methods, presuppositions, and conclusions of these disciplines . . . contradict those of Scripture, they must be abandoned."[37]

All Scripture Must Be Interpreted

Hermeneutics (from the Greek word *hermeneuō* meaning "to interpret") is the art and science of interpretation. In a general sense, hermeneutics can describe the interpretation of any text, from the Bible to the *New York Times*, or even "texts" communicating messages and ideas like popular movies or television shows (i.e., **general hermeneutics**). In a Bible college or seminary setting, one usually associates hermeneutics with the strategies taken up by interpreters to understand the meaning of biblical texts (i.e., **biblical hermeneutics**). Whether reading the Bible, the latest issue of *Superman*, or my Instagram feed, interpretation is always about understanding what authors are trying to do with their texts.[38]

According to Andrew Reid, faithful interpretation and application of the Bible involves "five looks" or approaches to the text.

1. *We begin the interpretation of Scripture by "looking up" to God, prayerfully receiving his Word in faith.* We acknowledge Scripture as the Word of God and ask for the illuminating activity of the Spirit to help us believe and apply the direction of the text.
2. *We then "look down" by doing the work of exegesis, trying to discover the meaning of individual texts.*

---

[36] Barrett, *God's Word Alone*, 344.
[37] Barrett, 345.
[38] Klein, Blomberg, and Hubbard, *Introduction to Biblical Interpretation*, 224 (see chap. 5, n. 16).

3–4. *We "look back" to the Old Testament and "look forward" to the New Testament by drawing the connection between individual texts and the grand narrative of Scripture.*

5. *We "look here" by applying the text to our present situation through systematic theology and Christian ethics.*[39]

For disciples of Jesus, the goal of biblical interpretation is to understand and apply the God-inspired meaning of Scripture. Sometimes this is easier said than done. In order to interpret the Bible correctly, we must become familiar with the literary forms of Scripture: its genres and distinct literary devices. Interpreters of Scripture must also make sense of the historical and social contexts of the Bible. We live in a much different world than biblical authors did, and we often struggle to understand the ancient social and historical contexts of the biblical text.

All Scripture Is God's Communicative Action

Authors and speakers string words and sentences together to convey meaning. Speakers and writers do more things with words than dispensing information. With words we can give *direction*, *appoint* someone to do a certain task, make a *promise*, ask a *question*, give *blessing*, *repent* of sin, *forgive* someone who has wronged us, *complain*, express *praise*, and a litany of other things.[40] Every text—whether it is the Bible, a novel, a movie, or a commercial—is someone's attempt at communicating through words.

Cambridge philosopher J. L. Austin (1911–1960) first developed **speech-act theory** as a way of describing the way we *perform certain*

---

[39] Andrew Reid developed this "five-look" approach, but Christopher Wright and Jonathan Lamb publish it in their *Understanding and Using the Bible* (Minneapolis: Fortress, 2015), 4–7. Trent Hunter and Stephen Wellum take up a slightly modified version of this approach in *Christ from Beginning to End: How the Full Story of Scripture Reveals the Full Glory of Christ* (Grand Rapids: Zondervan, 2018), 33–69.

[40] Anthony C. Thiselton, *New Horizons in Hermeneutics: The Theory and Practice of Transforming Biblical Reading* (Grand Rapids: Zondervan, 1992), 299.

actions with our words.[41] By yelling "Fire!" into a crowded space, an individual either *warns* people about impending danger or pulls a cruel (and illegal) *prank*.[42] With words properly backed by God and the local government, a minister changes the marital status of a happy couple when he pronounces them "husband and wife." With the support of the registrar's office and the authority given to him by the board of trustees, a college president can confer degrees upon students. God said, "Let there be light," and he caused light to come into existence (Gen 1:3). Each of these statements *change the world* with the words uttered.

Austin and his philosophical heirs recognized that we don't just utter words; we do things with words. In every speech-act, four things are happening simultaneously:

(a) Actual words are being spoken or written down (*locutionary acts*).
(b) Words are referring to things, whether they are real or fictitious (*propositional acts*).
(c) The author is trying to do something with her words, like stating a fact, warning, or making a promise (*illocutionary acts*).
(d) Words have an effect on their hearers, like understanding an idea, being warned, or obeying the speaker (*perlocutionary acts*).[43]

Every time I speak to my students, write an email, send a text message, or preach a sermon, these four elements come together. I am using written or spoken words (the **locutionary act**) that refer to something or someone (the **propositional act**) in order to communicate something (the **illocutionary act**) that provokes a response on the part of my hearer or reader (the **perlocutionary act**).

Every sentence, passage, book, and genre in the Bible is written with the *intention* to do something with its words. Every sentence conveys

[41] J. L. Austin, *How to Do Things with Words*, 2nd ed. (Cambridge, MA: Harvard University Press, 1975).

[42] Horton, *Christian Faith*, 119 (see chap. 2, n. 9).

[43] See John Searle, *Speech Acts: An Essay in the Philosophy of Language* (New York: Cambridge University Press, 1969), 24–25. For clarity, I have changed Searle's phrase *utterance act* to the more common designation of *locutionary act*.

purpose within the context of a passage, and every passage fits within the larger contexts of the book, the testament, and the canon. While every biblical text *reveals* something to us about God, God's communicative action in Scripture is much more diverse than revealing or disclosing information.[44] With his words, God makes covenants, makes promises, and comforts his people. The diversity of the canon implies a diversity of speech-acts. The central task of the interpreter is seeking to make sense of the divine-human speech-acts of Scripture.

All of God's communicative action ultimately points to Jesus. The Old and New Testaments are a unified divine witness of God's redemptive plan expressed through Christ Jesus. The Old Testament is "prophetic anticipation" of the Word made flesh in Jesus Christ (Luke 24:27; John 5:39). The New Testament is the "apostolic attestation," the Word of God present in Christ.[45] In the end, God has not communicated with us simply to give us information or a system of beliefs. He has spoken to us to redeem us and to make us a people for himself.[46]

KEY TERMS

biblical hermeneutics

clarity, of Scripture

general hermeneutics

hermeneutics

illocutionary act

illumination, of the Holy Spirit

inerrancy, of Scripture

inspiration, of Scripture

inspiration, verbal-plenary

locutionary act

perlocutionary act

propositional act

quadrilateral method

special hermeneutics

speech-act theory

sufficiency, of Scripture

---

[44] See Nicholas Wolterstorff, *Divine Discourse: Philosophical Reflections on the Claim That God Speaks* (New York: Cambridge University Press, 1995), 19–36. As Wolterstroff reminds us, not all God's speech is "revealing."

[45] Treier, "The Freedom of God's Word," 30.

[46] Horton, *The Christian Faith*, 122.

GOING DEEPER

Barrett, Matthew. *God's Word Alone: The Authority of Scripture—What the Reformers Taught . . . and Why It Still Matters*. Grand Rapids: Zondervan, 2016.

Dockery, David S. *Christian Scripture: An Evangelical Perspective on Inspiration, Authority, and Interpretation*. Nashville: B&H, 1995.

Hunter, Trent, and Stephen Wellum. *Christ from Beginning to End: How the Full Story of Scripture Reveals the Full Glory of Christ*. Grand Rapids: Zondervan, 2018.

Naselli, Andrew David. *How to Understand and Apply the New Testament: Twelve Steps from Exegesis to Theology*. Phillipsburg, NJ: P&R, 2017.

Vanhoozer, Kevin J. *First Theology: God, Scripture, and Hermeneutics*. Downers Grove, IL: InterVarsity Press, 2002.

Webster, John. *Holy Scripture: A Dogmatic Sketch*. New York: Cambridge University Press, 2003.

Wright, N. T. *Scripture and the Authority of God: How to Read the Bible Today*. New York: HarperCollins, 2013.

8

Tradition and Christian Theology

Tradition is the living faith of the dead, traditionalism is the dead faith of the living. And I suppose I should add that traditionalism is what gives tradition a bad name.
—Jaroslav Pelikan, *The Vindication of Tradition*

I recently heard a student grumble about the way some pastors and theologians frequently reference figures like Athanasius, Augustine, Anselm, Aquinas, Calvin, Luther, Wesley, and Spurgeon in their sermons and theological discussions. His objection was straightforward: "Why should I care what these dead men think when they are no authority over me? I have Scripture, and I can read it for myself. It is the only authority I need!"

People of faith can go to one of two unhelpful extremes with tradition. The first extreme is a rejection of tradition altogether sometimes associated with some "low-church" Christian groups whose mantra is "No creed but the Bible!" This statement, which, ironically, is a creed itself, comes from a misunderstanding of the Protestant doctrine of *sola Scriptura* ("Scripture alone"). Timothy George calls this anti-traditional, anti-creedal posture *nuda scriptura* ("bare scripture").[1] This position is sometimes described as naïve biblicism because its proponents are against the use of any language not explicitly stated in Scripture (e.g., Trinity, inerrancy, etc.).

The other extreme is elevating tradition to a place equal to or greater than the authority of Scripture in the formation of beliefs and practices. The *Catechism of the Catholic Church* openly endorses this joint authority of Scripture and Tradition: "Both Scripture and Tradition must be accepted and honored with equal sentiments of devotion and reverence."[2] This excessive devotion to tradition essentially makes it another source of revelation alongside Scripture, opening the door for extrabiblical doctrines. When Martin Luther challenged the sale of indulgences to reduce time in purgatory, he was essentially challenging this dangerous devotion to extrabiblical tradition.

In this chapter we will explore the various uses of tradition in Christian theology and discipleship. After defining tradition and making a case for its usefulness in doctrine, we will explore the various ways historical theologians approach the tradition and provide some basic instructions for researching tradition and using it in discipleship ministries.

What Is Tradition?

Tradition is a term with many different uses in Christian and theological literature, and much of the controversy surrounding the value of tradition is wrapped up with how we define it. Three uses of the word are important for studying historical theology.

First, tradition in the broadest sense refers to any information, custom, or belief that is transmitted from one individual or group to another. This definition of *tradition* closely reflects the etymology of the Latin (*traditio*

---

[1] Timothy George, "An Evangelical Reflection on Scripture and Tradition," *Pro Ecclesia* 9 (Spring 2000): 206.

[2] *Catechism of the Catholic Church*, 2nd ed. (New York: Doubleday, 2012), 31.

and *tradere*) and Greek (*parádosis* and *paradidómi*) from which it comes. These terms describe "handing over" a property or idea from one individual or group to another.[3] With tradition, we pass along deeply held beliefs or humbler things like family recipes or sports rituals. A lot of what we call "common sense" is wisdom passed down to us in the form of tradition. Tradition is the primary way people learn things apart from firsthand experience.[4]

The Christian faith itself is a tradition in this broad sense of the term, because it is a "faith that was delivered to the saints once for all" (a vertical transmission) and one that is transmitted from one disciple to another (a horizontal transmission). The Christian tradition builds on the religious tradition of Israel before it. Though Scripture is certainly more than a tradition transmitted from one generation to the next—it is the inerrant Word of God—it is itself part of the larger Christian tradition. The apostles understood they were transmitting a tradition through their writings.

Paul exhorted Timothy to cling to the apostolic tradition: "Hold on to the pattern of sound teaching that you have heard from me, in the faith and love that are in Christ Jesus. Guard the good deposit through the Holy Spirit who lives in us" (2 Tim 1:13–14). He explicitly called this pattern of sound teaching "tradition" in his second letter to the Thessalonian church: "So then, brothers and sisters, stand firm and *hold to the traditions* [*paradoseis*] *you were taught*, whether by what we said or what we wrote" (2 Thess 2:15, emphasis added). Paul celebrated the way the church at Corinth held "fast to the traditions" he delivered (*paredōka*) to them (1 Cor 11:2). He described the gospel itself as a tradition received and transmitted: "For I passed on [*paredōka*] to you as most important what I also received [*parelabon*]: that Christ died for our sins according

---

[3] See Yves Congar, *The Meaning of Tradition*, trans. A. N. Woodrow (San Francisco: Ignatius, 2004), 9–10. The Bible uses this literal meaning to talk about the handing over of Jesus to the authorities (Matt 27:18, 26; Mark 15:10, 15; John 19:16).

[4] See Anthony C. Thiselton, "Knowledge, Myth, and Corporate Memory," in *Believing in the Church: The Corporate Nature of Faith*, compiled by the Doctrine Commission of the Church of England (Wilton, CT: Morehouse-Barlow, 1981), 45–78.

to the Scriptures, that he was buried, that he was raised on the third day according to the Scriptures" (1 Cor 15:3–4).

Second, theologians can use tradition *to refer to the ongoing interpretation and application of Scripture throughout history.* The church fathers did not make the hardline distinction between Scripture and tradition because they perceived no difference in the substance of their teaching and apostolic tradition preserved in Scripture. In their minds, only heretics added to the doctrine of Scripture.[5] The tradition they received and passed along was "the proper and natural interpretation of Scripture."[6] The early theologians did not set out to add to biblical doctrine but to defend it in the face of false teachers like the Gnostics or the Arians who distorted it. The fifth-century Gallic theologian Vincent of Lérins (d. ca. 445) asserted true Christians affirm that "which has been believed everywhere, always, by all."[7]

Over time, Christian tradition developed as the church faced new challenges and new questions. The tradition developed not as a rejection of biblical authority, but as an attempt to understand what the Bible means and how it should be applied. As R. P. C. Hanson (1916–1988) observed, "theologians of the Christian Church were slowly driven to a realization that the deepest questions which face Christianity cannot be answered in purely biblical language, because *the questions are about the meaning of biblical language itself.*"[8] Christian theologians borrowed language from philosophy and coined new, non-biblical terminology to describe the God of the Bible, words like *immutable, Trinity, homoousion,*

---

[5] See Irenaeus, *Against Heresies* 3.2.1–2; Tertullian, *On the Prescription of Heretics* 38. For helpful overviews of early Christian beliefs about biblical authority and its relationship to tradition, see Keith A. Mathison, *The Shape of Sola Scriptura* (Moscow, ID: Canon, 2001), 19–48; Yves Congar, *Tradition and Traditions: A Historical and Theological Essay* (New York: Macmillan, 1966), 107–18.

[6] F. F. Bruce, *Tradition: Old and New* (Eugene, OR: Wipf and Stock, 2006), 116.

[7] Vincent of Lérins, *Commonitory* 2.5; *NPNF²* 11:132.

[8] R. P. C. Hanson, *The Search for the Christian Doctrine of God: The Arian Controversy, 318–381* (New York: T&T Clark, 1988), xxi.

and *perichoresis*. The philosophical Christian tradition continues to make use of the terms they invented.

Christian tradition can take many different shapes. The earliest form of tradition after the New Testament books were written was the "rule of faith" (*regula fidei*). The rule or "canon" was a summary of the apostolic message used to train converts into the Christian faith.[9] It also served as a measuring rod (hence the term "rule" or "ruler") for distinguishing between true doctrine and false doctrine. The rule was used in interpreting Scripture, and it also helped early Christians distinguish biblical Gospels from counterfeit ones like the Gnostic *Gospel of Thomas* or *The Secret Book of John*.[10]

Creeds and confessions are also important vehicles for transmitting interpretations of the Bible's doctrinal content from one generation to the next. The New Testament itself contains several early creeds or creedal fragments from the first-century church (Phil 2:5–11; 1 Tim 3:16; 1 Thess 4:14).[11] By the late second or early third century, Western Christians were reciting an early version of what came to be known as the Apostles' Creed.[12] The Apostles' Creed tells the grand narrative of Scripture in a short, portable fashion. It speaks of the triune God's creative activity, his saving activity in Christ, the ongoing activity of the Spirit in the church, and the future hope of all who serve him.

---

[9] For a helpful summary of the rule and its use in the first four centuries of Christianity, see Everett Ferguson, *The Rule of Faith* (Eugene, OR: Cascade, 2015).

[10] Bruce M. Metzger, *The Canon of the New Testament: Its Origin, Development, and Significance* (New York: Oxford University Press, 1987), 75–99; Lee M. McDonald, *The Formation of the Christian Biblical Canon*, rev. ed. (Peabody, MA: Hendrickson, 1995), 164–69.

[11] Michael F. Bird, *What Christians Ought to Believe: An Introduction to Christian Doctrine through the Apostles' Creed* (Grand Rapids: Zondervan, 2016), 18–21; J. N. D. Kelly, *Early Christian Creeds* (London: Longmans, 1950), 1–29; Vernon H. Neufeld, *The Earliest Christian Confessions*, New Testament Tools and Studies 5 (Leiden: Brill, 1963).

[12] Kelly, *Early Christian Creeds*, 100–204. This earlier iteration of the Apostles' Creed is also known as *Symbolum Apostolorum*.

The ecumenical creeds recognized universally by Christians were formulated in response to heresies that challenged the orthodox faith. The Nicene Creed was drafted by the Council of Nicaea in AD 325 in response to the Arian heresy that denied Jesus's true divinity (and his true humanity). Its later iteration, the Niceno-Constantinopolitan Creed, was formulated by the Council of Constantinople in 381 in response to the semi-Arians who denied the divinity and personhood of the Holy Spirit and the Apollinarians who denied the true humanity of Jesus.[13] The heresies of Nestorianism and Eutychianism propelled the Council at Chalcedon to write their creed in 451. The Chalcedonian Definition affirmed the trinitarian doctrine of Nicaea but further developed the doctrine of the person of Christ, stressing the relationship between the two natures of Christ in one person (what theologians call the *hypostatic union*).

Whereas the ancient creeds had universal recognition, the later Protestant confessions were descriptions of the distinctive doctrines taught in individual traditions. The first major Lutheran confession, the Augsburg Confession, was adopted and presented by German rulers in 1530. The Reformed tradition has numerous confessions of faith, including the Heidelberg Catechism (1563), the Belgic Confession (1566), and the Westminster Confession of Faith (1646). Baptists of different stripes have several confessions that reflect their convictions regarding doctrines like election, predestination, and human freedom. The General or Arminian Baptists had John Smyth's Short Confession (1610) and the Standard Confession (1660), among others. The Reformed Baptist creeds include the Second London Confession (1689), a Baptist revision of the Westminster Confession, and the Abstract of Principles (1858). Southern Baptists today use the Baptist Faith & Message 2000, which developed in a tradition following the New Hampshire Confession of Faith (1833).

The rich bounty of tradition also includes the sermons, commentaries, lexicons, and theological treatises written throughout history.

---

[13] A very thorough history of these events can be found in Hanson, *The Search for the Christian Doctrine of God.*

(Whether we like it or not, I guess theological blog posts will eventually be considered under this heading.) Until Jesus returns, the Christian tradition will continue to grow on earth because there is always a need to interpret and apply Scripture in every successive generation.

Finally, the term tradition *can refer to theological ideas added to Scripture that are given equal status with divine revelation.* Prior to the late medieval period, most Christian theologians recognized Scripture as a materially sufficient source of revelation, meaning it was the only necessary source of Christian revelation and doctrine. Tradition only interprets revelation; it is not itself a source of revelation. Heiko Oberman (1930–2001) called this once-sourced view of revelation **"Tradition I."** But some theologians in the late medieval period gradually came to understand tradition as another source of revelation alongside Scripture (a two-source theory of revelation Oberman dubbed **"Tradition II"**). These medieval churchmen claimed the teachings of the church were a necessary source of revelation in the development of doctrine. Many uniquely Roman Catholic doctrines and practices, such as the doctrine of purgatory and the perpetual virginity of Mary, were justified by Tradition II.[14]

Except for some of the so-called Radical Reformers, most Protestant Reformers held tradition in the sense of "Tradition I" in high regard. Luther frequently appealed to the creeds and the fathers in support of their interpretations of Scripture but denied tradition had "authority to establish new or different articles of faith."[15] John Calvin (1509–1564) called tradition an external aid "by which God invites us into the society of Christ and holds us therein."[16] Calvin acknowledged and celebrated "the early councils, such as those of Nicaea, Constantinople, Ephesus I, Chalcedon and the like, which were concerned with refuting errors—*in so*

---

[14] Alister E. McGrath, *Reformation Thought*, 3rd ed. (Malden, MA: Blackwell, 1999), 146–47; cf. Heiko A. Oberman, *Forerunners of the Reformation: The Shape of Late Medieval Thought*, trans. Paul L. Nyhus (New York: Holt, Rhinehart and Winston, 1966), 51–120.

[15] Martin Luther, "On the Councils and the Church," trans. Charles M. Jacobs and Eric W. Gritsch, in *Luther's Works*, vol. 41, ed. Jaroslav Pelikan (Philadelphia: Fortress Press, 1966), 105.

[16] Calvin used this phrase as the title of Book IV of the *Institutes*.

far as they relate to the teachings of the faith." Yet he could only revere them because he believed they "contained nothing but the pure and genuine exposition of Scripture, which the holy fathers applied with spiritual prudence to crush the enemies of religion who had then arisen."[17] For the Reformers and their evangelical heirs, tradition has a **ministerial authority** in the sense that it aids us in our interpretation of Scripture (much like a pastor or a teacher) but is denied **magisterial authority** that makes it the final word on Christian belief and practice.

Why Should We Study Tradition?

To study Christian theology is to enter a two-millennia-long conversation about the gospel and its implications for the mission and the practice of the church. When we study church history and historical theology, we are not simply reading "old books" by dead intellectuals. We are engaging our brothers and sisters in Christ, learning from their experiences, and wrestling through Scripture with them. As Karl Barth remarked:

> We cannot be in the Church without taking as much responsibility for the theology of the past as for the theology of our present. Augustine, Thomas Aquinas, Luther, Schleiermacher and all the rest are not dead, but living. They still speak and demand a hearing as living voices, as surely as we know that they and we belong together in the Church. They made in their time the same contribution to the task of the Church that is required of us today. As we make our contribution, they join in with theirs, and we cannot play our part today without allowing them to play theirs. Our responsibility is not only to God, to ourselves, to the men of today, to other living theologians, but to them. There is no past in the Church, so there is no past in theology. "In him they all live."[18]

---

[17] Calvin, *Institutes* 4.9.8.
[18] Karl Barth, *Protestant Theology in the Nineteenth Century*, trans. Brian Cozens and John Bowden (Grand Rapids: Eerdmans, 2002), 3.

In the same way we bear responsibility to hear living voices in the church today, we bear responsibility to hear what Jaroslav Pelikan (1923–2006) called "the living faith of the dead" in tradition.[19]

We are all shaped by tradition. Whether we know it or not, we are all products of our time and place in history. If we are Christians, we have been influenced by one Christian tradition or another. Whether it was a parent, a pastor, or a friend, someone shared the gospel with us—interpreting the Bible's grand narrative—and explained it to us in a clear and meaningful way. Someone in the tradition shared it with them, and someone in the tradition shared it with them, and so on and so forth. When Jesus prayed for the disciples in John 17, he also prayed for us: "those who believe in me through [the apostolic] word" (17:20). We are those who have believed in Jesus through the words of the disciples recorded in Scripture and the words of their disciples who passed it along. Our Christian worldview is indebted to faithful men and women of God in the past who interpreted the Bible and taught its truths to succeeding generations.

We need to understand how doctrine has developed in history. The more we study historical theology, the more we realize doctrine does not develop in a vacuum. Councils spelled out the doctrine of the Trinity when heretics denied it. Protestant Reformers unpacked justification by faith alone when the church had forgotten it. Evangelical theologians articulated biblical inerrancy when modernists attacked the Bible's authority and truthfulness. In the late twentieth and early twenty-first century, we needed a clearer definition of what it means to be "created . . . in the image of God . . . created . . . male and female" (Gen 1:27) as the culture began reevaluating sex, gender, and sexuality. The doctrines we cherish today grew out of practical, real-world needs faced by the people of God in every era. As the philosopher George Santayana (1863–1952) famously quipped, "Those who cannot remember the past are condemned to repeat it." To ignore the voices of church history is folly.

We must read the Bible in community with other believers. Hundreds of biblical commentaries line the walls of my office. I have access to

---

[19] Jaroslav Pelikan, *The Vindication of Tradition* (New Haven, CT: Yale University Press, 1984), 65.

thousands more on my laptop and mobile devices through my Bible software subscriptions. As a theologian in the broader Reformation tradition, I affirm the clarity of Scripture and the illuminating activity of the Holy Spirit, but rarely do I prepare for a sermon or a paper or article without consulting one of these commentaries on the biblical text. Why? Because I do not claim to be an expert on every facet of Scripture, and I always learn from other believers.

Scripture is too rich in meaning to ignore the writings, sermons, and insights of the community of God in the church. If this is true in the present age, why would it not also be true of the great cloud of witnesses who have gone before us? I do not have to appeal to tradition as a magisterial authority that lords over the Bible and my interpretation but certainly should envision it as a ministerial authority who comes along beside me and aids me in reading. With the Ethiopian eunuch I must ask, "How can I [understand the meaning of Scripture] . . . unless someone guides me?" (Acts 8:31). Tradition provides many guides who point me to Christ in the text.

We can learn from other traditions and interpretations of Scripture. There is also wisdom in reading widely across different theological traditions and cultural perspectives. Disagreement over doctrine stems from several causes but mainly from the various ways we as imperfect interpreters attempt to make sense of the biblical text.[20] Reading other traditions and cultures can humble us as we discover other people have good reasons for interpreting the Bible the way they do. On the pastoral and ecclesial value of hearing other traditions, Kevin Vanhoozer has asserted, "To the extent that it fosters humility in the biblical interpreter, theological diversity is surely to be welcomed."[21] Other traditions can teach us things we have failed to remember. Vanhoozer added, "It is a *pastoral* advantage to be able to draw on diverse theological voices: some congregations need to hear the reassuring Pauline message concerning justification; others need the challenge of James's call to prove faith by works."[22]

---

[20] See Putman, *When Doctrine Divides the People of God*, 37–174 (see chap. 2, n. 35).

[21] Vanhoozer, *The Drama of Doctrine*, 274 (see chap. 2, n. 2).

[22] Vanhoozer, 274 (see chap. 2, n. 2).

Four Approaches to Historical Theology

As a discipline, historical theology has far less uniformity than systematic theology. Historians cover the material of the Christian tradition in some vastly different ways. Consequently, no two historical theology surveys are exactly alike. Nevertheless, a few approaches useful for theological method can be identified.

The first approach is what some historians have labeled the **biographical or "great thinker" model**. The "great thinker" approach to Christian doctrine selects individual theologians throughout history and details their life, works, and key ideas. This approach has value in introducing students to the thought of major figures.[23] But as church historians James Bradley and Richard Muller have observed, this approach has some major shortcomings if one's goal is to understand the Christian tradition as a whole. First, it can be a repetitive way of teaching the history of doctrine since so many major figures in the same era have similar and overlapping ideas. It neglects the way these figures interact with and impact one another in their thinking. The larger problem with this approach is that it tends to reduce the history of ideas to "great" individuals and neglects the influence and impact of "lesser" minds.[24]

The second approach, labeled the **diachronic model** (from the Greek terms *dia*, meaning "through," and *chronos*, meaning "time"), traces individual doctrines throughout history. Diachronic approaches to historical theology often look like systematic theology textbooks in their arrangement. In his diachronic approach, Gregg Allison takes a doctrine like the atonement, summarizes its basic meaning, and then

---

[23] Helpful examples of this approach can be found in Michael Reeves, *Theologians You Should Know: An Introduction: From the Apostolic Fathers to the 21st Century* (Wheaton, IL: Crossway, 2006); Paul Foster, ed., *Early Christian Thinkers: The Lives and Legacies of Twelve Key Figures* (Downers Grove, IL: InterVarsity Press, 2011); Kenneth Richard Samples, *Classic Christian Thinkers: An Introduction* (Covina, CA: Reasons to Believe, 2019); Justo L. Gonzales, *A History of Christian Thought*, rev. ed. (Nashville: Abingdon, 2014).

[24] James E. Bradley and Richard A. Muller, *Church History: An Introduction to Research, Reference Works, and Methods* (Grand Rapids: Eerdmans, 1995), 30–31.

describes its treatment in four major periods of the church: the patristic period, the Middle Ages, the Reformation and post-Reformation, and in modern theology.[25]

Other diachronic works in historical theology are more focused, presenting an entire work on the history of a single doctrine. Two masterful examples immediately come to mind. Michael J. McClymond's recent two-volume work *The Devil's Redemption* is a detailed history and critical interpretation of universalist belief within the Christian tradition.[26] Alister McGrath wrote the most comprehensive history of the doctrine of justification to date in his book *Iustitia Dei*.[27]

I find volumes that take up this diachronic approach to be especially useful in preparing sermons or lectures. The systematic organization of these books makes it quite easy to look up references on what major figures throughout history have said about the theological topic in question. However, this model is not without its own deficiencies. While it can be useful in tracing the development of an individual doctrine, the diachronic approach often ignores the broader context in which a doctrine develops and can neglect the relationships between an individual doctrine held by a thinker and his or her larger system of belief.

A third approach is the **synchronic model** (from the Greek terms *syn*, meaning "together" or "with," and *chronos*, meaning "time"), which focuses on doctrinal development at given moments in the history of the church. Rather than focusing on a single doctrine throughout history or a single theologian, this method shows the organic relationship between ideas and their representative thinkers in a period or within a tradition. This approach shows the way in which doctrines develop alongside one another and in relationship to their time and place in history.[28]

---

[25] Allison, *Historical Theology*, 389–410 (see chap. 4, n. 15).

[26] Michael J. McClymond, *The Devil's Redemption: A New History and Interpretation of Christian Universalism*, 2 vols. (Grand Rapids: Baker, 2018).

[27] Alister E. McGrath, *Iustitia Dei: A History of the Christian Doctrine of Justification*, 4th ed. (Cambridge: Cambridge University Press, 2020).

[28] Bradley and Muller, *Church History*, 31–32.

For example, the third- and fourth-century development of the doctrine of the Trinity was not the result of any individual thinker or work but
the product of several factors at work over a period of time. Theologians
of the church responded to heretical deviations of the biblical teaching
that denied the true deity of Jesus Christ (Arianism) and the personal
distinction between the Father and the Son (Modalism). No one figure
dominated the councils that wrestled with these issues, and these issues
were closely related to other developing doctrines like the doctrine of the
Holy Spirit and the doctrine of salvation.

The relationship between the diachronic and synchronic methods of
historical theology parallels the relationship between systematic and biblical theologies. The synchronic model produces a more comprehensive
understanding of the developing tradition of the Christian faith because
it describes more fully the relationships of doctrines to each other and
their historical contexts. Yet the synchronic approach can be a pains-
taking process and is not as accessible for students who might need a
more basic grasp of how a single doctrine came to be formed. I tend to
use diachronic historical theologies in my systematic theology classes and
synchronic historical theologies in my history classes.

A fourth approach to historical theology gaining traction in some
evangelical circles is known as the **theology of retrieval**. Unlike the other
three modes, which are *descriptive* in nature, retrieval theology is deliber-
ately *prescriptive*. Theologians of retrieval employ tradition to address the
needs of the church today. According to some of its leading proponents,
retrieval is not so much a "method" of doing historical theology as much
as it is an "attitude of mind,"[29] a "theological sensibility,"[30] or a "*mode or
style of theological discernment* that looks back in order to move forward."[31]
In other words, there is no easy step-by-step process of doing theological
retrieval. Theologians of retrieval share a common interest in retrieving

---

[29] John Webster, "Theologies of Retrieval," in *The Oxford Handbook of
Systematic Theology*, ed. John Webster, Kathryn Tanner, and Iain Torrance (New
York: Oxford University Press, 2007), 584.
[30] Allen and Swain, *Reformed Catholicity*, 12 (see chap. 4, n. 16).
[31] Buschart and Eilers, *Theology as Retrieval*, 12 (see chap. 4, n. 28).

the theology of the past—including patristic and medieval theology often ignored by Protestants and evangelicals—for the present.[32]

Theologians of retrieval contend tradition has a regular place in our theological discourse: in our sermons, our Bible studies, our worship, and our public engagement. We should be reading the church fathers, medieval theology, Reformers, and theologians from other eras in history who have something to contribute to our dilemmas in the present. Our brothers and sisters in previous generations have wisdom from which we can glean when thinking about conflicts in the church, shallow worship, or spiritual disciplines.

Researching the Tradition

Whether you take up a biographical, diachronic, synchronic, or retrieval approach to historical theology, a few principles of research are necessary for attaining an accurate and charitable assessment of our theological forebears.

First, use the resources of church history to help you develop a preliminary understanding of the theologian's context. Though some may equate the disciplines, church history is far broader in its scope than historical theology. "Pure" church historians want to know more than doctrine or ideas. They want to know about the laity of the church, the preaching of the church, the practice of the church, and the church's relationship to the state. Church historians want to know not only what Christian figures believed but also what happened in the life of the church and why. This background is necessary for the study of historical theology. We cannot produce thick descriptions of the tradition without familiarity with the spiritual, social, and political contexts in which it took shape.

Uche Anizor has identified "three contextual dimensions" that help us establish the context of a theological work. The first context, *historical-cultural*, "considers what people and events are shaping the theologian's

---

[32] Gavin Ortlund, *Theological Retrieval for Evangelicals: Why We Need Our Past to Have a Future* (Wheaton, IL: Crossway, 2019), 17–22.

world."[33] This means assessing the author's worldview; societal structures like race, gender, and education; economics; political climate; and religious climate.[34]

The second context, the *ecclesial context*, is the confessional tradition that shapes the identity and thought life of a theologian.[35] Is the theologian Baptist, Reformed, Lutheran, Roman Catholic, Orthodox, Neo-Orthodox, or something else?[36] The theological distinctives of these traditions give you a quick window in how the theologian *might* think about certain topics, but theologians don't always toe the party line with their tradition. If they did, no dissension or disagreement would ever happen in the tradition.

The third context, the *polemical context*, "considers the debates and pressing theological issues of the theologian's time."[37] Second-century theologians did battle with Gnosticism. Sixteenth-century Reformers challenged the theological corruption of late medieval Catholicism. Theologians in the early twenty-first century are coming to terms with what Charles Taylor has called the "secular age"—ways in which Western culture has come to reject or reinvent religious beliefs.[38]

Second, the study of historical theology demands using the right sources. Not all sources are of equal value. It is helpful to distinguish between **primary sources**, **secondary sources**, and **tertiary sources**. Tertiary sources like church history or historical theology surveys provide a "big picture" of the figures and movements of history. As James Bradley and Richard Muller make note, these types of sources are helpful only to the degree

---

[33] Anizor, *How to Read Theology*, 29 (see chap. 5, n. 8).

[34] Anizor, 31.

[35] Anizor, 38–44.

[36] For helpful summaries of the doctrinal distinctives and respective approaches to theological method in these respective traditions, see M. James Sawyer, *The Survivor's Guide to Theology*, rev. ed. (Eugene, OR: Wipf & Stock, 2016), 239–469.

[37] Anizor, *How to Read Theology*, 29.

[38] Charles Taylor, *A Secular Age* (Cambridge, MA: Belknap, 2007). For a clear summary of Taylor's project, see James K. A. Smith, *How (Not) to Be Secular: Reading Charles Taylor* (Grand Rapids: Eerdmans, 2014).

that they help the researcher develop "an educated context for argument about the meaning and implication of primary sources."[39]

Secondary sources "are sources that offer information about an event but stand removed from it either in time or by a process of transformation of information."[40] In historical theology, secondary sources can include dissertations, monographs, biographies,[41] or academic journal articles. But one important warning for all these sources: history books are fallible human interpretations of events and ideas that are susceptible to error, prejudice, or misinterpretation. For this reason, read widely from credible academic sources to gain a critical outlook on these sources.

The most important resources in historical theology are primary sources. Primary sources are firsthand accounts or details written by those intimately involved. In one sense, all of the Christian tradition is made up of secondary and tertiary sources that interpret the primary source of Scripture, but when researching the thinkers of the past themselves, their works and documents are the primary sources.

Theological works written before the twentieth century are generally available at no cost somewhere on the internet or a research database, but not all these resources are of equal value. Sometimes these resources distort the original texts, either by misquoting, mistranslating, or shortening these works. Older translations, while usually free, often render ancient sources in stuffy King James–ish language that can be hard to follow. Students can expect to pay more (or use library copies of) newer translations of ancient resources, which usually have newer copyright dates. Critical editions of ancient sources can be found in series like the Loeb Classical Library published by Harvard University Press, which provides the original Latin or Greek source on one page and a literal translation into English on the next page.

---

[39] Bradley and Muller, *Church History*, 31–32.

[40] Bradley and Muller, 31–32.

[41] For example, well-documented biographies like Peter Brown's *Augustine of Hippo* (Berkeley: University of California Press, 1967), or George Marsden's *Jonathan Edwards: A Life* (New Haven, CT: Yale University Press, 2003) are invaluable for studying figures like Augustine or Edwards.

Students can find several English-language editions of *The Apostolic Fathers*, a collection of writings from first- and second-century theologians. The free versions are usually older translations, while the newer editions based on critical compilations of the Greek text are a little pricier. Students in advanced programs or postgraduate work are often required to read sources like these in the original Greek. Fortunately, there are several excellent Greek editions and readers of these sources.[42]

Some of the most important theological works of the past are exceptionally long—Augustine's *City of God* has over 400,000 words—but many others are quite short. I usually recommend students read works as large and complex as *City of God* with a critical commentary, but shorter writings can usually be read and understood on their own terms with a good translation in hand.

Entry-level students writing a paper on a theologian from history would do well to narrow their focus to a single work or a small group of works. The ambitious student may declare his desire to write on "Calvin's doctrine of the church," but this is the kind of topic an accomplished scholar could cover in two or three volumes—not one an MDiv student can realistically cover in fifteen pages. Students do not have time to read so broadly across the corpora of major figures when writing a paper for a course, so it is best for students to limit their topics to something more narrow, like "The Doctrine of the Church Expressed in Calvin's Commentary on Ephesians" or something derived from a specific section of a major work: "Calvin's Views on Church Discipline in the Institutes."

Third, closely read key sources. Lucretia Yaghjian recommends a "close reading" of theological works, which involves reading the text three times. On the first reading, she advises readers to *summarize* the work. The purpose of the first reading is understanding what the author is trying to do with a text, to understand the arguments of the author on her own terms.

---

[42] See Alan S. Bandy, ed., *A Greek Reader's Apostolic Fathers* (Eugene, OR: Cascade, 2018); Michael W. Holmes, ed., *The Apostolic Fathers: Greek Texts and English Translations*, 3rd ed. (Grand Rapids: Baker, 2007); Bart D. Ehrman, ed., *The Apostolic Fathers*, vols. 1–2, Loeb Classical Library (Cambridge, MA: Harvard University Press, 2003).

During this reading, the researcher should take copious notes and write down questions the source provokes.[43] Good questions have the potential of turning into good research problems for a paper or thesis. I will discuss this process in greater detail in the following chapters.

Whereas the first reading focuses on authorial intent, the second reading commended by Yaghjian, *categorization*, brings "your own agenda to the author's text" so you can "ask what you need to know to make a claim, to gather evidence for your claim, or to answer a substantive essay question."[44] If on your first reading you were only committed to grasping the stated purpose on the author, on your second reading, you are asking specific questions of the author that he or she may not directly address. Anytime you try to understand the assumption of the author or reconstruct her thinking on a subject, you have read on the level of categorization.

The third type of reading Yaghjian proposes is to *criticize* the work. Here she asks the reader to assess whether the thesis of the writing stands after multiple readings, whether the theological method practiced by the author is coherent, and whether the work has any large gaps. Yaghjian suggests readers offering their own objections to the author's work at this stage.[45] Historians must practice a healthy degree of skepticism as they seek to understand the past. Even the sources of history are often written with biases and agendas that require a critical reading.

Finally, evaluate the work theologically and spiritually. The Presbyterian theologian John M. Frame offered a list of practical helps for evaluating the works of other theologians, which I have adapted here for the study of historical theology:[46]

1. *Biblical fidelity.* Is the teaching of the theologian/tradition faithful to the content of Scripture or at least consistent with it?

---

[43] Lucretia B. Yaghjian, *Writing Theology Well: A Rhetoric for Theological and Biblical Writers*, 2nd. ed. (New York: Bloomsbury T&T Clark, 2015), 48.

[44] Yaghjian, 48.

[45] Yaghjian, 49.

[46] John M. Frame, *The Doctrine of the Knowledge of God*, A Theology of Lordship, vol. 1 (Phillipsburg, NJ: P&R, 1987), 369–70.

2. *Truth.* Are the author's ideas that are not explicitly found in Scripture true?

3. *Cogency.* Does the author demonstrate clear and good logic in his or her arguments?

4. *Edification.* Does this historical work edify or harm the body of Christ?

5. *Godliness.* Does the author display the spiritual characteristics consistent with the fruit of the Spirit or the fruit of the flesh? Does the theologian seek to honor God or slander, gossip, and justify sin?

6. *Importance.* Does the author present important and/or original ideas? Is he or she influential on the tradition that follows?

7. *Clarity.* Does the author define terms properly? Does the author make a clear case for his position?

8. *Profundity.* Does the author wrestle with difficult questions?

9. *Creativity.* Does the author write in a creative or compelling way?

As Dr. Frame has noted, the most important criterion in this list is *biblical fidelity.* Scripture is the only norming norm for evangelical theology, and tradition that does not comport with biblical authority must be critiqued or challenged.

Historical theology, like any other form of theology, requires intellectual virtues like teachability, curiosity, and attention to detail. Like systematic or biblical theologians, historians of theology have their own presuppositions or biases. They are selective in their use of sources and make interpretive judgments about them. Historians can offer varying degrees of probability, not certainty, but this need not result in cynicism toward the whole enterprise of historical study. Historical research is like "a *dialogue* between present and past, between historian and history."[47]

---

[47] James D. G. Dunn, *Jesus Remembered*, Christianity in the Making, vol. 1 (Grand Rapids: Eerdmans, 2003), 111.

The Use of the Tradition in Disciple-Making

In closing this chapter, I would like to suggest the use of historical resources not only in an academic setting but in the setting of a local church. Laypeople will be edified and encouraged to hear of God's work in the lives of past saints.

First, use the creeds and confessions of the church in corporate worship, group Bible studies, and in one-on-one disciple-making relationships. Creeds like the Apostles' Creed or the Nicene Creed can be educational and worshipful elements in our services when properly explained to their hearers. In the early church and in some traditions today, teachers instructed **catechumens**—new converts who were preparing for baptism—in the creeds before they were given full membership in the church. "New member" classes would do well to promote the same practice, walking people through the creeds of the church and the confessions of the faith celebrated by the church in which they are seeking membership.

Second, use illustrations from church history and historical theology in sermon and lesson preparation, especially when preaching and teaching on doctrinal topics. They may provide great insight for a doctrine or passage you are addressing. They also show how doctrines have been applied in the life of the church.

Third, offer courses in church history and historical theology in the local church. I have participated in several over the years in the format of midweek Bible study classes. These can appeal to the intellectually curious in your church, but they can also be of great practical value. When I pastored in southeast Louisiana, people in our churches greatly benefited from a historical understanding of the Reformation tradition because it helped them relate better to their Roman Catholic family members and neighbors.

Finally, encourage the people in your churches to read the primary sources of church history, especially those available as free resources online. What if our churches used *old books* in disciple-making in addition to all the new video-driven curricula many currently use? Granted, not every ancient, medieval, or Reformation-era book would be accessible or intelligible to everyone in our churches, nor would every source be of equal value. But many of the great works of the Christian tradition are accessible and should be read in our churches. Over a half century ago, C. S. Lewis made the same suggestion:

> This mistaken preference for the modern books and this shyness of the old ones is nowhere more rampant than in theology. Wherever you find a little study circle of Christian laity you can be almost certain that they are studying not St. Luke or St. Paul or St. Augustine or Thomas Aquinas or Hooker or Butler, but M. Berdyaev or M. Maritain or M. Niebuhr or Miss Sayers or even myself.[48]

The list of modern writers Lewis appeals to in the last sentence would be foreign to most laypersons in the church today, but imagine their names being replaced with the evangelical luminaries of our day like John Piper, Timothy Keller, or Jen Wilkin. We should be reading these people, but why don't we also encourage Christians to read older authors like Augustine, Aquinas, Anselm, Calvin, Luther, Arminius, and Wesley the same way we encourage them to read more recent writers? Lewis continued:

> Now this seems to me topsy-turvy. Naturally, since I myself am a writer, I do not wish the ordinary reader to read no modern books. But if he must read only the new or only the old, I would advise him to read the old. And I would give him this advice precisely because he is an amateur and therefore much less protected than the expert against the dangers of an exclusive contemporary diet. A new book is still on trial and the amateur is not in a position to judge it. It has to be tested against the great body of Christian thought down the ages, and all its hidden implications (often unsuspected by the author himself) have to be brought to light. Often it cannot be fully understood without the knowledge of a good many other modern books. . . . It is a good rule, after

---

[48] C. S. Lewis, introduction to *On the Incarnation*, by Athanasius, trans. and ed. by a Religious of the C.S.M.V. (Yonkers, NY: St. Vladimir's Seminary Press, 1977), 3.

reading a new book, never to allow yourself another new one till you have read an old one in between. If that is too much for you, you should at least read one old one to every three new ones.[49]

We should be reading an old book for every new book, or at least an old book every three new books. For Lewis, an *old book* was not last year's Bible Study curriculum. An old book was something from at least three hundred years ago. But in an age where every trend seems to be on the way out the door just as it comes in, we would even do well to encourage disciples to read books written a few generations ago too.

KEY TERMS

biographical or "great thinker" model

catechumens

diachronic model

magisterial authority (of tradition)

ministerial authority (of tradition)

primary sources

secondary sources

synchronic model

tertiary sources

theology of retrieval

tradition

Tradition I (one-source theory of revelation)

Tradition II (two-source theory of revelation)

GO DEEPER

Allison, Gregg R. *Historical Theology*. Grand Rapids: Zondervan, 2011.

Duesing, Jason G., and Nathan A. Finn, eds. *Historical Theology for the Church*. Nashville: B&H Academic, 2021.

Gonzales, Justo L. *A History of Christian Thought*. Rev. ed. Nashville: Abingdon, 2014.

---

[49] Lewis, 4.

Grenz, Stanley J. and Roger E. Olson. *20th-Century Theology: God and the World in a Transitional Age*. Downers Grove, IL: InterVarsity Press, 1992.

MacGregor, Kirk R. *Contemporary Theology: An Introduction: Classical, Evangelical, Philosophical, and Global Perspectives*. Grand Rapids: Zondervan, 2019.

Pelikan, Jaroslav. *The Christian Tradition: A History of the Development of Doctrine*. 5 vols. Chicago: University of Chicago Press, 1975–1991.

9

Philosophy and Christian Theology

Christian theology issues from the light of faith, philosophy
from the natural light of reason. Philosophical truths cannot
be opposed to the truth of faith, they fall short indeed, yet
they also admit common analogies; and some moreover
are foreshadowings, for nature is the preface to grace.
—THOMAS AQUINAS, *SUMMA THEOLOGICA*

T he Bible provides us with a clear, intelligible revelation by which we
understand God's redemptive purposes in the world. But in some
areas, its light is often more like a lamp in a dark room than sunlight
bursting through the windows. As "a lamp for my feet, and a light on my
path" (Ps 119:105), Scripture shows us what is most important to see, but
it does not illumine every mystery about God or his world. God does
many "great and unsearchable things" (Job 9:10) not detailed in Scripture.

Put more plainly, Scripture does not directly answer every theological
question it provokes: If God is all-good, all-powerful, and all-knowing, why

would he then allow evil in this world? How can God the Trinity be both three and one without logical contradiction? How does an eternal God relate to time? What does it mean for human beings to be made in God's image? Do human beings have free will, or is their every course of action predetermined by God? How does Christ relate to us in the Lord's Supper? Would Christ still have come into this world if human beings never sinned?

Through disciplines like philosophy, the natural sciences, or the social sciences, we can attempt to make sense of things in God's world that lie beyond the more focused light of special revelation. Philosophy uses the "weaker lights" of general revelation and natural reason to uncover mysteries about the nature of reality, knowledge, and the human constitution. Yet much of this important work is speculative and inconclusive, and with it, theologians often bumble around in the dark.[1]

The tools of philosophy can aid us in our search for answers to these questions, or at least help us recognize the underlying issues. While philosophy, known to medieval theologians as "theology's handmaiden" (*theologiae ancilla*),[2] can be useful in Christian doctrine, whatever results from philosophical reflection on God's self-revelation is always tentative and open to revision. Only Scripture is inerrant and infallible; philosophy rooted in general revelation and human reason is prone to error and mistakes. All philosophical ideas must be tested and subjected to Scripture, and those that clearly contradict it must be discarded or reworked.

But what is philosophy, and how do theologians use it? Philosophy, like theology, evades easy definition. As my philosophy teacher, Robert Stewart, routinely describes it, philosophy is "the art of telling people things they already know in a language they cannot understand." This description is not far from the truth. *Philosophy* literally means "the love of wisdom" (from the Greek *phileō*, meaning "to love," and *sophia*, meaning "wisdom"), but the "love of wisdom" tells us virtually nothing about what *philosophers do*.

---

[1] I want to thank my former student, Diana Bondurant, for this beautiful analogy.

[2] See Albert Henrichs, "Philosophy, the Handmaiden of Theology," *Greek, Roman, and Byzantine Studies* 9.4 (1968): 437–50.

Philosophers study big-picture questions about all human knowledge. They ask questions about **metaphysics** like "What is really real?" They ask questions concerning **epistemology**: "How can I know anything?" Philosophers employ the tools of **logic** to answer the question "How can I reason correctly?" They want to understand the nature of language and how it can be used to communicate meaning. The study of the **philosophy of religion** broadly examines religious beliefs like God, miracles, and evil.

Philosophy is also a **second-order discipline** that helps us make sense of other "first-order disciplines." As J. P. Moreland and William Lane Craig have illustrated, biology, a first-order discipline, studies living things. A second-order discipline like the philosophy of science can ask questions about the methods, goals, and assumptions of first-order disciplines like biology.[3] Theological method is a second-order discipline that investigates the meaning of theology and its central tasks; it is, in many respects, a philosophy of theology.

Perhaps the most beneficial aspect of philosophy for Christian theology is its function in clarifying, analyzing, and critiquing what we say about our subject matter. The scariest—yet most helpful—question a philosopher can ask you is "What do you mean?" Sometimes we need to be interrupted to hear this question, to slow down, and to think more carefully about what we are saying. The tools of philosophy can aid us in clearly communicating our ideas, defining our terms, and critically assessing the words and ideas of others. This chapter is an exploration of these themes, covering both objections to the use of philosophy in theology and its potential value in Christian discipleship.

Philosophy Can Help Disciples Defend Theological Claims

Christian theologians often use philosophy to aid in the apologetic task of defending Christian doctrine and truth claims. This apologetic

---

[3] Moreland and Craig, *Philosophical Foundations for a Christian Worldview*, 15 (see chap. 6, n. 29).

dimension can take several forms. *First, theologians have used philosophical tools and arguments to create common ground with nonbelievers as a precursor to gospel proclamation.* Thomas Aquinas spoke of truths known by "natural reason" that prepare a person to hear the truths of special revelation in the gospel and in Scripture.[4] With natural reason, we can establish rudimentary points of agreement with nonbelievers like logic, truth, and justice.

Traditional arguments for God's existence drawn from general revelation can serve as a precursor to Christian witness. These traditional arguments include arguments from causation (**cosmological arguments**), arguments from design (**teleological arguments**), arguments from morality (**moral law arguments**), and arguments from God's perfections (**ontological arguments**). Even if a conversation partner finds these arguments convincing, they only lead to general theistic belief in a God who caused all things to exist, a great Designer, a morally perfect being who is the ground of morality, or a being who is perfect in every conceivable way. These arguments do not necessarily lead to the God revealed in Jesus Christ; hence they are seen only as a prelude to gospel conversations.

Second, Christian theologians employ philosophy to demonstrate the logical coherence of traditional Christian beliefs. Atheists will often charge the concepts of classical theism with being incoherent or logically contradictory. For example, some philosophers have called the idea of God's **omnipotence** (i.e., God's quality of possessing all power) to be internally inconsistent or self-contradictory. You are probably familiar with this alleged paradox: Can God create a stone so heavy he cannot lift it?

Either way you respond to this "gotcha" question, your answer is going to imply there is something God cannot do. He is either incapable of creating the stone or incapable of picking it up. But as Christian philosophers observe, this dilemma asks God to perform a pseudo-task, like creating a square circle or a triangular square.[5] Few Christian theologians teach God can do absolutely anything, as Scripture teaches God cannot

---

[4] Thomas Aquinas, *Summa Theologica* 1.2.2.

[5] George I. Mavrodes, "Some Puzzles Concerning Omnipotence," *The Philosophical Review* 72.2 (Apr. 1963): 221–23; cf. Richard R. La Croix,

lie (Num 23:19; Titus 1:2; Heb 6:18) or be tempted by evil (Jas 1:13). For Thomas Aquinas, God cannot do the logically impossible, like creating a world where 2+2=5, because such would be a contradiction contrary to the true nature of omnipotence.[6] These responses do not prove God is omnipotent, but they show the atheistic argument to be of no consequence for the logical consistency of this Christian belief.[7] Christian theologians and philosophers strive to show the logical consistency of belief in God in areas like these. As Ronald Nash (1936–2006) recognized, "The concept of God found in Christian theism must pass the test of logical consistency."[8]

Third, theologians use philosophical arguments to defend the historical reliability of Christian revelation. The historicity of the miracle accounts in the Bible has been a subject of great philosophical scrutiny since the dawn of the Enlightenment in the late seventeenth century. Philosophers like Baruch Spinoza (1632–1677) and David Hume (1711–1776) mounted arguments against the possibility and probability of miracles like Jesus's resurrection. For Spinoza, a pantheist, miracles are logically impossible because (1) they are violations of the law of nature established by God and (2) God cannot violate his own will.[9] For Hume, no number of testimonies or accounts is sufficient to establish or prove miraculous events, and consequently, no rational person should subscribe to the Christian faith built on miracle accounts.[10]

Christian apologists, theologians, and philosophers have disputed all points. C. S. Lewis challenged the assumption shared by Spinoza and Hume that miracles are violations of the law of nature, instead calling

---

"The Hidden Assumption in the Paradox of Omnipotence," *Philosophy and Phenomenological Research* 38.1 (Sep. 1977): 125–27.

[6] Thomas Aquinas, *Summa Theologica* 1.25.3.

[7] Mavrodes, "Some Puzzles Concerning Omnipotence," 223.

[8] Ronald H. Nash, *The Concept of God: An Exploration of the Contemporary Difficulties with the Attributes of God* (Grand Rapids: Zondervan, 1983), 12.

[9] Benedict de [Baruch] Spinoza, *Tractatus Theologico-Politicus* (London, 1682), 120–41.

[10] David Hume, *An Enquiry Concerning Human Understanding*, §10, "Of Miracles."

them divine interruptions of nature that produce results within nature. According to Lewis, miracles that initially interrupt nature eventually end up conforming to the laws of nature:

> If God creates a miraculous spermatozoon in the body of a virgin, it does not proceed to break any laws. The laws at once take it over. Nature is ready. Pregnancy follows, according to all the normal laws, and nine months later, a child is born. . . . Miraculous wine will intoxicate, miraculous conception will lead to pregnancy, inspired books will suffer the ordinary processes of textual corruption, miraculous bread will be digested. The divine art of miracle is not an art of suspending the pattern to which events conform but of feeding new events into that pattern.[11]

Biblical scholar N. T. Wright added that the whole supernatural/natural distinction is a flawed product of the Enlightenment—not a view held by the earliest Christians. Rather than seeing the miracles of Jesus as supernatural, the worldview of the New Testament insisted "The world is charged with the grandeur of God."[12]

Richard Swinburne has answered Hume's charge that no amount of testimony could provide sufficient proof for the truthfulness of miracle accounts. The testimony of reliable sources can also evidence an interruption of the normal laws of nature unless we have clear reason *not* to believe these accounts.[13] It only takes one counter-instance, namely the resurrection of Jesus, to establish that the rule "dead men stay dead" can be broken. The testimony of one may not constitute sufficient evidence, but the testimony of "over five hundred brothers and sisters at one time" (1 Cor 15:6) might suffice.

---

[11] C. S. Lewis, *Miracles* (San Francisco: HarperCollins, 2000), 94–95. For a variation on this argument, see George I. Mavrodes, "Miracles and the Laws of Nature," *Faith and Philosophy* 2.4 (Oct. 1985): 333–46.

[12] Wright, *The New Testament and the People of God*, 97 (see chap. 2, n. 36).

[13] Richard Swinburne, "Miracles," *Philosophical Quarterly* 18 (1968): 320–28; cf. Richard Swinburne, *The Concept of Miracle* (New York: MacMillan, 1970).

Philosophy Can Provide Key
Concepts for Theology

Philosophy may provide conceptual elements useful for understanding the revealed content of Christian theology. Many of the most important phrases in Christian theology are borrowed from philosophy: terms like *substance* when speaking about the doctrine of the Trinity; *libertarian freedom* or *compatibilism* when talking about human freedom and responsibility; and *divine simplicity* when talking about the nature of one God without divisions or parts.

Of the application of philosophical concepts like these to theological conversations I must make two important caveats. *First, it would be naive to assume these terms or ideas are "biblical" in the sense of being directly taught by Scripture.* Many of these concepts probably would have been alien to the human authors of Scripture. If we hopped in a time-traveling DeLorean and went back to the year AD 54 to ask Paul a question about whether Jesus was the "same substance" (Gk. *homoousion*) as the Father, as argued by the theologians at the fourth-century council of Nicaea in AD 325, the apostle probably would have given us weird looks (especially after seeing our flying time machine land in his general area). Though he was well trained in rhetoric and familiar with Greek philosophical sources (Acts 17:28; 1 Cor 15:33; Titus 1:12), Paul probably would have been unfamiliar with the terms and concepts debated at Nicaea.[14]

Consequently, do not expect to find these philosophical concepts in a straightforward exegesis of New Testament texts. By using these philosophical concepts, *we are trying to interpret Scripture theologically by better understanding the divine subject matter addressed in biblical texts.* Just because the concept of Jesus as *homoousion* would have been foreign to Paul does not mean we are contradicting his writing. As David Yeago has shown, when we affirm Jesus is the "same substance" with the Father, we are using a philosophical framework to expound on the same judgment

---

[14] William P. Alston, "Substance and the Trinity," in *The Trinity: An Interdisciplinary Symposium on the Trinity*, ed. Stephen T. Davis, Daniel Kendall, and Gerald O'Collins (New York: Oxford University Press, 2000), 179–201.

Paul made in Scripture: Jesus is equal in power and glory to the Father and worthy of the same reverence and worship (Phil 2:6).[15]

Second, philosophical concepts used in Christian theology are always subjected to the clearer authority of Scripture. While it may be valuable to ponder these concepts, the silence of Scripture on these matters means they do not hold authority over us. We can argue for the theological coherence of a doctrine like divine simplicity or divine timelessness, but because of their speculative nature, they are third- or fourth-tier matters that we should not impose on other believers as a litmus test for orthodoxy. Theologians who employ philosophical categories must be careful not to present them as having "the same degree of authoritativeness" attributed to first-tier doctrines.[16]

Philosophy Can Clarify Theological Truths

The growth of **analytic theology** in recent decades has given philosophy new life in Christian theology. In the past, philosophers of religion dealt with questions like the existence of God, the problem of evil, and miracles from the perspective of general theism rooted in natural revelation. Philosophical theology was thought to "discuss the existence, essence, and attributes of God but not the doctrine of the Trinity . . . the problem of evil but not the doctrines of sin and grace."[17]

By contrast, contemporary proponents of analytic theology use philosophy to examine traditional Christian doctrines found in special revelation.[18] Analytic theology is seen as a type of systematic theology rooted

---

[15] David S. Yeago, "The New Testament and Nicene Dogma: A Contribution to the Recovery of Theological Exegesis," in *Theological Interpretation of Scripture: Classic and Contemporary Readings*, ed. Stephen E. Fowl (Cambridge, MA: Blackwell, 1997), 87–100.

[16] Erickson, *Christian Theology*, 66 (see chap. 1, n. 18).

[17] Richard A. Muller, *The Study of Theology: From Biblical Interpretation to Contemporary Formation* (Grand Rapids: Zondervan, 1990), 138.

[18] Thomas H. McCall, *An Invitation to Analytic Theology* (Downers Grove, IL: InterVarsity Press, 2015), 15–16.

in Scripture.[19] It can give conceptual clarity to Christian doctrines such as the attributes of God, the inspiration of Scripture, original sin, the virginal conception of Jesus, the incarnation, the nature and the extent of the atonement, and the future resurrection of believers.[20]

Thomas McCall has provided a useful overview of what analytic theology is and isn't in his recent introduction on the subject. He denies analytic theology is just another form of natural theology or apologetics and affirms its spiritual merits. But most importantly, he calls attention to the way analytic theologians employ the style of analytic philosophy to describe and analyze Christian doctrine. *Analytic theologians give formal expressions to Christian doctrines in precise, clear, and logically coherent propositional statements.* They weigh every word carefully and strive not to weigh theological language down with unnecessary metaphors or hidden assumptions. Then they proceed to assess the cogency and coherence of these theological statements.[21] Clarity, McCall observed, does not mean "easy," but speaks to the way in which the philosopher or theologian spells out claims and assumptions with rigor.[22]

One issue analytic theologians have grappled with is God's relationship to time. Biblical authors describe God as the "eternal God" (Deut 33:27 ESV; Rom 16:26) and the "King eternal" (1 Tim 1:17). The psalmist declared, "Before the mountains were brought forth, or ever you had formed the earth and the world, from *everlasting to everlasting* you are God" (Ps 90:2 ESV, emphasis added). God is the "one who lives forever and ever" (Rev. 4:9). Yet none of these biblical descriptions explain *eternity*

---

[19] See William J. Abraham, "Systematic Theology as Analytic Theology," in *Analytic Theology: New Essays in the Philosophy of Theology*, ed. Oliver D. Crisp and Michael C. Rea (Oxford: Oxford University Press, 2009), 54–69; Crisp, *Analyzing Doctrine*, 15–32 (see chap. 4, n. 4).

[20] Oliver Crisp, the most prolific analytic theologian working today, has written books on nearly all these subjects. For a small sample of these works, see Crisp, *Divinity and Humanity* (New York: Cambridge University Press, 2007); Crisp, *God Incarnate* (New York: T&T Clark, 2009); and Crisp, *Approaching the Atonement* (Downers Grove, IL: InterVarsity Press, 2020).

[21] McCall, *An Invitation to Analytic Theology*, 17–18; cf. Michael C. Rea, introduction to *Analytic Theology*, 3–6.

[22] McCall, *An Invitation to Analytic Theology*, 19.

or how God relates to time itself. Is God timelessly "atemporal"—outside of time but present to every moment simultaneously—or is God "temporally everlasting"—experiencing temporal succession like past, present, and future alongside his creatures?[23]

The question has interesting implications for our understanding of creation, predestination, God's foreknowledge, and God's immutability.[24] But since the Bible does not directly address God's relationship to time, we can appeal to outside resources like philosophy and theoretical physics for guidance, which can help us understand the nature of time itself.[25] Following the work of John McTaggart (1866–1925), philosophers and scientists usually fall into one of two camps on this problem: the A-theory of time, which suggests time as we presently experience it is real, and the B-theory of time, which indicates the experience of time passing is an illusion.[26]

If we apply these philosophical concepts to Christian theology, we have at least two broad options for conceiving of God's relationship to time (though many have offered mediating positions between these two opposites). If the B-theory of time is true, then the "past," "present," and "future" exist simultaneously. If the passing of time is only an illusion, God is "timeless" and does not experience the passing of time like his creatures. He is present *to* time but not present *in* time with us (much like he is present *to* creation in his omnipresence and immensity). This is the

---

[23] Gregory E. Ganssle, introduction to *God and Time: Four Views*, ed. Gregory E. Ganssle (Downers Grove, IL: InterVarsity Press, 2001), 12–13.

[24] Ganssle, 13–24.

[25] For useful summaries of the scientific and philosophical debates surrounding the nature of time, see Scientific American, *A Question of Time: The Ultimate Paradox* (New York: Scientific American, 2017), eBook; Craig Callender, ed., *The Oxford Handbook of Philosophy of Time* (New York: Oxford University Press, 2011).

[26] J. M. E. McTaggart, *The Nature of Existence*, vol. 2 (Cambridge: Cambridge University Press, 1927), 9–31; cf. McTaggart, "The Unreality of Time," *Mind* 17 (1908): 457–74. The terms "A-theory" and "B-theory" first appear in Richard M. Gale, "McTaggart's Analysis of Time," *American Philosophical Quarterly* 3, no. 2 (1966): 145–52.

"classical" view of God's relationship to time held by major figures like Augustine and Thomas Aquinas. For some theologians who hold to the B-theory, creation exists eternally alongside the eternal Creator, and Jesus has eternally been the incarnate God-man.[27]

If the A-theory of time is true, God is in time with us, experiencing the passing of time in a very real "now." God is "everlasting" but not timeless. Christian philosopher Nicholas Wolterstorff advocates for this view of God in time, contending that it is the most consistent with the narratives of the Bible that depict God taking different courses of action in response to different human situations.[28] Some A-theorists embrace open theism—the idea that God's omniscience does not include knowledge of future events involving free creatures. Open theists argue God is in the present moment with us and the future has not yet been actualized.[29] For numerous philosophical and theological reasons, Christian theologians like me find this latter option internally incoherent and inconsistent with Scripture and tradition.[30]

Again, any concept not directly derived from the Bible is open to criticism and revision in Christian theology. Some concepts applied to Christian theology are more helpful than others. They must be assessed and evaluated. These concepts may also change over time given the philosophical climate of the theologian.

---

[27] See Paul Helm, *Eternal God: A Study of God without Time*, 2nd ed. (New York: Oxford University Press, 2011).

[28] Nicholas Wolterstorff, "Unqualified Divine Temporality," in Ganssle, *God and Time: Four Views*, 187–213.

[29] William Hasker, *God, Time, and Knowledge* (Ithaca, NY: Cornell University, 1989).

[30] See Benjamin H. Arbour, *Philosophical Essays against Open Theism* (New York: Routledge, 2018); Millard J. Erickson, *What Does God Know and When Does He Know It?: The Current Controversy over Divine Foreknowledge* (Grand Rapids: Zondervan, 2006); Bruce A. Ware, *God's Lesser Glory: The Diminished God of Open Theism* (Wheaton, IL: Crossway, 2000).

Philosophy and Worldview Analysis

With the tools of philosophy, we can also train disciples to assess their worldviews and the worldviews of others. Every worldview includes a grand narrative, truth claims about our ultimate questions, practices driven by our beliefs, and affections that direct our course of action. But how can we have confidence in our own worldview or critique the world-views of others? Robert Stewart offers five helpful criteria for evaluating and critiquing worldviews.[31]

Coherence. Coherence is "freedom from contradiction."[32] For a world-view to be coherent, it must be free from contradictions. No one can coher-ently believe the earth is flat *and* believe the earth is round because these two beliefs are outright contradictions. While coherence is necessary for the truthfulness of a worldview, coherence alone is not a sufficient condition for a worldview being true. A person may hold a set of noncontradictory beliefs about what it means to live on a flat earth, but simply holding those beliefs does not make them true if the world is not really flat.

Correlation. A worldview must be more than internally coherent; it must correlate with the world as we experience it. Does our worldview match up with our experience of reality? The belief that the world is flat does not correlate with our visual perceptions. The earth casts a round shadow on the moon, not a flat line. We can see more when we climb to the top of a tall structure than we can from the bottom of a structure because being high up can remove visual obstacles created by the curva-ture of the earth. When it comes to questions about the truthfulness of our religious beliefs, does life experience correlate more closely with God at work in our lives or a world devoid of God?

Comprehensiveness. How well does the worldview in question account for *all of life?* Stewart wrote, "Worldviews that don't address all areas of life are partial and incomplete. Therefore worldviews that effectively

---

[31] Robert B. Stewart, "The Insufficiency of Naturalism: A Worldview Critique," in *Come Let Us Reason: New Essays in Christian Apologetics*, ed. Paul Copan and William Lane Craig (Nashville: B&H Academic, 2012), 81–83.

[32] Stewart, 81.

address more areas of life are preferable to those that address fewer."[33] Atheists cannot account for human consciousness or the perception that we have minds independent of our brains. Like Job's friends, prosperity preachers who believe in a "health and wealth" gospel cannot account for why a faithful Christian would endure suffering. A worldview does not have to address every single unknown question, but the more it can account for, the better.

Consistency. Can the worldview in question be lived out consistently? Can we operate in every area of life as if all our beliefs are true, or must we act as if some of our beliefs are not true? For example, a postmodern individual may say, "I don't believe in objective truth. Truth is merely what we want it to be." Yet faced with the prospect of a life-threatening illness, this same individual would want his physician to give him medical advice that corresponds to his very real condition. The same postmodern who says "texts have no meaning other than the interpretation we give them" will want his pharmacist to read for the intended meaning of his doctor's prescription. Worldviews must be livable.

Commitment. This is the existential question of worldview analysis. Can we wholeheartedly commit ourselves to a worldview? Is it worth my all? Jesus says this kind of commitment is a prerequisite for discipleship: "If anyone wants to follow after me, let him deny himself, take up his cross daily, and follow me. For whoever wants to save his life will lose it, but whoever loses his life because of me will save it" (Luke 9:23–24).

KEY TERMS

analytic theology

cosmological arguments

epistemology

logic

metaphysics

moral law arguments

omnipotence

ontological arguments

philosophy of religion

second-order discipline

teleological arguments

---

[33] Stewart, "The Insufficiency of Naturalism," 82.

GO DEEPER

Copan, Paul. *Loving Wisdom: A Guide to Philosophy and Christian Faith.* 2nd ed. Grand Rapids: Eerdmans, 2020.

Cowan, Steven B. *The Love of Wisdom: A Christian Introduction to Philosophy.* Nashville: B&H Academic, 2009.

Levering, Matthew. *Proofs of God: Classical Arguments from Tertullian to Barth.* Grand Rapids: Baker, 2016.

McCall, Thomas H. *An Invitation to Analytic Theology.* Downers Grove, IL: InterVarsity Press, 2015.

10

Experience and Christian Theology

So Christianity tells me; and So I find it, may every real
Christian say. I now am assured that these things are so:
I experience them in my own breast. What Christianity
(considered as a doctrine) promised is accomplished in my
soul. And Christianity, considered as an inward principle,
is the completion of all those promises. It is holiness and
happiness, the image of God impressed on a created spirit, a
fountain of peace and love springing up into everlasting life.
—JOHN WESLEY, *THE LETTERS OF THE REV. JOHN WESLEY*

Everyone has a worldview that shapes the way we live in and interact with the world, but few people stop to think critically about
what they believe. Because we are creatures wired with feelings, emotions, and affections, we often feel our way through decision-making
and belief formation rather than reasoning through these matters. Our
decisions about what we will eat and how we will dress have more to
do with our feelings and preferences than our logic. People often make

major life decisions based on gut feelings alone, frequently resulting in disastrous consequences.

We also learn from our experiences. Negative experiences are some of life's best teachers. Experience may teach us not to grab the cookie sheet from the oven without wearing oven mitts. The outcome of foolish investments can make us wiser with our income in the future. Past relationship mistakes can help us learn new behaviors with our friends, our family members, or our romantic partners. Positive experiences that result in a feeling of accomplishment or reward can also direct our beliefs, thoughts, and actions.

But what of spiritual feelings and religious experiences? What role, if any, do they play in forming our beliefs about God, his world, and what he desires from our lives?

Few people come to faith in Christ through an appeal to reason alone. Conversion stories usually include a strong sense of the Holy Spirit at work in our hearts. Through the Spirit's conviction, we came face to face with the ugliness of our sin. He made the Word of God come alive to us. The glory of Christ shone in the eyes of our hearts, and we yearned for him and the life only he gives.

While the Christian life is *experiential* and *heart-stirring*, it cannot be reduced to experiences or feelings of our heart. Some throughout church history have reduced religion to their *impressions* or *sensations* of God. Others have added to God's Word by claiming *additional revelation* that goes beyond the bounds of Scripture or is outright contradictory to it. In the "post-truth" culture of the West in which we now live, many have made living their "own truth" the summum bonum (i.e., the highest good) of their lives. "I have to do what is best for me. I have to do what I know *feels* right."

On the one hand, there is a danger of elevating personal religious experience to a place of authority that surpasses Scripture. On the other hand, a faith devoid of all experience with God is useless. As Jesus mourned the hypocrisy of the scribes and Pharisees, he warned them, "You are like whitewashed tombs, which appear beautiful on the outside, but inside are full of the bones of the dead and every kind of impurity. . . . On the outside you seem righteous to people, but inside you are full of hypocrisy and lawlessness" (Matt 23:27–28). The same warning applies to theologians today who have an intellectual works righteousness but hardened hearts dead to sin. As we have seen already, holistic Christian discipleship involves *right thinking* (orthodoxy), *right acting* (orthopraxy), and *right feelings* (orthopathy). Christian doctrine changes our minds, as well as our feelings and experiences.

In this chapter, I define religious experience, detail historical perspectives on the role of experience in theology, and conclude by offering practical instruction about the role of experience in disciple-making today.

The Role of Experience Across Theological Traditions

The word *experience* comes from Latin terms meaning "to try" (*experiri*) and "a trial, proof, experiment; knowledge gained by repeated trials" (*experientia*). We use *experience* in a similar way today. When we tell our friends that they "must experience" a favorite dish, book, or movie, we want them to try it because we believe it can be a positive life event for them. A person who has tried many things or learned through firsthand knowledge is called *experienced* (e.g., "an experienced pastor," "an experienced teacher").[1] Since Plato, philosophers, skeptics, and intellectuals of every stripe have argued that personal experience provides more certainty in the pursuit of knowledge than secondhand information.[2] Experience, in short, "can be understood as a source of knowledge deriving from a direct perception or apprehension of reality."[3]

Two types of experience play roles in religious belief: (1) *empirical* experiences derived from the senses that can serve as evidence for the

---

[1] McGrath, *A Passion for Truth*, 71 (see chap. 2, n. 2); McGrath, *Christian Theology*, 5th ed. (Malden, MA: Wiley-Blackwell, 2011), 146.

[2] Plato, *Meno* 96b–98d.

[3] Robert K. Johnston, "Experience, Theology Of," in *Evangelical Dictionary of Theology*, 2nd ed., ed. Daniel J. Treier and Walter A. Elwell (Grand Rapids: Baker, 2001), 428.

rationality of faith claims and (2) *existential* experiences that take place in the "inner life" of individuals.[4] Empirical experience has had some apologetic value in supporting the truth claims of Christianity. For example, New Testament scholar Craig Keener has compiled numerous anecdotal accounts of miracles and miraculous healings in Asia, Africa, Latin America, the Caribbean, and the West that offer support to the plausibility of ongoing supernatural activity in the world today.[5] Gary Habermas and J. P. Moreland use *empirically verifiable* near-death experiences in support of the Christian notion of immortality.[6]

Existential experience, on the other hand, describes the "inner life of individuals, in which those individuals become aware of their own subjective feelings and emotions."[7] Knowledge of this existential experience is not observable from the outside but drawn from introspection of one's private thoughts and feelings. Religious experiences in this vein involve having direct impressions of God that cannot be verified by empirical means.[8]

William James (1842–1910), one of the most influential figures of late-nineteenth- and early-twentieth-century psychology, created a detailed account of these kinds of existential experiences in his 1902 work, *Varieties of Religious Experience*. In this book, he detailed the experiences of religious mysticism—aspects of religion that seem beyond reasonable

---

[4] Donald A. D. Thorsen, *The Wesleyan Quadrilateral: Scripture, Tradition, Reason, and Experience as a Model of Evangelical Theology* (Grand Rapids: Zondervan, 1990), 203–4.

[5] See Craig S. Keener, *Miracles: The Credibility of the New Testament Accounts* (Grand Rapids: Baker, 2011), 264–358; 426–600.

[6] See Gary Habermas and J. P. Moreland, *Beyond Death: Exploring the Evidence for Immortality* (Eugene, OR: Wipf & Stock, 2004). These accounts are not like the "heaven tourism" books that give subjective accounts of going to heaven and describing it. Rather, they are based on data of objectively observable data, such as people describing things going on in the hospital room or in other parts of the hospital while they are in an unconscious state.

[7] McGrath, *Christian Theology*, 146 (see chap. 1, n. 22).

[8] Thorsen, *The Wesleyan Quadrilateral*, 204.

explanation or expression. James depicted religious experiences of this kind in four ways.[9]

1. We usually cannot fully comprehend or express our religious experiences. James called this the *ineffable* quality of religious experience.
2. Our experiences are *noetic* (from the Greek word *nous*, meaning mind). In other words, religious experiences often *shape what we believe*. They can serve as a kind of authority for faith and practice. Some people base their moral judgments on their experience, whether it is a feeling or something they claim God told them to do.
3. James also described religious experiences as *transient*, meaning they are short-lived. Some claim a moment in which they felt God speaking to them, or others have claimed momentary spiritual gifts like the gift of tongues or special prophetic knowledge.
4. Religious experiences are also *passive*, meaning they are beyond the control of the individual experiencing them. Reformed notions of irresistible grace and regeneration before conversion also fit in this category of religious experience.

All these categories of religious experience can describe an experience with the Holy Spirit that is consistent with Scripture and orthodoxy, but they can also describe spiritual experiences contrary to sound teaching and practice.

People who perceive God speaking to them often take those perceptions as having authority over the direction and course of their lives. Religious fanatics and cult leaders are not the only ones who claim such experiences. When ordinary Christians say things like, "I was convicted by the Holy Spirit for my sin in this area," or "I sense the Lord leading me to take on this ministry," they are describing instances of existential experience. I cannot objectively *prove* to others the work of the Holy Spirit in my life or the direction I sense he is giving me.

---

[9] McGrath, *Christian Theology*, 147; William James, *The Varieties of Religious Experience: A Study in Human Nature* (New York, 1902), 380–81.

But what value, if any, does talk of experience with God have in Christian doctrine? Alister McGrath has identified two basic approaches to this question:[10]

1. Experience provides a foundational resource for Christian theology.
2. Christian theology provides a framework within which human experience may be interpreted.

According to the first approach, experience is a key authority for religious beliefs. The second approach does not minimize or negate religious experience but states Scripture (and its interpretation in Christian theology) has authority over our experiences. We make sense of our experience by Christian doctrine rather than having our doctrine determined by our experiences.

As theology lecturer Simeon Zahl has observed, our view of experience's role in Christian theological method is tied closely to our doctrine of the Holy Spirit.[11] The Spirit is the source of our own religious experiences, and our views on his ongoing work in the life of the church affect the degree to which we consider experience to be of doctrinal value. If we believe the Spirit's primarily revelatory work to be limited to the apostolic age, then we will primarily see Christian theology as the interpreter of human experience. If, on the other hand, we follow Pentecostal and charismatic theologians who contend the Spirit is still performing the same works in the world today that he did during the apostolic era, we will see experience as a crucial resource for what we believe. Theologians throughout modern history usually have taken up one or the other of these two perspectives.

Wesley on the Role of Experience

John Wesley, the founder of Methodism, was one of the first evangelical theologians to give extended attention to the role of religious experience

---

[10] McGrath, *Christian Theology*, 147.

[11] See Simeon Zahl, *The Holy Spirit and Christian Experience* (New York: Oxford University Press, 2020).

in theological method.[12] In the early 1730s, Wesley had gained a reputation around Oxford University as a Christian intellectual well versed in the Greek New Testament and Anglo-Catholic theology. His adherence to discipline and a rigid moral code earned him and his associates the nickname "The Holy Club" or "The Methodists." But Wesley didn't feel peace about his salvation until May 24, 1738, when he had what came to be known as his "Aldersgate experience."

> In the evening I went very unwillingly to a society in Aldersgate Street, where one was reading Luther's preface to the Epistle to the Romans. About a quarter before nine, while he was describing the change which God works in the heart through faith in Christ, I felt my heart strangely warmed. I felt I did trust in Christ, Christ alone, for salvation: And an assurance was given me that He had taken away *my* sins, even *mine*, and saved *me* from the law of sin and death.[13]

This experience would shape Wesley's theology and practice for the rest of his life. For Wesley, religious experience provides a kind of apologetic, reassuring the believer of the truthfulness of Christian doctrine and the assurance of his or her salvation.[14]

Wesley also saw Christian experience as key in believers developing spiritual discernment. He distinguished the *natural senses* with which we hear, see, smell, taste, and touch from the *spiritual senses* with which we perceive God. With these spiritual senses, we can discern good from evil, discern spiritual objects, and apprehend the things of God.[15] These spiritual senses are given to a person (or restored to their original working order) when he is born again by the Spirit of God.[16] This subjective discernment will always be consistent with the Scriptures the Spirit inspired.

---

[12] Thorsen, *The Wesleyan Quadrilateral*, 216–21.

[13] From Wesley's journal on Wednesday, May 24, 1738, in John Wesley, *The Works of John Wesley*, 3rd ed., ed. Thomas Jackson (Grand Rapids: 1979), 1:103.

[14] Oden, *John Wesley's Teachings*, 1:112–13.

[15] Oden, 1:113; Thorsen, *The Wesleyan Quadrilateral*, 205–6.

[16] Oden, *John Wesley's Teachings*, 1:115.

But Wesley also emphatically warned against abuses of experience in religion. He used the mystic theologian and philosopher Emanuel Swedenborg (1688–1772) as an example of giving experience too high a place in doctrinal formation. Swedenborg denied the doctrine of the Trinity detailed in Scripture and tradition because he claimed to have had spiritual experiences in which he conversed regularly with angels and spirits who corrected him in areas of doctrine. Wesley insisted that whatever spiritual experiences Swedenborg had that led him to contradict the claims of Scripture were not of the Holy Spirit who inspired the biblical authors, but "the spirit of darkness."[17] Wesley also criticized the so-called enthusiasts of his day who, claiming to be under the direct inspiration of God, suspended the use of "scripturally informed reasoning" in order to justify the claims they made from their religious experiences.[18]

Pentecostalism, Charismatic Theology, and Third-Wave Evangelicalism

Birthed out of the Wesleyan tradition, Pentecostal and charismatic movements place a considerable emphasis on the role of Christian experience in doctrinal formation and practice.[19] Though other experience-driven, revivalist movements had emerged across Europe, Australia, and other parts of the United States in the mid- to late-nineteenth century, modern **Pentecostalism** traces its origin to 1901, when Methodist evangelist Charles Fox Parham (1873–1929) challenged his students at the Bethel Bible School in Topeka, Kansas, to seek "the baptism of the Holy Spirit."

Parham explicitly linked this baptism of the Holy Spirit with the practice of speaking in tongues (**glossolalia**). One of Parham's students, African American pastor William J. Seymour (1870–1922), would go on to lead the Los Angeles–based prayer meetings known to history as the

---

[17] John Wesley, "Thoughts on the Writings of Baron Swedenborg," in *The Works of John Wesley*, 3rd ed. (Grand Rapids: Baker, 1979), 13:447–48.

[18] Oden, *John Wesley's Teachings*, 1:117; Thorsen, *The Wesleyan Quadrilateral*, 216.

[19] F. Dale Bruner, *A Theology of the Holy Spirit* (Grand Rapids: Eerdmans, 1970), 21.

Azusa Street Revival (1906–1909). These prayer meetings were known for emotional, spontaneous experiences with participants speaking in tongues. These meetings became a hub for the emerging Pentecostal movement as curious visitors from around the world gathered to experience the revival made known by Seymour's publications.[20]

With an emphasis on experience in the Holy Spirit and the miraculous gifts, the **charismatic movement** swept through Protestant churches of every stripe and Roman Catholic churches in the 1960s and 1970s. Charismatics often maintained many of the characteristics of their home denominations (e.g., polity, worship culture, etc.) but added several of the distinctive doctrines and practices of Pentecostalism, such as the baptism in the Spirit accompanied by tongues. Both Pentecostal and charismatic Christians have emphasized the ongoing role of prophecy in the church, as well as signs, visions, and dreams. The charismatic theologian J. Rodman Williams (1918–2008) called these prophetic experiences an additional means of revelation but stressed that this "revelation is subordinate or secondary to the special revelation attested to in the Scriptures."[21]

Unfortunately, some of the most visible and popular offshoots of Pentecostal and charismatic theology give greater priority to sensational and emotional religious experiences than Scripture. Late-twentieth-century charismatic movements like the so-called Toronto Blessing and Brownsville Revival (also known as the Pensacola Outpouring) emphasized unusual, emotion-filled "manifestations of the Spirit" more akin to paganism than biblical Christianity: "holy laughter," being "slain in the Spirit," barking, animal noises, and "holy intoxication." The fact that these "manifestations" of the Spirit are not in Scripture did not deter their proponents who emphasized experience with God over the Bible.[22]

---

[20] See Geoffrey R. Treloar, *The Disruption of Evangelicalism: The Age of Torrey, Mott, McPherson, and Hammond,* A History of Evangelicalism, vol. 4 (Downers Grove, IL: InterVarsity Press, 2017), 61–63.

[21] J. Rodman Williams, *Renewal Theology: Systematic Theology from a Charismatic Perspective,* 3 vols. (Grand Rapids: Zondervan, 1996), 1:43.

[22] For a helpful analysis of these so-called revivals, see Hank Hanegraaff, *Counterfeit Revival: Looking for God in All the Wrong Places,* rev. ed. (Nashville: Word, 2001).

Another movement, identified as **"third-wave evangelicalism,"** encourages the use of the miraculous gifts and prophecy today but differs from Pentecostalism (the "first wave") and the charismatic movement (the "second wave") in its acknowledgment that baptism in the Spirit is concurrent with conversion.[23] Unlike many Pentecostal and charismatic counterparts, third-wave evangelicals in the Reformed tradition put an emphasis on the sufficiency of Scripture (in the sense of an adequate source of revelatory knowledge) but nevertheless leave room for other experiential means of knowing God's will.

Evangelical theologian Wayne Grudem, one of the leading proponents of third-wave evangelicalism, has argued extensively for an ongoing gift of prophecy, which he defined as "telling something that God has spontaneously brought to mind."[24] While Grudem counts this gift of prophecy as a "revelation" in the broader sense, he does not count it as authoritative in the same sense as Scripture.[25] Third-wave evangelicals appeal to Paul's instruction in 1 Thess 5:19–22 in support of their position: "Don't stifle the Spirit. Don't despise prophecies, but test all things. Hold on to what is good. Stay away from every kind of evil."

The Experiential Dimension of Liberal Protestantism

In the classical, formal sense, liberal Protestant theology represents a tendency to regard "many traditional beliefs as dispensable, invalidated by modern thought, or liable to change."[26] Theologians in the liberal

---

[23] Allison, *Historical Theology*, 449 (see chap. 4, n. 15); C. Peter Wagner, *The Third Wave of the Holy Spirit* (Ann Arbor: Vine, 1988).

[24] Grudem, *Systematic Theology*, 1050; cf. 1049–61 (see chap. 1, n. 17); Wayne Grudem, *The Gift of Prophecy in the New Testament and Today* (Wheaton, IL: Crossway, 2000); Grudem, *The Gift of Prophecy in 1 Corinthians* (Eugene, OR: Wipf and Stock, 2000). See also C. Samuel Storms, "A Third Wave View," in *Are the Miraculous Gifts for Today? Four Views*, ed. Wayne Grudem (Grand Rapids: Zondervan, 1996), 173–223.

[25] Grudem, *Systematic Theology*, 1056–61.

[26] Gary Dorrien, *The Making of American Liberal Theology: Imagining Progressive Religion 1805–1900* (Louisville: Westminster John Knox, 2001), xix.

Protestant tradition may hold different beliefs, but what all liberal theologians have in common is anti-dogmatism: a tendency to question, reject as authoritative, or redefine the primary doctrines of the historic Christian faith. They usually reject the supernatural inspiration of the Bible and aspire to read it through a critical or reconstructive lens. For our purposes here, what is most important to note is that liberal theologians in the classical sense tend to minimize the role of external authorities like Scripture or creeds and confessions in theological formation and emphasize individual human experience and reason. They feel the "liberty" to transform doctrine to conform to their experience of contemporary culture.

Liberal theologians emphasize theology "from below" rather than "theology from above," meaning they start with human experience rather than written revelation. Religious experience, contemporary culture, or context become the final criteria by which theologies are judged, not Scripture or tradition. Scripture has its place to be sure but is generally regarded as a fallible expression of ancient religious experiences. In liberal theology, revelation is an ongoing activity of God that human beings can discern from their personal experiences.

Friedrich Schleiermacher (1768–1834), known by many as "the father of modern theology" or "the father of liberal Protestant theology," spearheaded this move toward liberal, experience-driven theology. Discontented with traditional theology rooted in biblical revelation and Enlightenment natural theology rooted in reason, Schleiermacher redefined religion to be "the feeling of absolute dependence."[27] Influenced by **romanticism**, a cultural and intellectual movement that swept across Europe during the late-eighteenth and early-nineteenth centuries, Schleiermacher rejected rationalistic forms of theology and focused on the individual, experiential aspects of faith.[28]

---

[27] Roger E. Olson, *The Journey of Modern Theology: From Reconstruction to Deconstruction* (Downers Grove, IL: InterVarsity Press, 2013), 129.

[28] For more on the history of romanticism, see Arthur O. Lovejoy, *Essays in the History of Ideas* (Baltimore: John Hopkins University Press, 1948), 228–53.

Liberal theologians often subscribe to the experiential-expressive theory of doctrine described in chapter 2, reducing doctrinal statements to symbolic expressions of religious sentiment. The creeds and confessions of the church are reduced to expressions of our religious experience. Because doctrines are merely symbolic interpretations of religious feelings, they are prone to change over time and from context to context. What is constant and universal about religion are questions about human origins, meaning, and immortality. The Christian belief in the resurrection becomes merely one expression of this universal hope. As a result, liberal theologians tend to embrace religious pluralism, the idea that all faith traditions are equally valid expressions of the human longing for God and immortality.

Liberation Theology

Liberation theology is a term used to describe several prominent late-twentieth-century Roman Catholic and Protestant movements that redefined the gospel and the mission of the church to address the social, economic, and political concerns of "oppressed" peoples such as ethnic minorities and the poor. For liberation theologians, we do not need salvation from God's judgment toward our sin but rather salvation from oppressive political structures like capitalism that keep the poor in their poverty. Latin American and black liberation theologies were the most prominent forms of liberation theology in the late twentieth century, but others, such as feminist theology, womanist theology, and "queer theology," have also gained some traction in universities and mainline Protestant seminaries.

Like Schleiermacher's liberal theology, liberation theology "made human feelings and human sensitivity a source of divine revelation that can be placed alongside Scripture."[29] For Gustavo Gutiérrez, the Roman Catholic priest who first developed Latin American liberation theology,

---

[29] Harold O. J. Brown, "What Is Liberation Theology?" in *Liberation Theology*, ed. Ronald Nash (Milford, MI: Mott Media, 1984), 11.

theology is "critical reflection on praxis."[30] Instead of emphasizing the content of God's self-revelation, Gutiérrez believes theology should reflect on what the church is doing politically for the poor. For James Cone, the father of black liberation theology, black experience, black culture, and black history are foundational sources for theology.[31]

Moral Relativism and the Sexual Revolution

The heirs of Enlightenment-era liberal theology in our postmodern "anything goes" milieu often adhere to a form of **moral relativism**, the belief that morality is merely a social construct that may vary from place to place or from individual to individual. The sexual revolution that began in the 1960s encouraged people to "find themselves" by doing whatever they wanted with their bodies. They rejected divine revelation regarding human sexuality and replaced it with "the autonomous individual's right to self-definition."[32] For moral relativists under the sway of the sexual revolution, everything we have always presumed about sex and gender is open to radical reorientation. When this moral relativism came home to the church, it led to relaxed views on divorce, cohabitation, and eventually, same-sex relationships and transgenderism.

Many who reject traditional Christian interpretations of biblical passages prohibiting same-sex erotic behavior (e.g., Rom 1:24–27; 1 Cor 6:9–11) make experience, not the biblical text, the final authority over belief and practice. The Roman Catholic New Testament scholar Luke Timothy Johnson openly admitted this approach to doctrine: "*We appeal explicitly to the weight of our own experience* and the experience thousands of others have witnessed to, which tells us that to claim our own sexual orientation is in fact to accept the way in which God has created us. By so doing, *we explicitly reject as well the premises of the scriptural*

---

[30] Gustavo Gutiérrez, *A Theology of Liberation*, trans. Caridad Inda and John Eagleson (Maryknoll, NY: Orbis, 1973), 6.

[31] James Cone, *A Black Theology of Liberation* (Maryknoll, NY: Orbis, 2012), 22–41.

[32] Wax, *Eschatological Discipleship*, 135 (see chap. 3, n. 16).

statements condemning homosexuality—namely, that it is a vice freely chosen, a symptom of human corruption, and disobedience to God's created order."[33]

Experience, Theology, and Discipleship

Doctrine and experience relate to one another in paradox. Experience can lay the groundwork for and confirm the truths of doctrine, but it must not have final say in the way we form our beliefs or walk with God. Yet theological beliefs that do not transform our personal experience or walk with God are of little value in the Christian life. We should actively seek to experience God in prayer, the illumination of his Word, and Spirit-empowered ministry. From here, we can draw some basic conclusions about the relationship between religious experience and theology in Christian discipleship.

First, all theology is experiential to some degree. Our experiences shape us, and we should learn from them. Our culture and our upbringing shape the worldviews with which we encounter the gospel. Our experience can color the interpretive framework with which we read the Bible and prompt many of our theological questions.

Second, to be more effective as communicators of theological truth, we must seek to understand the experiences of others. For me, this means I must pay close attention to brothers and sisters in Christ of different nationalities, ethnicities, or cultural backgrounds. Unlike many of my black brothers and sisters in Christ, I have never experienced mean-spirited racial slurs or discriminating behaviors. I also have little personal acquaintance with the collectivist culture in which many of my Chinese and Korean students were reared. While experiences do not *determine* the objective truths of Scripture, they can color the way we receive them. These experiences also shape the ministry needs of the Christian church today.

Third, our experience of God can provide assurance of our salvation and the truthfulness of the gospel. The Spirit gives us an inward testimony of Christ

---

[33] Luke Timothy Johnson and Eve Tushnet, "Homosexuality and the Church: Two Views," *Commonweal,* June 15, 2007, http://commonwealmagazine .org/homosexuality-church-1, italics mine.

(John 15:26). John told us, "The Spirit is the one who testifies, because the Spirit is the truth" (1 John 5:6). God himself gives us a testimony of his activity through Christ (1 John 5:9–11). This inward testimony helps us recognize who we are in Christ: "The Spirit himself testifies together with our spirit that we are God's children" (Rom 8:16).[34] Because we have received this Spirit of adoption, "we cry out, 'Abba, Father!'" (Rom 8:15). As William Lane Craig explained, this inner witness of the Holy Spirit provides for believers a self-authenticating witness to the truthfulness of Christianity that is consistent with reason and evidence.[35]

Finally, believers can be blessed by the experiences of other believers in their testimonies. Testimony can even serve a role in belief formation. Much of the New Testament is the apostolic testimony of the disciples of Jesus, but the testimony of contemporary Christians can also inform my beliefs about God's ongoing activity in the world. Testimonies of answered prayers, miracles, and dramatic conversions can be both informative and encouraging. Testimonies from missionary frontiers detail experiences unusual to my American evangelical experience, such as dreams and visions of Jesus in the Muslim world.

Yet for all these positive things we could say about experience, there are three warnings I want to underscore in closing. *First, we should be wary of lifeless and Spirit-less doctrine.* Doctrine divorced from the heart-rending and obedience-giving work of the Holy Spirit is useless and dead. David Hamilton (1663–1721), Queen Anne's personal physician, anonymously wrote of this Spirit-less Christianity: "Without inward religion, and an inward change upon the will and the affections, the person who merely professes faith is without life, like a dead carcass parted from the soul which animates it. . . . A mere profession in Christ without the Spirit's work is for show, nothing more than shadow. A picture of a

[34] John Wesley, "The Witness of the Spirit," pt. 2, in *The Works of John Wesley*, Bicentennial Edition, vol. 11, ed. Gerald R. Cragg (Nashville: Abingdon, 1987), 167; quoted in Oden, *John Wesley's Teachings*, 1:111; cf. Rom 8:16.

[35] William Lane Craig, *Reasonable Faith: Christian Truth and Apologetics*, 3rd ed. (Wheaton, IL: Crossway, 2008), 43–52.

man is not a real man, just like a professing believer without the work of the Spirit is no real Christian."[36]

Second, we should be concerned about textless enthusiasm. For Wesley, Hamilton, and other eighteenth-century Christians, "enthusiasm" was no compliment. It spoke of an excess of emotion or religious experience divorced from God's revelation in Scripture and reason. Enthusiasts claim to speak on God's behalf or to be empowered by God but defy his Word with practices and teachings foreign to it. Enthusiasts elevate immediate revelation above biblical revelation. They add to Christian doctrine with speculative and inventive ideas.

Cult leaders and false teachers have claimed new revelation from God. Personalities like Joseph Smith Jr. (1805–1844), Jim Jones (1931–1978), and David Koresh (1959–1993) all claimed to have received new revelations from God before founding their religious movements (and meeting early, violent deaths). Even in our own evangelical circles, some have claimed to receive extrabiblical revelation like road trips to heaven or hearing additional words from Jesus not recorded in Scripture. They also have conveniently found ways to monetize these additional revelations through the sale of books, devotionals, calendars, and coffee mugs!

I don't rule out the possibility that God *could* speak directly to individuals (though this is clearly not the ordinary way he communicates his will to us) or the prospect of someone having deep-seated convictions in their heart about what they should do (we all do). I am, however, concerned about anyone who would claim to hear from God about something contrary to Scripture or something extrabiblical they would enforce on the consciences of others. Please don't tell me "thus saith the Lord" unless what you tell me can be found in God's Word. From our experience with the Spirit, one may say, "*I sense* the Lord guiding me to do this," or a pastor may say, "*I feel* like this is the will of the Lord for our church." But these *impressions* of God's activity are not inerrant, nor are they binding on other believers apart from similar direction of the Spirit in their

---

[36] [David Hamilton], *The Inward Testimony of the Spirit of Christ to His Outward Revelation* (London, 1701), 33. I have updated the language and rearranged some of the original phrasing for clarity.

lives. Pastors often lead their churches as they sense the Spirit leading or guiding them (e.g., to go on a mission trip, to plant a new church, or to relocate). Individuals wrestle with the calling and direction of the Spirit in their lives. But make note: the Holy Spirit will never guide us as individuals or as a group in a way that is directly contrary to the words of Scripture that he inspired.

Third, we should be on guard against the deceitfulness of our hearts. The effects of sin on the mind also taint our affections and feelings. Over the years, I have heard professing believers say things like, "I know God wanted me to leave my wife and pursue a relationship with this other woman." "I know the Bible says this is wrong, but in my heart of hearts, I know I'm doing the right thing." "I know God loves me and isn't trying to change me into something I am not." "I have to live *my truth*." Yet any individual who makes his or her feelings the ultimate authority on belief and practice is treading extremely dangerous waters.

In the words of the proverb, "The one who trusts in himself is a fool, but one who walks in wisdom will be safe" (Prov 28:26). As the prophet Jeremiah warned the people of Judah, "The heart is more deceitful than anything else, and incurable—who can understand it?" (Jer 17:9). Our own sinful hearts are the source of our temptations: "Each person is tempted when he is drawn away and enticed by his own evil desire" (Jas 1:14). The heart of flesh is at war with God and resists submission to his instruction (Rom 8:7).

The only way we can guard against self-destructive, feelings-driven religion is through Scripture: "For the word of God is living and effective and sharper than any double-edged sword, penetrating as far as the separation of soul and spirit, joints and marrow. *It is able to judge the thoughts and intentions of the heart*" (Heb 4:12, emphasis added). We must continually exercise repentance, guarding against self-deception. We must pray like the psalmist:

> Search me, God, and know my heart;
> test me and know my concerns.
> See if there is any offensive way in me;
> lead me in the everlasting way. (Ps 139:23–24)

May our worldviews never be reduced to our preferences or feelings. May God cast light on the dark corners of our hearts, and through his Word, expose sin and unbelief.

In conclusion, religious experience does not dictate the meaning of Scripture. Scripture gives meaning to experience, and experience confirms biblical truth. The effective communication and application of biblical truth requires listening to the experiences of our ministry context. Experience has its place in Christian doctrine and discipleship, but it is not a final authority.

KEY TERMS

charismatic movement
glossolalia
liberation theology
moral relativism

Pentecostalism
romanticism
third-wave evangelicalism

GO DEEPER

Grudem, Wayne. *The Gift of Prophecy in the New Testament and Today.* Wheaton, IL: Crossway, 2000.

Schreiner, Thomas R. *Spiritual Gifts: What They Are and Why They Matter.* Nashville: B&H, 2018.

Storms, C. Samuel. "A Third Wave View." In *Are the Miraculous Gifts for Today? Four Views*, edited by Wayne Grudem, 173–223. Grand Rapids: Zondervan, 1996.

Zahl, Simeon. *The Holy Spirit and Christian Experience.* New York: Oxford University Press, 2020.

11

A Procedure for Theology

Open my eyes so that I may contemplate
wondrous things from your instruction.

—PSALM 119:18

Very few works written in theological method offer their readers a
concrete, repeatable methodology for doing theology. After all, as
Bernard Lonergan (1904–1984) observed, "method is not a set of rules
to be followed meticulously by a dolt."[1] Theologians have good reason
for this aversion to the procedural. Theology is not a mechanistic, paint-
by-numbers exercise. It is more of an art than a precise science, more like
wisdom than *technical know-how*.[2] Theology is both an *art-like science* and
a *science-like art*. It is like science in the way it resembles the scientific
method used to identify problems, formulate and test hypotheses, and

---

[1] Bernard Lonergan, *Method in Theology*, Collected Works of Bernard
Lonergan 14 (Toronto: University of Toronto Press, 2017), 3.
[2] See Daniel J. Treier, *Virtue and the Voice of God: Toward Theology as Wisdom*
(Grand Rapids: Eerdmans, 2006).

draw conclusions. It is like art in the way it forces us to be creative, to be wise, and to improvise.

However, no one learns an art without some type of concrete instruction. Every student of the piano must learn the keys and the sounds they make, how to read notes, the timings, rhythms, and the progressions of music. They learn how to play the sheet music before them. A pianist must first learn the rules before she can riff the keys in improvisation. The same is true of the painter, the craftsman, the writer, *and* the theologian. Understanding the process and mechanics of theology is essential to practicing its art form.

Wisdom is not a set of rules but a developed sense of judgment and discernment that enables good decision-making. Yet human beings foster this wisdom through direct instruction and life experience. As I write this, I have two small children in my home. I will often tell them "the fear of the LORD is the beginning of knowledge" (Prov 1:7), but at this juncture in their little lives, neither of them is capable of making complex moral decisions. For the time being, they need direct *commands*, instructions they are capable of obeying at this stage in their moral, mental, emotional, and spiritual developments. Instructions rehearsed and implemented make a person wise (Prov 10:17).

The same is true with students of the theological disciplines. Beginning students in biblical interpretation, pastoral ministry, preaching, and theology need clear direction that will help them make good and wise decisions down the road. As an exegete and a preacher, I learned much from the methods presented in my hermeneutics and preaching classes in Bible college and seminary, though I by no means still follow the "checklist" approaches to biblical interpretation and sermon preparation I was taught in those classes. For me, familiarity with the resources of Bible study and the skills needed to use those resources in preaching have been the long-term benefits of those courses of study. Eventually, I formed my own habits for biblical interpretation and sermon preparation.

Students of theology will need to do the same thing—to move from a method like the one presented here to their own habit of study. Here I present *a way to study theology*. It is not the only way or even necessarily the best way to study theology, but it does reflect the focus on worldview-forming discipleship discussed to this point. My purpose is simply to give students a sketch for how they can study theology and prepare to present their findings, whether it is in a church or an academic setting. I here incorporate everything I have written to this point about worldview and its core elements (grand narrative, truth, practice, and affections). My aim is to help students proceed through these steps in theological research and be prepared to apply them in their ministry settings.

Twelve Steps for Effective Theological Study

1. Regularly read and prayerfully meditate on the written Word of God.

This is not so much a "step" in the process of Christian theologizing as much as it is a prerequisite, a habit every devoted disciple of Jesus must take up. Though many have tried, a systematic theologian *cannot* be faithful to the theological task without regularly feasting on the Word of God. We should be weary of "textless" approaches to theology devoid of interaction with Scripture. Such approaches to theology quickly devolve into speculation without any firm grounding in divine revelation.[3]

Annual reading plans can take readers through the Bible multiple times a year, once a year, or once over a few years.[4] While there is great value in reading large chunks of Scripture in short periods of time—it helps make connections across the canon—there is also a place for more intensive studies of individual books that help you focus on the details

---

[3] Graham Cole offers a helpful warning against "textless doctrine" in *Faithful Theology: An Introduction* (Wheaton, IL: Crossway, 2020), 19–38.

[4] One popular plan developed by Robert Murray M'Cheyne (1813–1843) involves reading four chapters a day and will take readers through the Old Testament once over the course of year and twice through the New Testament and the Psalms. Joe Carter offers a calendar-free version of a Bible reading plan in his book, *The Life & Faith Field Guide for Parents* (Eugene, OR: Harvest House, 2019), 73–77.

and key ideas of their authors. Whether you opt for an annual reading plan or closer readings, be consistent and make observations about what you read in the text. Keep a journal that helps you sort through the ideas we will talk about in this section: (a) the main idea of the text, (b) how the text fits in the grand story of Scripture, (c) its theological truths, (d) its practical instruction, and (e) its devotional value.

2. Engage the biblical text, tradition, and culture with listening ears and thoughtful questions.

Every theological investigation begins with a conversation, or more precisely, every theological investigation begins with butting in to an ongoing conversation that started long before we arrived at the party. The questions we ask stem from overhearing the discussion already going on, and we can only contribute to the discussion by listening to and responding to the voices of Scripture, of the tradition, and from other outside influences.

Some of our theological questions pop up when we are wrestling with baffling biblical passages that present no simple or obvious explanations.

- What is the "blasphemy of the Holy Spirit" Jesus spoke of in Mark 3:28–30?
- What is the gift of "tongues" described in 1 Corinthians 12–14?
- What does Paul mean by the "righteousness of God" in 2 Cor 5:21?
- What is the meaning of the "thousand years" in Rev 20:1–6?

If you come across an idea or concept in Scripture you do not understand or would like to understand more fully, make note of it. Keep a running list of questions you would like to explore.

Other questions surface through the reading of theology. Theology requires a lot of reading, engaging, and responding to the ideas of other theologians and scholars. When it comes to reading theology, my first advice is to read widely and deeply—from within your theological tradition and without. Read old books and new ones. Read journal articles. Read from the best representatives of positions with which you don't agree. Whatever you read, read charitably and critically. Take copious notes and ask questions!

- Does Jesus eternally submit to the will of the Father, or was his submission to the Father limited to the incarnation event?
- What is the relationship between divine sovereignty and human responsibility or freedom in the Scriptures?
- Which traditional practice of baptism most closely adheres to the instruction of Scripture—*credobaptism* (i.e., the baptism of believers only) or *pedobaptism* (i.e., the baptism of infants)?

The more broadly you read in theology and its sister disciplines like philosophy and hermeneutics, the more questions you will uncover.

Experience is not a final authority on doctrine, but it can prompt important theological queries. Our personal experiences provoke questions, as do the testimonial experiences of others.

- How can the Bible and Christian theology help us achieve racial reconciliation?
- Some people from other religions seem so nice. Can I be confident the Christian faith is really "the only way" to God?
- I have a close friend who once openly professed faith in Christ but who later claimed to have become an atheist. Did that person "lose his salvation" or was he never truly saved in the first place?

Culture can prompt significant theological developments as well. The civil rights movement forced American Christians in the 1950s and 1960s to reflect on what it means to be one human race made in the image of God. The legalization of abortion in all fifty states with *Roe v. Wade* in 1972 led to questions about the dignity and worth of pre-born human beings. Now we are having open discussions about what it means to be made male or female.[5] As Christians committed to the sufficiency and truthfulness of Scripture, we are convinced that the

---

[5] Kevin J. Vanhoozer, "A Drama-of-Redemption Model," in *Four Views on Moving beyond the Bible to Theology* (Grand Rapids: Zondervan, 2009), 191–97.

Bible—not culture or experience—ultimately provides the framework by which we must address these issues. In the words of the apostle Paul, "We demolish arguments and every proud thing that is raised up against the knowledge of God, and we take every thought captive to obey Christ" (2 Cor 10:4b–5).

3. Collect all the biblical materials relevant to the question or problem, and then sort them by priority.

Whether your question comes from Scripture, tradition, reason, culture, or experience, you must consider ways in which the Bible might directly or indirectly address it. All biblical texts relevant to the question must be collected and examined.[6]

But how exactly does someone new to Christian theology go about discovering ways in which the Bible addresses our concerns? The more familiar a reader is with the content of Scripture, the easier this step becomes, but there are helpful tools available for this step:

- A trusted **mentor, teacher,** or **pastor** may be a helpful source in getting started.
- **Concordances** may be a helpful place to begin your search for biblical texts, but they are usually limited to the specific words found in the Bible, meaning they would exclude important theological terms like *Trinity, inerrancy,* and *eschatology.*
- Students more well versed in biblical languages may benefit from detailed **Hebrew and Greek dictionaries** like the *New International Dictionary of Old Testament Theology and Exegesis* and the *New International Dictionary of New Testament Theology and Exegesis,* both of which include comprehensive lists of where key Hebrew and Greek terms can be found across the Bible. However, these resources, like concordances, are usually limited to words explicitly used in the Bible.

---

[6] Erickson, *Christian Theology,* 53–56 (see chap. 1, n. 18).

- **Confessions of faith** can also be a valuable resource. Since the Reformation era, most confessional statements have included "proof texts" (*dicta probanta*) or Scripture references that point readers back to biblical passages that support their theological claims. "Proof texts" may have a negative connotation for some, but they do serve an important function for helping people discover relevant biblical materials. Proof-texting is not inherently problematic if the theologian takes the time to do the proper work of exegesis to back up these references.[7]

- **Theological dictionaries,** such as the *Evangelical Dictionary of Theology*, provide encyclopedic summaries of doctrines and their development, detailing key biblical texts related to the topic.[8]

- **Systematic theology textbooks** can be a place to start when looking for texts pertinent to a doctrinal topic, but they are rarely complete in the references they include and can overlook important passages.

- **Topical Bibles and topical Bible guides** arrange the topics of the Bible systematically and usually offer detailed lists of passages relevant to theological topics. *Nave's Topical Bible* is a classic, trusted source that has been revised and updated on several occasions. Books like *The Complete Topical Guide to the Bible* (2017) and *Topical Analysis of the Bible* (2012) provide detailed lists of biblical references for every category and subcategory in systematic theology.[9]

---

[7] See R. Michael Allen and Scott Swain, "In Defense of Proof-Texting," *JETS* 54, no. 3 (September 2011): 589–606; cf. Allen and Swain, *Reformed Catholicity*, 117–42 (see chap. 4, n. 16).

[8] Presently, I believe the standard in this area to be Daniel J. Treier and Walter A. Elwell's *Evangelical Dictionary of Theology* (see chap. 10, n. 3).

[9] Martin H. Manser, Alister McGrath, J. I. Packer, and Donald J. Wiseman, *The Complete Topical Guide to the Bible* (Grand Rapids: Baker, 2017). See also Walter A. Elwell, ed., *Topical Analysis of the Bible: A Survey of Essential Christian Doctrines* (Peabody, MA: Hendrickson, 2012).

Many of these tools are available on your preferred Bible software. While they are all helpful for different reasons, remember that these resources, like any other work in Christian theology, are products of biblical interpretation. Consequently, they are fallible, are prone to theological biases, and are open to correction or revision. There may also be key biblical texts overlooked by these resources that may be discovered through your own close reading of the biblical text.

Theologians, pastors, and students do not always have time to study every passage related to a theological topic in detail, so it is a good practice to prioritize four to six passages that are the most important to cover in your time and writing constraints. One may focus on a passage based on the frequency with which it is used in other treatments of the doctrine. For instance, almost every systematic discussion of the deity of Jesus will include key texts like John 1:1–18; Phil 2:5–11; Col 1:15–23; and Heb 1:1–4, though many other passages could be cited. If we were to take up the debated question "Can a believer who has been genuinely converted lose his salvation?," we would need to work through texts related to eternal security like John 6:35–40; 10:27–30; and 2 Tim 1:12, as well as texts used to defend apostasy like Heb 6:4–6; 2 Pet 2:20–22; and Gal 5:1–5. The scope of the project—whether it is a paper, a sermon, a dissertation, or a book—will always drive the number of passages that can be selected.

4. Using the tools of biblical hermeneutics, determine what it is the authors are trying to do with the relevant biblical texts.

The end goal in biblical interpretation, as with the interpretation of any other text, is to *understand the intended meaning of the authorship of the text*. Medieval interpreters called the author's intended meaning the *literal sense* of the text. What is the *author trying to do with his words*? In the case of Christian theology, our focus is rarely on a single text. We are doing hermeneutical multitasking, often interpreting several related texts at the same time. Our goal is not simply to know what *a human author of Scripture* is doing with *a single text*. We are trying to make sense of what the *divine–human authorship of Scripture is doing across multiple texts*.

First, discern the genres of the texts in question. A **genre** is a form or type of communication and expression used in a medium like literature, music, or film. A basic grasp of the rules of a genre is essential for properly interpreting it. Christopher J. H. Wright and Jonathan Lamb ask their readers to "imagine if somebody landed on our planet unaware of the *advertisement* genre. And they thought everything they read in the advert[isements]—on the walls or buses or on TV—were all simple and true statements of fact, which they were supposed to believe at face value. They would end up with some very strange beliefs about the human race!"[10] Though we have to be taught not to believe everything we see advertised on TV, a rudimentary understanding of advertising will keep us from buying everything we see.

The Bible is a library of sixty-six books that contains several genres: narratives, law, poetry, prophetic literature, wisdom literature, epistles, parables, and apocalyptic literature. Each genre is governed by a different set of interpretive guidelines, and readers of the Bible need to become familiar with how each type of literature works. Introductory biblical hermeneutics textbooks are valuable guides for making sense of these genres.[11] Some genres give direct instruction to the readers; some genres provide bare historical description; and other genres, like poetry and apocalyptic literature, provide imaginative ways of thinking about God and his activity in the world. Familiarity with the rules of a genre can help the theologian distinguish between metaphors and literal language, and between descriptive and prescriptive texts.

Second, slowly and carefully read the immediate context of each relevant text. The immediate context for a verse or passage is usually marked off by

---

[10] Wright and Lamb, *Understanding and Using the Bible*, 23 (see chap. 7, n. 39).

[11] For non-academics and laypersons, I recommend Fee and Stuart, *How to Read the Bible for All Its Worth* (see chap. 3, n. 27). For students of the Bible with academic interests, Klein, Blomberg, and Hubbard's *Introduction to Biblical Interpretation* (see chap. 5, n. 16) is an excellent choice, as is Osborne, *Hermeneutical Spiral* (see chap. 4, n. 32).

headings in contemporary Bible translations. Jesus's statement "You did not choose me, but I chose you" (John 15:16a) is often used as a proof-text for the doctrine of unconditional election. In the CSB, 15:16 falls in a section (15:9–17) under the heading "Christlike Love." Read the unit and pay close attention to verbs and repeated nouns. When 15:16 is read in context, it becomes clear that Jesus's primary purpose is *not* to describe the doctrine of election but to instruct his disciples in the kind of love they should have for one another: a love that reflects the self-sacrificial love of God the Son (15:13). Jesus loved the disciples as the Father had loved him (15:9a). He instructed them to remain in his love by keeping his commandments (15:9b–10, 14) and loving one another (15:17).

Third, more advanced students of the Bible familiar with Hebrew and Greek will work to make sense of the passages in their original grammatical context. Students who seek to study the Bible in its original languages (Hebrew, Greek, and Aramaic) are in a far better place to grasp the various nuances of the words of Scripture (**semantics**), how those words relate to one another in their various forms (**morphology**), and the grammatical structures of biblical texts (**syntax**). Students who are not as familiar with biblical languages can rely on the work of quality critical commentaries by Old Testament and New Testament scholars who unpack these issues for them.[12]

Fourth, gather information on the historical context and cultural background of the passages. Historical factors like authorship, date, and intended audience can be crucial for understanding the message of the book. Readers cannot fully grasp the theological claims of the Bible without some understanding of its "social context"—the worldviews, behaviors,

---

[12] Less technical, more "user-friendly" critical commentaries include the new Christian Standard Commentary from B&H Academic and its predecessor, the New American Commentary. The New International Commentary on the Old Testament (NICOT) and the New International Commentary on the New Testament (NICNT) from Eerdmans and the Baker Exegetical Commentaries on the Old and New Testaments are also personal favorites. The online resource https://www.bestcommentaries.com/ provides community rankings of individual commentaries and sorts them into groups by theology, level of technical expertise needed, and pastoral or devotional application.

institutions, and customs of the biblical world. For example, many New Testament passages are better understood in the light of Second Temple Judaism—the worldview, religion, culture, and society that developed between the Old and New Testaments. Students can glean this information from secondary sources like critical biblical commentaries, Old Testament and New Testament introductions, and Bible dictionaries and encyclopedias. Newer resources are usually better because they often include detailed and up-to-date information about recent archaeological discoveries and developments in the field.[13]

Fifth, make sense of each relevant passage in its larger literary context. The author's intended meaning cannot be seized without attention to the larger **literary context** of a verse, passage, sequence, or book. The literary context is the way a passage logically fits into the passages around it. Jesus's teaching on Christlike love (John 15:9–17) makes more sense when read in the larger context of his final instructions to the disciples before his betrayal (13:1–16:33). Seek to understand the role the immediate context plays in the larger context of the whole book. For this task, Grant Osborne recommends reading and charting the flow of thought in a whole book of Scripture.[14] Find common threads between the paragraphs and sections of the text.[15] When the text is read in its literary context, theological themes throughout the book start to become evident.

Finally, establish the main purpose of the texts in question. What is the "big idea" of the passage? What *information* does the text communicate? Most importantly, what is the author trying to do? Remember the four elements of the speech-act discussed in chapter 7:

- the words written or spoken (the *locutionary act*) that account for the words used, the grammar, and the syntax of a passage
- the persons, places, and things to which the text refers (the *propositional* act)

---

[13] Osborne, *The Hermeneutical Spiral*, 37–38.
[14] Osborne, 40–45.
[15] Donald S. Whitney, *Spiritual Disciplines for the Christian Life*, rev. ed. (Colorado Springs, CO: NavPress, 2014), 66.

- the purpose of the writing (the *illocutionary act* or *speech-act*) that accounts for what the author is trying to do (i.e., inform, command, promise, bless, etc.)
- the intended effects of the writing on the hearer (the *perlocutionary act*) that account for how the message is received

From the passage, determine what the divine-human authorship of the passage wants readers to do in response (e.g., to remember something, to obey, to pray). The primary purpose of most historical books in the Old Testament is not to teach moral lessons but to help God's people *remember* his work in their midst. Old Testament law *regulated* the community of Israel; for New Testament readers, it points to our ultimate need for Christ. New Testament letters *address needs* in the early church. Apocalyptic literature like the book of Revelation serve both as *hope* for the believer and a *warning* for those who do not know Jesus.

5. Place the theological theme of these texts in the larger story of Israel or the church and then in the grand narrative of Scripture fulfilled in Christ.

After you have employed the tools of hermeneutics to establish the main point of the passages related to your theological topic, you will need to relate the texts to biblical theology. Biblical theology takes its shape from the grand narrative of the Bible.[16] From Genesis to Revelation, the "salvation history" of the Bible unfolds like one big, interconnected story in five acts:

- Act 1: God *creates* the world and everything in it from nothing. He created man and "crowned him with glory and honor" (Ps 8:5b). Humanity rebels against him, plunging the world into darkness and despair.

---

[16] See Klink and Lockett, *Understanding Biblical Theology*, 93–107 (see chap. 4, n. 6). I have adopted and adapted the approach to biblical theology described by Klink and Lockett as BT3: Biblical Theology as Worldview Story.

- Act 2: God elects the people of *Israel* to be the instrument through which he will reveal his name, his law, his wisdom, and his promises to the world. Israel's sin keeps them from fulfilling their mission, but God promises a coming Suffering Servant who will fulfill the promises he made to them.

- Act 3: God sends *Jesus* the Messiah, who announces the kingdom of God and who carries out his redemptive plan in the world. On the cross, Jesus takes the punishment for sin that rightly belongs to sinful humanity. In the climax of human history, Jesus is raised from the dead, becoming the firstfruits of our own future resurrection (1 Cor 15:20).

- Act 4: God creates a new people, the *church*, from Jews and Gentiles alike who are tasked with carrying out the Great Commission given by Jesus and empowered by the Holy Spirit to do so. This is the "incomplete" part of the biblical story in which we presently live our lives.

- Act 5: God will bring history to an *end* with the glorious return of Jesus the Messiah, the consummation of the kingdom, and the establishment of a new heaven and a new earth free of sin, pain, suffering, and death (Rev 22:1–5).

The unified witness of Scripture is an unfolding or **progressive revelation**, meaning God has gradually disclosed more and more of himself over the course of history. While the authors of Scripture lived in various stages of this unfolding revelation, they spoke about God and his world in a coherent way within a shared worldview.

Every unit of text has some relationship to God's work in the life of Israel (Old Testament theology) or God's work in the life of the church (New Testament theology). Both levels connect to the arc of the biblical story (biblical theology). Narrative passages take place like "scenes" in the five acts of the biblical story. Every act ultimately points to Christ. Israel's story across the Old Testament anticipates Jesus by raising the questions only he can answer. Non-narrative passages like laws, psalms, prophecies, and epistles are only properly understood in the contexts of Israel's story or the church's story and the grand, overarching story of the Bible.

In assessing the biblical theology of a text, look for unique theological themes or emphases the text offers, such as God's loving-kindness, the righteousness of God, or the kingdom of God. Themes in biblical theology tend to be narrower than the categories of systematic theology. In order to grasp how the text or theological theme fits in the story of Scripture, we will need to understand how this point relates to the *whole book* and the *corpus of an author* (i.e., all the books by a single author). Then we will need to relate that idea to the *Testament* in which it is located (i.e., Old or New Testament).

The final and most important step of biblical theology is making sense of a biblical theme across the whole *canon*. "All Scripture is a testimony to Christ, who is Himself the focus of divine revelation," so our goal is to make sense of how the text, typology, or theme—whether it is in the Old Testament or the New—ultimately relates to the gospel of God's redemptive plan in Christ.[17] We achieve this final step by recognizing the text's place in the five acts of Scripture and noting how it serves the overall story of the Bible. How does this passage reveal Jesus Christ? If it is an Old Testament text, does it (1) directly prophesy about Jesus, (2) present a typology of Jesus, or (3) evidence an encounter with the preincarnate Christ?

6. Identify theological truths either explicitly stated by the biblical authorship or presumed by the author.

The Bible is not a systematic theology written in a single voice, but a library of books written in several genres and with distinct voices. Instead of speaking from a single voice and a single genre, "God spoke . . . at different times *and in different ways*" (Heb 1:1, emphasis added).[18] Consequently, a Christian theology dedicated to making disciples who

---

[17] See Naselli, *How to Understand and Apply the New Testament*, 239–43 (see chap. 4, n. 14). Naselli uses the topic of holiness across the Bible to make the connections between the theology of the Old Testament and its fulfillment in Christ.

[18] See Vanhoozer, *Drama of Doctrine*, 272–76 (see chap. 2, n. 2). Vanhoozer calls Scripture "plurivocal and polyphonic" (272).

learn to think like the Bible must do more than mine it for facts. We must seek to understand and obey the Bible in its own life-transforming terms. However, we cannot neglect the direct truth claims of Scripture or overlook the worldview beliefs of biblical authors.

We are seeking to understand what God has disclosed about himself through the human authors of Scripture. Because they wrote under the inspiration of the Holy Spirit, this step means *discerning the stated and unstated theological beliefs of all biblical authors* and *restating them for our contemporary setting.* In other words, we are trying to understand the worldviews of the Bible and train people in the present to think like biblical authors do. The discerning reader of Scripture can *reconstruct the theological framework* of the text by asking questions from the categories of systematic theology:

1. The doctrine of God (theology proper)—who is God in this passage?
2. The doctrine of humanity (theological anthropology)—who are human beings in this passage?
3. The doctrine of Christ (Christology)—what does this passage say about the person and work of Christ?
4. The doctrine of salvation (soteriology)—what does this passage explain about salvation and redemption?
5. The doctrine of the Spirit (pneumatology)—what does this passage teach about the Holy Spirit?
6. The doctrine of the church (ecclesiology)—what does this passage say about the new covenant people of God?
7. The doctrine of last things (eschatology)—what does this passage say about the future God has planned for us?

7. Isolate the practices the biblical authors encourage readers to take up, either in his explicit instructions or in the implications of what they are saying or doing in the text.

Medieval biblical interpreters referred to this step as discerning the "tropological" or moral sense of the text. A significant portion of

Scripture contains God's commands for his people. Some biblical authors focus on the character of the disciple. Other portions of Scripture provide general principles for wise living under the leadership of the Holy Spirit. As disciples, we want to pay close attention to the speech-acts of Scripture, *responding in obedience* to what God is doing and saying through the biblical text. In the long run, we desire for the text to reshape and renew our character as followers of Jesus. A few guiding questions may help us work through the practical direction of a passage.

What is the genre of the text? Genre is important for discerning practical instructions in Scripture. The Mosaic law offers a series of divine commands given to Israel with the purpose of maintaining the covenant community. It includes basic moral laws binding on all people for all time, civic regulations specific to the governance of the cities and tribes of Israel, and ritual instructions for the worship of Israel. Moral instructions like the Ten Commandments "are understood to have permanent validity."[19] Prophetic literature reinforces the law by showing its application in changing situations faced by the kingdom. Wisdom literature like the Proverbs gives guidance to readers by helping them think through the consequences of wise and foolish practices. Old Testament narratives are not prescriptive but provide illustrations for the rewards of obedience and the consequences of sin.

Jesus's teachings in the Gospels provide clear instruction for the new covenant community that produces obedience and a change of character. Narratives like Acts can provide principles for Christian mission but primarily serve to tell the story of the work of the Spirit in the church. The New Testament epistles contain direct statements and instructions given to the people of God living in Act 4 of the divine drama.

Who is the intended audience of the text, and at what moment in salvation history is the practical direction given? This question is useful in distinguishing between instructions specifically meant for Israel's civil governance

---

[19] Mark F. Rooker, *The Ten Commandments: Ethics for the Twenty-First Century* (Nashville: B&H Academic, 2010), 192.

(e.g., laws about food, slavery, agriculture, capital punishment) and commands that continue to have direct relevance for Christians in the New Testament (e.g., the Ten Commandments). Most instructions written to the New Testament church have direct bearing on us in the present, though some statements seem to be specific to a moment in time and culture (e.g., Paul's direction to Timothy to drink wine for his stomach problems in 1 Tim 5:23; the instruction to greet one another with a holy kiss in 1 Thess 5:26). The hard work of hermeneutics helps us distinguish between permanent and context-specific directions.

What type of ethic does the passage employ? Does the passage give a direct command from God (divine command ethics), a type of moral instruction that shows the consequences of our actions, whether good or bad (consequentialist ethics), or instruction meant to grow us in our character and virtue (virtue ethics)? Occasionally a biblical passage can contain multiple ethical approaches at once. Consider Paul's instruction to families from Eph 6:1–3: "Children, obey your parents in the Lord, because this is right. **Honor your father and mother**, which is the first commandment with a promise, **so that it may go well with you and that you may have a long life in the land.**"

Paul told children (presumably adult children and their offspring) to honor their parents. He did so by the *divine command* of Deut 5:16. Because God commands this, we have a duty to obey. Paul also stated we should obey parents because it is the right thing to do (Eph 6:1). In so doing, he appealed to the *virtue of the act*. Paul also ensured a *good result* for obedience to this commandment: things will go well for you, and you will have long life in the land (6:2–3).

8. Work to harmonize the theological and practical truths of the relevant texts with other theological statements and ideas throughout Scripture.

Biblical authors may write with different emphases that reflect the act of the divine drama in which they find themselves, but they do so under the inspiration of the Holy Spirit, who cannot disagree with himself. In its diversity, the Bible presents us with an "organic unity" among the acts of the grand narrative. The systematic theologian wants to see how these truth claims "fit" together into a coherent whole. A guiding principle is what the Reformers called the *analogy of faith* (*analogia fidei*): Scripture helps us interpret Scripture. The clearer parts of Scripture help us understand the more difficult parts.

One approach begins by sorting relevant passages into groups of related texts (and subgroups if necessary). Many systematic theologians organize the pertinent biblical texts into sections of the canon, like this:

- The Pentateuch on sacrifice and atonement
- The Prophets on sacrifice and atonement
- The Gospels on Jesus's sacrifice and atonement
  — The Synoptic Gospels (i.e., Matthew, Mark, and Luke)
  — The Gospel of John
- The Pauline letters on Jesus's sacrifice and atonement
- The Catholic letters on Jesus's sacrifice and atonement
  — Petrine Literature (1 and 2 Peter)
  — Hebrews
  — The Letters of John

This is a helpful way for beginning students in theology to sort materials, but it is not the only way. A more advanced approach takes up the observation of "patterns" across the biblical text.[20] New Testament doctrines build on Old Testament concepts or ideas. New Testament authors clearly construct their concept of Christ's sacrifice with reference to Old Testament patterns about God's nature, human sin, and the sacrificial system.[21]

The task of harmonization requires attention to the unity of the Bible's truth and the diversity of its witness. Truths across Scripture will not contradict one another, but biblical authors do vary in their emphases and

---

[20] This approach is explained and well illustrated in Matthew Y. Emerson, *"He Descended to the Dead": An Evangelical Theology of Holy Saturday* (Downers Grove, IL: InterVarsity Press, 2019), 11–17.

[21] See Erickson, *Christian Theology*, 733–36.

their respective presentations of truth. The theologian must make sense of these differences. For example, why do the Synoptic Gospels treat the life of Jesus differently than the Gospel of John, and how do their presentations of Jesus cohere with one another? Do Paul and Jesus present the same gospel message? All biblical authors speak to the same reality—God's work in Christ—but underscore various aspects of that reality.

Work to understand how the various theological truths of Scripture relate to one another. In other words, ask what the implication of the doctrine is for other doctrines. How does Christ's atonement relate to our doctrines of the Trinity, God's attributes, humanity, sin, the incarnation of Christ, salvation, the work of the Holy Spirit, the church, and last things? The more you think through these types of questions, the more specific they will become. How does God's eternality relate to his work in predestination? How can Jesus be truly God—who is omniscient—and still seemingly lack knowledge of certain things (Matt 24:36; Luke 2:52)? How can Jesus be truly man—who was tempted (Matt 4:1–11; Mark 1:12–13; Luke 4:1–13)—and still be God, who James tells us is "not tempted by evil" (Jas 1:13)?

Work to resolve apparent contradictions in the Bible. While there are no genuine contradictions in Scripture, there are Bible difficulties we must work to resolve. For example, James asserted that Abraham was justified by works and not by faith alone (Jas 2:20–24), but Paul insisted Abraham was justified by faith and not works (Rom 4:1–5). Yet in this case, Paul and James were using the terms "works" and "justify" in distinct senses.[22]

9. Consult the resources of tradition, reason, and other cultural perspectives in order to enhance your understanding of the biblical text and its doctrinal truths.

Remember, the Reformation principle of *sola Scriptura* does not mean a Christian worldview and theological framework cannot be informed by

---

[22] See Putman, *When Doctrine Divides the People of God*, 179–81 (see chap. 2, n. 35).

other sources than Scripture. Additional sources from tradition, reason, and culture can aid in the interpretation of biblical texts.

Read creeds, confessions, and classic resources in tradition. Ask how the doctrine was treated in patristic Christianity (c. 100–600), the medieval church (600–1500), the Reformation and the post-Reformation (1500–1750), and in modernity (1750–present).[23] Use the tools discussed in chapter 8 to discover how the tradition speaks to the theological question you have raised. Secondary sources like historical theology textbooks and systematic theologies can point you to valuable primary sources from across the tradition. Commentaries like the *Ancient Christian Commentary on Scripture* and the *Reformation Commentary on Scripture* collect various ancient and Reformation-era interpretations of biblical texts and arrange them by books and chapters of the Bible. These resources are extremely helpful in analyzing the passages relevant to your theological inquiry.

Read the work of contemporary biblical scholarship. Read from the best commentaries available on the passages you are studying.[24] Preaching commentaries are of some value in sermon preparation, but also take the time to read **critical commentaries** by Old and New Testament scholars who are thoroughly trained in the languages and background of biblical books. Glean what you can from biblical-theological treatments of the topic.

Read the work of other systematic theologians—past and present alike. Read the pertinent sections from systematic theology textbooks. Read the primary sources from ancient, medieval, and Reformation Christianity.

---

[23] This fourfold group of chronological categories for historical theology comes from Allison, *Historical Theology*, 12 (see chap. 4, n. 15).

[24] When students ask me which commentary series is the best to buy, I normally do not recommend any one series but suggest that students search out the best commentaries available for the particular book of the Bible they would like to study. Which commentaries are quoted the most frequently? Which commentaries provide the best historical resources? I find the website http://www.bestcommentaries.com to be a helpful source in finding these. It ranks commentaries by book of the Bible, provides reviews, and distinguishes between technical and non-technical commentaries.

If you need help finding these sources, secondary sources like historical theology textbooks can help point you to those relevant to your topic. Read **monographs** from contemporary theologians that focus on specific doctrines.

Read scholars and Christians from other theological traditions. To reiterate what was said above, take the insights of other theological traditions seriously. Reading broadly safeguards us from simply confirming our own views or the views of our tradition.[25]

Read scholars and Christians from other cultures. I do not encourage seminary students or laypersons to read other cultural perspectives on the Bible because doctrinal truth changes from culture to culture or because culture ultimately determines the meaning of biblical texts. As I have argued to this point, neither of these statements is true. However, there is significant value in reading the perspective of Christians in other cultures. First, we are fallible interpreters who can misunderstand the meaning of texts. Second, reading other cultural perspectives sheds light on how the Spirit is helping other believers in other contexts apply Scripture.

Read the work of philosophical theologians and philosophers of religion. Remember, philosophical and analytic theologians do not always use the standard tools of biblical exegesis, but they do use philosophical tools to analyze key biblical ideas. They often bring a much-needed clarity to the theological meaning of the biblical text.

10. Rank doctrines according to their importance.

Not every doctrine is of equal importance for belief or practice. Christian theologians often rank doctrines according to their urgency for the church. R. Albert Mohler Jr., renowned for his "doctrinal triage," uses the illustration of an emergency room triage to separate those who need immediate treatment (e.g., gunshot victims) from those who will be waiting for hours to see a doctor (e.g., those who have the sniffles). According to Mohler, some doctrinal disagreements demand immediate attention

---

[25] See Putman, *When Doctrine Divides the People of God*, 151–71.

(i.e., faith-denying heresies), while others can wait out the process of discipleship and seasons of disagreement.

Doctrinal ranks like the triage sort doctrines into primary, secondary, or tertiary categories. In his discussion of the doctrinal triage, Gavin Ortlund offers four categories of doctrine:

- First-rank doctrines that are "*essential* to the gospel."
- Second-rank doctrines that are "*urgent* for the church (but not essential to the gospel)."
- Third-rank doctrines that are "*important* to Christian theology (but not essential to the gospel or necessarily urgent for the church)."
- Fourth-rank doctrines that are "*indifferent*" because they are "theologically unimportant."[26]

Ortlund's ranking of doctrines distinguishes between first-rank beliefs essential to becoming a Christian, second-rank doctrines that divide local churches or congregations, third-rank doctrines that, while important, are not enough to divide Christians in local church fellowships, and fourth-rank doctrines that are theologically insignificant.

One of the key steps in the process of "doing" systematic theology is ranking doctrines according to their importance. For ranking doctrine into categories like these, I use three tests: (1) the hermeneutical test, (2) the gospel test, and (3) the praxis test. I have written extensively about these elsewhere, but I will expound on them briefly for you here.[27]

The hermeneutical test is a way of assessing doctrines most clearly stated in Scripture. While all Scripture is "clear" in the sense that it is intelligible or capable of being understood, not everything in Scripture is equally easy to understand.[28] Doctrines that are more clearly understood by Christians across different traditions are usually first-rank, essential doctrines. These include but are not limited to the deity of Jesus, his

---

[26] Gavin Ortlund, *Finding the Right Hills to Die On: The Case for Theological Triage* (Wheaton, IL: Crossway, 2020), 47.

[27] See Putman, *When Doctrine Divides the People of God*, 218–39.

[28] The Westminster Confession of Faith 1:7.

resurrection from the dead, salvation by grace through faith alone, and the return of Jesus.

The more disputed second-, third-, and fourth-rank doctrines usually stem from the more debated passages in the Bible. While Christians all agree Jesus is returning, they disagree about when and where. While we all affirm that the Bible teaches predestination, we disagree about the meaning of Scripture on how and why God predestines believers.[29]

The gospel test ranks doctrines in relationship to the gospel message. It begins by asking, "What is the gospel? And what must I believe in order to become a Christian?" The goal of such a test is not to reduce doctrine to the least common denominator but to distinguish between the gospel itself and other doctrines that either support the gospel or are practical implications of it.[30] For this test, I rely heavily on the work of Michael Wittmer, who distinguishes between doctrines Christians *must believe*, doctrines Christians *must not reject*, and those doctrines Christians *should believe*.[31] Upon conversion, a Christian *must believe* Jesus is Lord (Rom 10:9). While a new Christian is not expected to have a clear grasp on the doctrine of the Trinity, she *must not reject* it. Finally, Christians *should believe* in doctrines such as biblical inerrancy or God's knowledge of future events, even if they are not required for salvation. These doctrines are not part of the gospel, but they buttress the gospel message.

The final test is the praxis test, which asks, "What doctrines are vital for fellowship and partnership in ministry?"[32] Christians may recognize other believers as true brothers and sisters in the faith while still having disagreements that keep them from ministering together in the same congregation. Many of these disagreements relate to the practice of a local church. Someone who has strong convictions about credobaptism (i.e., the baptism of believers alone) will struggle to join with a church

---

[29] For a helpful categorization of doctrines that sorts them according to biblical clarity, see Erickson, *Christian Theology*, 65–66; cf. Putman, *When Doctrine Divides the People of God*, 220–25.

[30] Putman, 225–32.

[31] Michael E. Wittmer, *Don't Stop Believing: Why Living Like Jesus Is Not Enough* (Grand Rapids: Zondervan, 2008), 15–20.

[32] Putman, *When Doctrine Divides the People of God*, 233; cf. 232–39.

that practices pedobaptism (i.e., the baptism of infants). These doctrinal matters, while urgent or important (what Ortlund calls "second-rank" or "third-rank" matters), do not prevent us from co-laboring in public ministry with believers who disagree with us on these matters. Bible-believing and gospel-preaching Baptists, Presbyterians, and Methodists could partner together in a citywide ministry or in a joint evangelistic effort, despite their practical disagreements in ecclesiology.

One more note about ranking doctrine: when you shepherd a local congregation, the people in the pews look to you as an expert authority on biblical and doctrinal matters. Many of their theological opinions will be shaped by how you answer their questions. For this reason, it is of great importance that you *explain why Christians disagree* on certain doctrinal topics, and what topics afford us room for theological disagreement. Boldly preach the Christian hope of the second coming of Christ. Make a case for your own interpretation of the events surrounding his return, but also grant freedom for disagreement on third- and fourth-rank doctrinal differences.

11. Determine the way the doctrine directs our affections in worship, prayer, and self-reflection.

The affective dimension of Christian theology is often neglected in favor of the cognitive and propositional elements, but as Paul Hiebert insisted, "In the Christian worldview, *feelings are as important as truth in our understanding of God, ourselves, and our relationships to one another.* Comparatively little theological reflection has been accorded to the affective dimension. Much more is needed."[33] A brief set of diagnostic questions can help us think about the affective implications of a text or a doctrine.

How does this theological truth lead me to prayer and worship? The Psalms tell us to "Praise him for his powerful acts; praise him for his abundant greatness" (Ps 150:2). We praise God for (1) what he does and has done, and (2) who he is in his attributes. What does the passage or

---

[33] Hiebert, *Transforming Worldviews*, 291, italics mine.

doctrine teach us about God's activity in the world and in salvation history? What does the passage teach us about the greatness of God? Fixate on these things and give thanks to the Lord for who he is. Pray Scripture back to God by turning the Bible's language *about* God *toward* God:

- "[You are my] God, [you are] the faithful God who keeps his gracious covenant loyalty for a thousand generations with those [of us] who love [you] and keep [your] commands" (Deut 7:9).
- "God [you are] faithful; [I was] called by [you] into fellowship with [your] Son, Jesus Christ our Lord" (1 Cor 1:9).
- "[You have] rescued [me] from the domain of darkness and transferred [me] into the kingdom of [your] Son [whom you] love. In [your Son Jesus] [I] have redemption, the forgiveness of sins" (Col 1:13–14).

Meditate on these things and give thanks to the Lord for who he is. As J. I. Packer has defined it, meditation on the truth of God "is the activity of calling to mind, and thinking over, and dwelling on, and applying to oneself, the various things that one knows about the works and ways and purposes and promises of God. It is an activity of holy thought, consciously performed in the presence of God, under the eye of God, by the help of God, as a means of communion with God."[34]

How does this truth help me confront my sinful desires and passions? Does the truth expose an area of personal weakness in my life? Paul wrote that "those who belong to Christ Jesus have crucified the flesh with its passions and desires" (Gal 5:24). We are called to crucify our sinful longings—to put to death the indwelling sin that keeps us from obedience to Christ. There is a significant correlation between the way our minds think about obedience and the way we practice obedience. *Metanoeó*, the most frequently used word in the New Testament for "repentance" (Matt 3:2; 4:17; 11:20; Mark 1:15; Luke 13:3, etc.), is a word that literally means "to change one's mind." We must repent of our sin by changing the way we think about it. Reflect on the sovereignty and holiness of God. Meditate

---

[34] Packer, *Knowing God*, 23 (see chap. 5, n. 1).

on the sanctifying work of the Spirit in your life. Ask God to help you hate your sin the way he does and to stir your affections for the things that please him.[35]

How does this truth promote emotional wellness? It is easy to become dejected, depressed, anxious, or bitter, but let Scripture be your first line of counsel. When meditating on the Word, seek the peace, joy, and comfort offered to followers of Christ. Let the faithfulness of God displayed in the grand story of Scripture sink into your own life story. Let your theological convictions about God's character help you trust him more and to be patient and wait on his perfect timing in all things.

12. Present your theological discovery in a contextually appropriate manner for the purpose of shaping the worldviews of disciples.

Without a clear and relevant presentation of Christian doctrine fitting to the context in which the theologian, pastor, or teacher is ministering, doctrine cannot be effective in making disciples. As a pastor, it is valuable for me to know the people I shepherd and their struggles in order to more effectively relate to them in my preaching. This relevant, contextual presentation of doctrine is the subject we will need to address next.

KEY TERMS

concordances
confessions of faith
critical commentaries
genre
Hebrew and Greek dictionaries
literary context
mentor, teacher, or pastor
monographs

morphology
progressive revelation
semantics
syntax
systematic theology textbooks
theological dictionaries
topical Bibles and topical Bible
  guides

---

[35] See Kris Lundgaard, *The Enemy Within: Straight Talk about the Power and Defeat of Sin* (Phillipsburg, NJ: P&R, 1998), 79–89.

PART FOUR

Practices

Delivering the products of Christian theology

12

Contextualizing Doctrine

I have become all things to all people, so that I
may by every possible means save some.
—1 CORINTHIANS 9:22

Whether we are preaching, teaching, or writing, the way we communicate doctrine is just as important as the process by which we formulate it. It does not matter how much we know or how precise we are in our use of theological language if our intended audience cannot make sense of what we are trying to say. Having solid biblical content and rigorous logic does not guarantee discipleship is always taking place, particularly if the doctrinal instruction is not compelling in its presentation and meeting the needs (both felt and real) of its hearers. Poorly communicated truth cannot provoke the people of God to love and good works. Doctrine that does not connect with its hearers falls short of its purpose in disciple-making.

Christian truth proclaimed in the context of disciple-making must be shared in such a way that it is meaningful and relevant to its hearers, no matter their background or station in life. Since the 1970s, theologians and **missiologists** (i.e., scholars of Christian missions) have called this task **contextualization**.[1] As Timothy Keller has noted, contextualization does not mean "giving people what they want to hear" but rather "giving people *the Bible's answers*, which they may not at all want to hear, *to questions about life* that people in their particular time and place are asking, *in language and forms* they can comprehend, and *through appeals and arguments* with force they can feel, even if they reject them."[2]

While this term *contextualization* may be relatively new in the history of Christian thought, its practice is as old as time itself. God gave clear and intelligible instruction to our first parents, even though they disobeyed it. The law he gave to the Israelites had regulations and provisions specific to their cultural setting. The prophets applied the law to a people in and out of exile. In the incarnation, the Son of God became a man who lived in a real place and time in history. In the footsteps of their Master, the earliest Christians learned how to express the good news of Jesus in ways both Jewish and Gentile hearers could relate to it and respond.

This chapter is about making the content of Christian doctrine relatable and compelling to the culture and context to which the Lord assigns us, wherever that might be and in whatever capacity we are called to serve. Whether in Jerusalem, Athens, Nashville, New York, or Nineveh, you are called to express Christian truth in a relatable and loving way to the people you are called to serve.

---

[1] See Ray Wheeler, "The Legacy of Shoki Coe," *International Bulletin of Missionary Research* 26.2 (2002): 77–80; Justin Ukpong, "What Is Contextualization?" *Neue Zeitschrift für Missionswissenschaft* 43 (1987): 161–68; David J. Bosch, *Transforming Mission: Paradigm Shifts in Theology of Mission* (Maryknoll, NY: Orbis, 1991), 420–23; David J. Hesselgrave and Edward Rommen, *Contextualization: Meanings, Methods, and Models* (Grand Rapids: Baker, 1989), 27–35.

[2] Timothy Keller, *Center Church: Doing Balanced, Gospel-Centered Ministry in Your City* (Grand Rapids: Zondervan, 2012), 89, italics in original.

Two Problematic Approaches to Contextualization

Theologians, pastors, and missionaries face two extremes when it comes to the task of giving a contemporary expression of Christian teaching for their contexts. They can either underestimate the important role context plays in interpreting and communicating biblical truth, or they can allow their non-Christian context or culture to dictate or control what they believe and teach. Millard Erickson calls those who make the former mistake "transplanters." Transplanters presume we can uproot the historically rooted message of the Bible and drop it in another culture or demographic without any adaptation or indigenization.[3] The latter group, which William Hordern critically labeled "**transformers**," believes traditional Christian beliefs and practices must be changed to be relevant to their context.[4]

Transplanters

Transplanters often overlook the dissimilarities between the cultures of the biblical world and their own. New York journalist A. J. Jacobs humorously illustrated the "transplanter" mindset in his 2007 bestseller *The Year of Living Biblically*. In this amusing experimental memoir, Jacobs, a self-described agnostic from a non-religious Jewish family, chronicles his attempt to follow the Bible's instructions as literally as possible for one year.[5]

After reading the Bible through for the first time, Jacobs compiled a seventy-two-page checklist of laws and instructions he found in this cursory reading and proceeded to act on as many as possible. He mothballed everything polyester in his closet so as not to violate the Torah's prohibition against wearing clothing with two kinds of material (Lev 19:19).

---

[3] Erickson, *Christian Theology*, 73–75 (see chap. 1, n. 18).

[4] William Hordern, *New Directions in Theology Today*, vol. 1, *Introduction* (Philadelphia: Westminster, 1966), 141–42; cf. Erickson, *Christian Theology*, 76.

[5] A. J. Jacobs, *The Year of Living Biblically: One Man's Humble Quest to Follow the Bible as Literally as Possible* (New York: Simon and Schuster, 2007).

He quit shaving so he wouldn't violate Levitical instructions about beard grooming (Lev 19:27; 21:5). He even walked around New York City in a biblical-era getup like a costume from *The Ten Commandments* movie. In his effort to follow Num 15:32–36, Jacobs tried his hand at politely "stoning" Sabbath-violators in Central Park with small pebbles. Though he was intending to lampoon the literalism he perceived to be at the center of religious fundamentalism, he inadvertently demonstrated how biblical and theological illiteracy can result in the misapplication of Scripture. His experiment shows the Bible cannot be rightly obeyed without being interpreted in its original historical-cultural context and then properly applied to the context of the reader.[6]

Good hermeneutical practices are essential to understanding the teaching of the Bible and applying it to contemporary settings. For example, one needs to understand that not every instruction from the biblical world is normative for every successive context.[7] The civic and ceremonial laws given to Israel were distinct instructions to those living in a theocratic government under the old covenant. Laws regarding capital punishment for religious offenses are not applicable in secular states like ours. Many of the laws about animal sacrifices and dietary restrictions are no longer relevant in the new covenant (Acts 10:9–15; Heb 9:11–12). Nonetheless, the Old Testament remains authoritative for believers living in the new covenant because it is an important witness to God's acts in salvation history and because it contains principles still applicable for holy living today.

Even the New Testament contains incidental, context-limited instruction not directed toward all Christians in every time and place. For example, no Christian doctor is expected to prescribe wine to all his patients with stomach ailments, even if Paul made this personal suggestion to Timothy in a world without Pepto-Bismol (1 Tim 5:23). When Paul told slave masters to deal with their slaves fairly (Col 4:1), he did not

---

[6] To his credit, Jacobs did consult Bible scholars, historians, and religious leaders as he conducted this experiment. Yet his piecemeal approach to the laws and instructions of the Bible never really put him in contact with the big picture of the Bible. See Vanhoozer, "A Drama-of-Redemption Model," 152–53 (see chap. 11, n. 5).

[7] Vanhoozer, 154–55.

intend to enshrine slavery as a permanent human institution. Instead, he spoke about how Christians could act and react lovingly and wisely given the harsh realities of their present context.

Transplanters don't generally go to the comical excesses detailed in Jacobs's book, but they are skeptical about attempts to contemporize the message of the Bible. A small minority deny any need to present biblical and theological truth in a contextually or culturally specific manner. Many transplanters push back against contextual theology out of the concern that it changes the essence of timeless Christian truth. By refusing to contextualize Christian truth, they can distort it.[8] Like Paul's Jewish opponents in Galatia who expected Gentiles to take up Jewish cultural practices before coming to faith in Christ, transplanters naively presume their distinctive cultural practices must be assumed by those whom they convert and disciple.[9] Over the years, well-meaning Christians have told me to wear suits and ties because "God wants us to give him our very best." "Our very best" just happens to be reflective of their own culturally conditioned fashion preferences. Transplanters confuse the timeless truth of the gospel and biblical doctrine with particular cultural expressions.

Transformers

The 1980s animated TV series *Transformers* (and the terrible film series based on it) was about a race of giant robots from the planet Cybertron who could transform into different vehicles, such as muscle cars, eighteen-wheelers, or jets. The good guys were the Autobots, and the bad guys were the Decepticons (as if they could be anything but villains with a name like that). Theological "transformers" are not robots from

---

[8] David J. Hesselgrave, "Syncretism: Mission and Missionary Induced?" in *Contextualization and Syncretism: Navigating Cultural Currents*, Evangelical Missiological Society 13, ed. Gaylin Van Rheenen (Pasadena, CA: William Carey Library, 2006), 81–82.

[9] M. David Sills, "Paul and Contextualization," in *Paul's Missionary Methods: In His Time and Ours*, ed. Robert L. Plummer and John Mark Terry (Downers Grove, IL: IVP Academic, 2012), 197.

Cybertron but theologians who change Christian beliefs to make them more palatable to their cultural contexts. Instead of seeking to transform the culture with biblical truth, transformers (or theological Decepticons?) allow cultural norms to transform their theological beliefs.

Transformers practice what Gailyn Van Rheenen calls **theological syncretism**: "the conscious or unconscious reshaping of Christian . . . beliefs . . . through cultural accommodation so that they reflect the dominant culture."[10] **Syncretism** can occur on the mission field when a missionary or convert uncritically integrates a cultural or religious practice into their Christian framework. "Folk religion" may blend Christian beliefs with native customs and beliefs, like the ongoing practice of ancestor worship or adding Jesus to a pantheon of other deities.[11]

One of the more controversial outreach strategies to Islamic peoples among evangelical missionaries has been the development of "insider movements," which actually encourage Muslim converts to Christ to stay in mosques, maintain their Muslim identity, and retain Muslim practices they view as compatible with Christian belief.[12] Missionaries who support this strategy contend it is similar to Paul's strategy for reaching Jews in synagogues. They also insist this tactic is best for the safety of Muslims coming to faith in Christ, especially in totalitarian contexts where Christianity is illegal. Yet even well-intentioned advocates of these insider movements often overlook the dangers of such a contextual approach.

---

[10] Gailyn Van Rheenen, "Syncretism and Contextualization: The Church on a Journey Defining Itself," in *Contextualization and Syncretism: Navigating Cultural Currents*, Evangelical Missiological Society 13 (Pasadena, CA: William Carey Library, 2006), 7.

[11] One prevalent example of religious syncretism is the Day of the Dead (*Día de los Muertos*), a Mexican national holiday, an amalgamation of millennia-old indigenous rituals honoring the dead and the Roman Catholic observance of All Saints' Day.

[12] For a collection of arguments in favor of insider movements, see Travis Talman, ed., *Understanding Insider Movements: Disciples of Jesus within Diverse Religious Communities* (Pasadena, CA: William Carey Library, 2015). A collection of essays more critical of insider movements is available in Ayman S. Ibrahim and Ant Greenham, eds., *Muslim Conversions to Christ: A Critique of Insider Movements in Islamic Contexts* (New York: Peter Lang, 2018).

Muslim practices are sacramental in Islam and inseparable from belief, which stresses submission to Allah and the teachings of his prophet Muhammad. Some insider movement converts even read the Qur'an alongside the Bible as part of their religious practice,[13] but the Qur'an outright denies biblical truths like the divinity of Jesus and the doctrine of the Trinity (Qur'an 4:171; 5:72–75, 116).

Theologians who openly champion liberal theology practice a type of theological syncretism that accommodates Christian belief to academic and cultural fads. Liberal theologians throughout the last two centuries have had diverse emphases and methods, but they hold a few things in common. First, they reject traditional views of biblical authority and make culture, experience, or a philosophy the final criterion by which belief systems should be judged.[14] Second, their theology is *modern* because of their "preference for the new over the traditional."[15] Third, their theology is *liberal* because they consider themselves entitled to "the free criticism of all theological claims."[16] Not even the historic tenets of Christian orthodoxy are beyond their scrutiny.

Transformers maintain that the "faith once received" (see Jude v. 3) must be changed in order to be made more sensible and tolerable for people who oppose the gospel.[17] The Bible repeatedly cautions against the dangers of distorting the truth by conforming it to the culture (Rom 12:2). God warned Israel not to comingle with pagan nations and appropriate the worship of their idols and gods (e.g., Exod 20:3; 23:13; Deut 5:7; 6:14; 11:16; 2 Kgs 17:41). New Testament authors combated false teachers who introduced heresies and pagan practices into the life of the

---

[13] Phil Parshall, "Danger! New Directions in Contextualization," *Evangelical Missions Quarterly* 34.4 (1998): 404–10.

[14] Bernard Ramm, "Liberalism," in *Baker's Dictionary of Theology*, ed. Everett F. Harrison, Geoffrey W. Bromiley, and Carl F. H. Henry (Grand Rapids: Baker, 1960), 322–23; cf. Hesselgrave and Rommen, *Contextualization*, 146.

[15] Ramm, "Liberalism," 322.

[16] Ramm, 322.

[17] John Shelby Spong, *Why Christianity Must Change or Die: A Bishop Speaks to Believers in Exile: A New Reformation of the Church's Faith and Practice* (San Francisco: HarperCollins, 1998).

local church (Col 2:8, 18). Paul advised Timothy about false teachers who are "always learning and never able to come to a knowledge of the truth" (2 Tim 3:7). They have a guise of Christian truth but are "deceiving and being deceived" (2 Tim 3:13). Believers committed to the historic Christian faith and the full truthfulness of Scripture find the transformer approach to contextualization unacceptable.

Faithfully and Meaningfully Communicate Christian Truth

Both the transplanter and transformer approaches to contextualization fall short. Between these two positions, William Hordern has called for a middle way, the "translator" approach.[18] The **translator** is both faithful to the message of Scripture and cognizant of her need to make that message intelligible to a specific context or setting without changing its essence. In sum, contextualization is "the attempt to communicate the message of the person, works, Word, and will of God in a way that is faithful to God's revelation, especially as it is put forth in the teachings of Holy Scripture, and that is meaningful to respondents in their respective cultural and existential contexts."[19]

While the gospel message does not change, the method of proclaiming the gospel may vary from context to context and audience to audience. Paul illustrated this in his ministry to Jews and Gentiles. He expressed an intentional desire to adapt to the context where he served in order to reach the people there:

> To the Jews I became like a Jew, to win Jews; to those under the law, like one under the law . . . to win those under the law. To those who are without the law, like one without the law . . . to win those without the law. To the weak I became weak, in order to win the weak. I have become all things to all people,

---

[18] Hordern, *New Directions in Theology*, 1:142; Erickson, *Christian Theology*, 77–80.

[19] Hesselgrave and Rommen, *Contextualization*, 200.

so that I may by every possible means save some. Now I do all this because of the gospel, so that I may share in the blessings. (1 Cor 9:20–23)

Paul's sermons in Acts make excellent case studies for contextual gospel presentations.[20] Paul did not focus his ministry on any single ethnic group or culture. He did not give a "Gentile theology" or a "gospel for Jewish people," nor did he start affinity-group congregations for targeted interests. Instead, he preached an unchanging gospel to all people but contextualized his expression of it for every setting, situation, and audience.[21]

When Paul proclaimed the gospel to Jewish audiences, he was speaking to a group with a shared frame of reference rooted in the narrative of the Old Testament (Acts 13:16–41). He did not have to convince the Jews in Antioch that Yahweh is the one true God (13:16). They all agreed on the basic plot of Scripture: that God elected Israel and called them out of Egypt (13:17); that God gave Israel the Promised Land after years of wandering in the wilderness (13:18–19); and that God installed David as the king over Israel (13:20–22). Paul addressed their common hope and expectation that God would send a redeemer through the line of David (13:23–25) and asserted that Jesus of Nazareth was the fulfillment of that promise (13:26–38). Paul made similar arguments elsewhere to those who also presupposed Scripture's authority (17:1–3, 10–11). He ended with a call to repentance that addressed their tendency to trust the law of Moses for their justification before God (13:38–41).[22]

Unlike his presentation to Jewish audiences, Paul's proclamation of the gospel to the Gentiles did not include shared assumptions about Israel's God. In his address to the city of Lystra (Acts 14:15–17), Paul had to correct the assertion of the crowd that he and Barnabas were pagan

---

[20] See Eckhard J. Schnabel, *Early Christian Mission,* vol. 2, *Paul and the Early Church* (Downers Grove, IL: InterVarsity Press 2004), 1293–1475; cf. Schnabel, *Paul the Missionary: Realities, Strategies, and Methods* (Downers Grove, IL: InterVarsity Press, 2008), 155–208.

[21] Schnabel, *Paul the Missionary,* 306–7.

[22] Schnabel, 156–62; Schnabel, *Early Christian Mission,* 1380–85.

gods Hermes and Zeus in human form (14:8–12). Instead of speaking to their shared assertions about God, he spoke to their shared humanity and described the God who created them (14:15). He bemoaned the fallen human condition wrought by sin and perpetuated by pagan worship (14:16) but also spoke of the common grace and general revelation God has given all people everywhere (14:17). Paul made scriptural allusions (14:15; cf. Exod 20:11; Ps 146:6) but did not quote the Scripture extensively because his hearers did not yet share his belief in biblical authority.[23] Before he could speak to this polytheistic audience enamored with folk religion about the gospel of Jesus Christ, he needed to persuade them there was one God, the "living God," and that this God cared deeply for them regardless of their erroneous beliefs.[24]

Paul's sermon at Areopagus to a group of cultured pagan philosophers (Acts 17:22–31) differed in style from his sermon to the folk pagans in Lystra. His rhetoric began with a commendation of the audience, appreciative of their interest in religious things (17:22). He attempted to make a point of contact with their altar of worship to "an Unknown God" (17:23). Though he did not extol their worship of pagan deities, he said they rightly acknowledged a God whom they still did not yet know, the Lord of heaven and earth who created all things (17:24a).

Paul first confirmed points of agreement he had with the Epicureans and Stoics who were present, even quoting their poets and philosophers (17:28).[25] He contrasted this unknown God with the gods they served

---

[23] Schnabel, *Paul the Missionary*, 166.

[24] Schnabel, 162–68; Schnabel, *Early Christian Mission*, 1116–19.

[25] Scholars debate the origin of the phrase "for in him we live and move and have our being" (*en autō gar zōmen kai kinoumetha kai esmen*) in Acts 17:28a. Many attribute it to Epimenides, the sixth- or seventh-century BC poet also cited in Titus 1:12. The latter quotation, "For we are also his offspring" (*gar kai genos esmen*), comes from the third-century BC poet Aratus (*Phenomena* 5). See Ben W. Witherington III, *The Acts of the Apostles: A Socio-Rhetorical Commentary* (Grand Rapids: Eerdmans, 1997), 529–30; cf. Betril Gärtner, *The Areopagus Speech and Natural Revelation*, Acta seminarii neotestamentici upsaliensis 21, trans. Carolyn Hannay King (Uppsala: Almquist & Wiksells, 1955), 179–98; Edouard Des Places, "'Ipsius enim et genus sumus' (Act 17,28)," *Biblica* 43.3 (1962): 388–95; Mark J. Edwards, "Quoting Aratus: Acts 17, 28," *Zeitschrift für*

(17:24b–29). He then proclaimed God was calling for all people everywhere to repent and turn to him (17:30) and has established a day of judgment through Jesus Christ, whom he raised from the dead (17:31). When Paul stressed the bodily resurrection from the dead—something absurd to pagan philosophers who denied the goodness of the body— most of the crowd dismissed him (17:32–33). Some, however, came to faith in Christ (17:34).

In all these contexts, Paul demonstrated a commitment to the faithful and meaningful expression of gospel truth, no matter the audience or environment. First, Paul was well acquainted with Scripture and Christian truth—something that came with his formal training in Judaism and his personal time with the Lord (Gal 1:14–18). Second, when Paul entered a new place, he sought to understand the people and their culture. Third, he engaged in constructive dialogue with his audiences in which he expressed points of agreement and confronted cultural beliefs and practices that were contrary to revealed truth. Paul affirmed aspects of culture useful for introducing people to Christ and was countercultural where the gospel conflicted with culture.[26] Finally, in places where he had success, Paul helped establish indigenous churches that provided an ongoing gospel presence (Acts 14:21–23; 2 Tim 2:2).

The ministry of Paul provides a useful pattern for thinking about contextualizing theology. Contextualization, like any ministry to a new and challenging setting, is normally a long-term task that requires hard work, perseverance, and the ability to think on one's feet. For the sake of clarity, however, I want to talk about this process in a more procedural way. I do not think about this as a one-and-done, surefire method for contextual theological teaching but rather as a biblical and practical

---

die neutestamentliche Wissenschaft und die Kunde der älteren Kirche 83.3 (1992): 266–69.

[26] Dean Flemming, "Paul the Contextualizer," in *Local Theology for the Global Church: Principles for an Evangelical Approach to Contextualization*, ed. Matthew Cook, Rob Haskell, Ruth Julian, and Natee Tachanpongs (Pasadena, CA: William Carey Library, 2010), 11–13.

(yet incomplete) process for communicating and appropriating Christian truth for your ministry setting.

Exegete Your Audience

The successful translator of biblical truth has a good grasp on the hearers or readers he is addressing. Exegete your audience and the culture of which they are a part.[27] *Recognize that some things about your audience are universal, biblical, and theological givens.* No matter where they live, no matter what culture they come from, no matter how old they are or how educated they may be, the people you encounter are people who were made in God's image (Gen 1:27–28). God created them to know him and to reflect his glory (Isa 43:7), but they are also sinners, born into this world corrupted by sin and depravity (Ps 51:5; Eccl 7:20, 29; Rom 5:12; Eph 2:1–3). The good news of the gospel is that Christ died for sinners, even when they were undeserving of his love (Rom 5:1; 1 John 1:8–10).

Be sensitive to the cultural context of your immediate audience. I have pastored in rural and urban settings, and while the same kind of personalities that live in one church tend to live in another, their ways of life can be poles apart. The illustrations about gridiron football used in the Southern United States will not stick in other cultures. Literary allusions or analogies that would stimulate a highly educated audience have less appeal in a blue-collar congregation. Outside the United States, believers in Majority World churches face distinct challenges virtually unknown to Western Christians. All these factors shape the way we apply and illustrate our texts and the way we frame our theological categories.

Be mindful of the knowledge base and education level of your audience. My children's sermons do not sound like the messages I write for adults, though I usually try to be mindful of children who are listening to the sermons with their parents and vice versa. I do not talk about Christian doctrine with my first-semester theology students on the same level as

---

[27] Paul G. Hiebert, *Anthropological Reflections on Missiological Issues* (Grand Rapids: Baker, 1994), 88–89.

I will when I am speaking to a room full of PhD-credentialed theologians. Laypersons often deal with anxiety about Christian doctrine that we must seek to alleviate, not by impressing them with our knowledge but by speaking about doctrine in such a way that it meets their real and perceived needs.[28]

Timothy Keller recommends preachers use "accessible or well-explained vocabulary," especially in sermon settings where they will address outsiders unfamiliar with technical terminology or "evangelical subcultural jargon."[29] Seek a common language that a diverse group of hearers will understand.[30] Inaccessible language excludes hearers from receiving the Word of God and can send the message that those who cannot understand it aren't welcome.[31] In writing and teaching Christian theology, we cannot (and should not) completely avoid the use of our rich doctrinal vocabulary, but we should always take time to make sure it is well explained and illustrated if our intended audience is not familiar with it.

Consider the spiritual conditions of your primary audience. Is your primary audience made up of nonbelievers, new or immature believers, or strong and maturing believers?[32] If they are nonbelievers, what kind of spiritual receptivity do they exhibit? Are they antagonistic toward the gospel, hesitant about the gospel but not antagonistic, somewhat receptive to the gospel, or are they "low-hanging fruit," ready to receive the gospel if we will ask?[33] If they are believers, do they display a teachable spirit and a hunger to learn, or are they stifled in their spiritual growth by

---

[28] Helmut Thielicke, *A Little Exercise for Young Theologians*, trans. Charles L. Taylor (Grand Rapids: Eerdmans, 1962), 3–5.

[29] Timothy Keller, *Preaching: Communicating Faith in an Age of Skepticism* (New York: Viking, 2015), 103, 105.

[30] Matthew D. Kim, *Preaching with Cultural Intelligence: Understanding the People Who Hear Our Sermons* (Grand Rapids: Baker, 2017), 27–28.

[31] Keller, *Preaching*, 106.

[32] Keller, 182.

[33] These questions come from the faith stages described in Thom S. Rainer, *The Unchurched Next Door: Understanding Faith Stages as Keys to Sharing Your Faith* (Grand Rapids: Zondervan, 2003), 20–21.

ongoing sin or personal challenges? The smaller the audience, the more focused the teaching or writing can be. The wider the audience, the more likely the preacher or teacher will need to be sensitive to all these groups and consider the various ways the biblical text or doctrinal topic will meet their needs.[34]

Engage Your Ministry Context

The process does not end with analyzing our setting. We cannot make disciples without talking to the people in our ministry context about Jesus! When he first arrived in Corinth, Paul had a day job as a tent-maker (Acts 18:3) but spent every Sabbath "reasoning" (*dielegeto*) in the synagogue trying "to persuade both Jews and Greeks" to believe the good news about Jesus (18:4). Like Paul, we want to engage in constructive theological dialogue in "such a way that God's Word speaks prophetically to that context."[35]

Start by contrasting their worldview with the grand narrative of Scripture summed up in the gospel. Begin by affirming your shared assumptions and concerns. Make the case that nothing outside of Christ—whether it is politics, science, or hedonism—can remedy this broken world. Articulate the Bible's story in a way that addresses the universal worldview questions, plainly describing God's creative purpose for the world and human beings, the problem of sin, and the redemption bought by Jesus.

Address unique circumstances faced by your cultural context. Christians in every culture and in every generation face new questions and dilemmas.[36] This is true on the mission field when a new convert must decide whether she should continue honoring her deceased ancestors in their family traditions. This is likewise true in a Western context grappling with the ramifications of the sexual revolution when the broader culture shuns traditional views on gender roles, sexuality, and marriage. We must

---

[34] Keller, *Preaching*, 182–83.

[35] Ashford and Whitfield, "Theological Method," 51 (see chap. 1, n. 2).

[36] Clark, *To Know and Love God*, 114 (see chap. 1, n. 8); cf. Robert J. Schreiter, *Constructing Local Theologies* (Maryknoll, NY: Orbis, 1985), 6–12.

offer gospel hope to seemingly hopeless situations and confront the cultural idols that keep people from enjoying God's blessings in their lives.

The British historian of missions Andrew Walls made a helpful distinction between the "pilgrim" principle and the "indigenizing" principle, or what Timothy Tennent calls the "universal" and the "particular" in the Christian gospel.[37] The gospel itself is the universal principle, the unchanging element that unites all believers (pilgrims) throughout history in their respective contexts, despite differences in language, culture, and personal backgrounds. The indigenizing principle is the way in which the gospel impacts the peculiar challenges faced in each cultural context.[38]

Wisdom is needed when responding to indigenous cultural beliefs and practices. What distinctive cultural practices can be affirmed and retained? Which should be corrected and revitalized? Which must be confronted and rejected?[39] Transplanters tend to snub all cultural practices that are not like their own, and transformers uncritically embrace cultural beliefs and practices. Translators attempt to speak prophetically by applying biblical truth to unique cultural beliefs and practices, many of which are not directly addressed by Scripture.

We can begin by identifying the theological and ethical nonnegotiables detailed in the Bible.[40] These come from explicit statements in or direct inferences from Scripture. Where Scripture plainly speaks, the matter is settled. The New Testament repeatedly, explicitly condemns fornication (*porneía*), or sex between persons outside of the confines of a marriage between one man and one woman (1 Cor 5:1, 9; 6:9; 7:2; Gal 5:19; 1 Thess 4:3). The Bible, as we have seen already, condemns

[37] Andrew Walls, *The Missionary Movement in Christian History: Studies in the Transmission of the Faith* (Maryknoll, NY: Orbis, 1996), 7–9; Timothy C. Tennent, *Theology in the Context of World Christianity* (Grand Rapids: Zondervan, 2007), 11–14.

[38] Tennent, *Theology in the Context of World Christianity*, 12.

[39] Flemming, "Paul the Contextualizer," 11–15.

[40] A. Scott Moreau, "Contextualization, Syncretism, and Spiritual Warfare: Identifying the Issues," in *Contextualization and Syncretism: Navigating Cultural Currents*, 64–65.

same-sex erotic behavior. Consequently, sexual practices outside of God's design for marriage should be universally rejected, no matter the time or place.

The more difficult questions come with social and ethical issues that Scripture does not address directly. What is a "biblical" stance on buying lottery tickets or participating in fantasy football leagues with monetary prizes? Though Scripture does not offer an explicit position on gambling, it does show us how to be wise with our money. How might biblical theology inform our positions on gun control, climate change, and affirmative action? Christians who share a desire to see human flourishing may disagree with one another about what public policies best produce those ends. We can reason from Scripture but have the freedom to disagree about how to apply the Bible to these matters.

Whatever the cultural circumstances, our end goal is clear: to make disciples who are transformed by biblical truth, who are learning to think biblically about the world around them, and who are striving to live faithfully as followers of Jesus. Pastors, missionaries, and theologians can model this by studying the Bible together with our people.[41] In so doing, we implicitly remind them that the Bible, not experience or culture, is the ultimate authority on discerning the will of God in these cultural practices.

Conclusion

As Christian theologians, pastors, teachers, evangelists, and other leaders working in various ministry contexts, we need to be intentional about expressing truth in ways that fit the needs of our hearers. Theology rooted in revelation can provide sound answers to the existential questions raised by our culture, but culture should not control the conversation because

---

[41] Hiebert, *Anthropological Reflections on Missiological Issues*, 89; Clark, *Know and Love God*, 114.

it does not always ask the right questions.[42] We want Scripture to direct and have the final say in the discourse.

A final word of warning: overemphasis on meeting local needs can lead to a parochial theology that is too limited in its scope or focus.[43] Though theology should be expressed in a way that is meaningful to a local context, the content of theology should not be restricted to a local context. Biblical authors addressed specific contexts, but their message still translates into other settings. One of the dangers that many liberation and postmodern theologies face is an overly narrow focus on the local context that neglects what God is doing in other places and among other people. The essential content of the gospel does not change from one culture to another. As the apostle Paul argued, the gospel "is the power of God for salvation to *everyone who believes*, first to the Jew, and also to the Greek" (Rom 1:16, emphasis added).

Whether you are preaching doctrinal sermons or writing papers or blog posts, keep your intended audience in mind. Know about them and relate to them. Only the truth spoken in love can produce maturity in the lives of believers (Eph 4:15–16). Be like Jesus, who was full of grace and truth (John 1:14). And finally, as Paul told the Colossian Christians, "Act wisely toward outsiders, making the most of the time. Let your speech always be gracious, seasoned with salt, so that you may know how you should answer each person" (Col 4:5–6).

KEY TERMS

contextualization
missiologists
syncretism
theological syncretism

transformers
translators
transplanters

---

[42] Stanley J. Grenz and Roger E. Olson, *20th-Century Theology: God and World in a Transitional Age* (Downers Grove, IL: InterVarsity Press, 1992), 119–22.

[43] Patricia Harrison, "Bridging Theory and Training," in *Local Theology for the Global Church*, 210–12.

GO DEEPER

Bosch, David J. *Transforming Mission: Paradigm Shifts in Theology of Mission*. Maryknoll, NY: Orbis, 1991.

Keller, Timothy. *Center Church: Doing Balanced, Gospel-Centered Ministry in Your City*. Grand Rapids: Zondervan, 2012.

Schnabel, Eckhard J. *Early Christian Mission*, vol. 2. Downers Grove, IL: InterVarsity Press, 2004.

————. *Paul the Missionary: Realities, Strategies, and Methods*. Downers Grove, IL: InterVarsity Press, 2008.

Tennent, Timothy C. *Theology in the Context of World Christianity*. Grand Rapids: Zondervan, 2007.

Walls, Andrew. *The Missionary Movement in Christian History: Studies in the Transmission of the Faith*. Maryknoll, NY: Orbis, 1996.

13

Writing a Theological
Research Paper

> Writing systematic theology is hard.
> —OLIVER CRISP, *ANALYZING DOCTRINE*

If you are in a Bible college or seminary, you more than likely will be required to write a theological research paper at some point in time. Some students have a knack for writing papers. They enjoy the "thrill of the hunt" in research, tracking down resources, and putting their big ideas to paper. Others muster the same excitement for writing a paper as they do for a root canal. Whether you are in the former, admittedly geekier crowd, or the latter, probably more common one, I want you to remember why you are doing this in the first place. Writing research papers can be an act of worship to the God who created human language and expressed himself in it. Writing research papers is also a ministry to everyone you will ever serve in a local church, regardless of whether they ever see anything you write.

While you might not always have to write formal academic papers, writing is a vital skill for Christian ministry you need to hone for the sake of God's people. Every week as a pastor, I write sermons, devotions, and personal notes to church members who need me to be able to state God's truth for them in a clear and compelling way. I need to be able to make rational and convincing arguments for my decisions as a pastor or administrator. As a theology professor, I write emails, lecture notes, and articles. Learning how to write good papers in a formal setting makes me better at communication in more informal settings. Academic writing trains you in how to think well, establish your main point clearly, and make compelling cases for your point-of-view.

A well-crafted academic paper resembles a well-crafted sermon. The best papers, like the best sermons, invite the reader in with an enticing *introduction* and a clearly articulated *main idea*. They make *arguments* and use *data* to support their case. They use *illustrations* to help their audience understand and apply key concepts. The best theological papers even elicit a *response* on the part of their readers. After all, the end goal of all Christian theologizing is growth as disciples of Jesus.

The goal of this chapter is to help students compose well-developed and logically cohesive theological papers. My hope is that you can integrate the methodological research procedures covered in previous chapters into this chapter, which specifically addresses the writing process itself. While my focus here is on writing papers in systematic theology, many of the principles laid out here are applicable to paper writing in other related disciplines in the theological family tree.

Find the Right Topic

One of the most challenging parts of the writing process can be choosing your topic. You may feel pressure to impress. You may worry about the library having the books you need. You may even have grandiose ideas about a fifteen-page paper that will change the world of theology forever. Let me ease your burden here: "there is nothing new under the sun" (Eccl 1:9b). Besides, if you write something too new in theology, you run a good risk of writing something heretical. Rather than reinventing the wheel, think about writing *a good paper* on a familiar topic with *your unique voice* for *your ministry context*. Focus more on learning for yourself and your distinct calling as a minister of the gospel—not discovering the next big thing in theology or biblical studies.

Choose a topic that builds on your training and background knowledge.[1] With all my degrees in Christian ministry, biblical studies, and theology, I probably will not be writing an article about foreign trade policy or molecular biophysics any time soon. Write what you know, or at least what you can learn within a reasonable amount of time. If you are in an introductory theology course, you can build on what you have studied in the course and the knowledge you have acquired in the discipleship ministries of the local church. If you are in a more advanced course, you may be expected to build on a wider base of knowledge established in earlier coursework.

Choose a topic you can write about within your allotted time frame. Writing a good fifteen- to twenty-page paper usually requires a *close reading* of two to three books and familiarity with the contents of several others. As discussed in chapter 8, Lucretia Yaghjian recommends students read their sources three times: once to summarize, once to categorize, and once to criticize.[2] This requires significant time dedicated to your research. As a student, the first thing I did when receiving a syllabus was mark the date in my calendar when my major paper was due. I would try to commit four to six weeks for working on that major paper, which meant doing some creative scheduling as I worked around other assignments for the class and assignments for other classes. Whatever way you schedule your research and writing time, you need to ensure you do not bite off more than you can chew in the research process.

---

[1] Umberto Eco, *How to Write a Thesis*, trans. Caterina Mongiat Farina and Geoff Farina (Cambridge, MA: The MIT Press, 2015), 7.

[2] Yaghjian, *Writing Theology Well*, 48–49 (see chap. 8, n. 43).

244 The Method of Christian Theology

Choose a topic on which you can find quality resources in a timely manner.[3] Closely related to the previous suggestion, you need to be able to put your hands on the pertinent resources quickly when researching to write. Once you have a topic in mind, you can usually find several books on that topic located in the same section of your library. Comb the footnotes of those books to look for frequently repeated sources. Acquire those books or articles from your library or an online source. Online journal databases your school subscribes to can provide a gold mine of additional sources as well.

Choose a topic that evokes your passions and interests. The topic might address a need in your life or your ministry context. The topic may be controversial. The topic might be of great importance to defend or critique. Your level of interest in the topic will keep you engaged and stimulate creative thought. For students preparing to write their master's theses or dissertations, great interest in the topic is crucial because of all the time they will spend with it in the writing process.

Choose a topic that can interest others. No one is going to find a topic that will appeal to everyone, but you can find a topic that will interest the narrow audience you have in mind. Of course, part of your challenge in writing the paper is to be able to "sell it" to your readers—to explain its importance to them in a way they can see its value. This involves taking a broad topic and creating a specific problem with a practical outcome or consequence tied to it.

In a systematic theology class, you will more than likely be tasked with writing on one of the following topics. From this list, you can find a broader topic from which you later can tighten your focus. This will probably require you to read what various systematic theologies say about the subject. You need to make note of the scholars quoted or addressed in the chapters related to your topic. Check out books you find in the footnotes. This will situate you in the topic and prepare you for the next level.

---

[3] Eco, *How to Write a Thesis*, 7; Wayne C. Booth et al., *The Craft of Research*, 4th ed. (Chicago: University of Chicago Press, 2016), 33.

Theological Method
- Definitions of theology
- Doctrinal language
- Sources of theology
- Process of theology

The Doctrine of Revelation
- General revelation
- Special revelation
- Doctrine of Scripture

God (Theology Proper)
- The existence of God
- The attributes of God
- The Trinity
- Creation
- Providence

Humanity (Anthropology)
- The creation of humanity
- The image of God
- The constitution of humanity
- Human sexuality

Sin (Hamartiology)
- The nature of sin
- The transmission of sin
- The scope and effects of sin

Christ (Christology)
- The person of Christ
  — The deity of Jesus
  — The humanity of Jesus
  — The incarnation
  — The union of the two natures

- The work of Christ
  — The offices of Christ
  — The atonement
  — The resurrection
  — The ascension

Salvation (Soteriology)
- The order of salvation
- The beginning of salvation (election, conversion)
- The objective aspects of salvation (union with Christ, justification)
- The subjective aspects of salvation (regeneration, sanctification)
- The completion of salvation (eternal security, apostasy)

The Holy Spirit (Pneumatology)
- The person of the Spirit
- The activities of the Spirit
- The gifts of the Spirit

The Church (Ecclesiology)
- The nature of the church
- Church government
- Church ordinances (baptism, Lord's Supper)

Last Things (Eschatology)
- Individual eschatology (heaven, hell, intermediate state)
- Cosmic eschatology (the return of Christ, final judgment, restoration of creation)

Unless you are tasked with writing a general summary of one of these doctrines, you will likely need to focus the topic even further. One way you can tighten your focus is to concentrate on a recent debate over the topic or the stance of a denomination or faith tradition on the topic. You may consider assessing how a theologian from history or a contemporary biblical scholar has treated the topic. For example,

- Augustine on original sin
- Hugo Grotius (1583–1645) on the atonement
- The fourth-century development of trinitarian doctrine
- Jacob Arminius on the order of salvation
- Pentecostal perspectives on the gift of prophecy

Yet even these topics need to be narrowed further. As the authors of *The Craft of Research* observe, "A topic is probably too broad if you can state it in four or five words."[4] Once you have a broader topic that holds your interest, you need to develop a problem related to that topic you will explore for your readers.

Creating Problems for Your Readers

Finding the problem means you need to ask the So what? question. Beyond your own interest in the research question, why would others think this is a question worth asking? Your task is to help the reader understand its importance by connecting it to concerns important to them.

Researchers deal with two kinds of problems: **practical problems** and **conceptual problems**. A practical problem is a problem that affects our well-being; it robs us of our joy or causes us pain in a tangible way.[5] Practical problems force us to research an issue. A practical problem might be "I can't stream from Hulu right now." If my Hulu connection is not working, I will research how to fix it, lest I miss out on the trendy new reality show everyone is buzzing about on social media. More than likely, the solution involves (1) repairing my internet connection by resetting my router, or (2) paying my Hulu or cable bill.

---

[4] Booth et al., *The Craft of Research*, 37.
[5] Booth et al., 50.

A conceptual problem, by contrast, is a research problem in an academic sense: "we simply do not *understand* something about the world as well as we would like."[6] The relationship between conceptual and practical problems resembles the process of discovering theological questions described in chapter 11:[7]

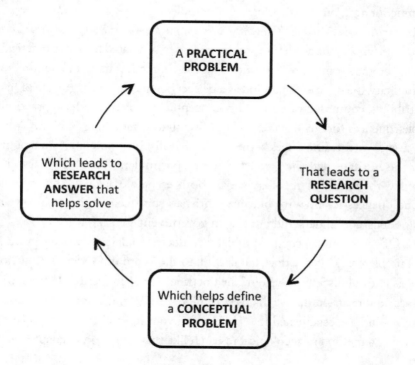

Both practical and conceptual problems have a situation or condition "with *undesirable* consequences caused by that condition."[8] The practical condition may be an illness that causes the consequence of bodily affliction or pain. The practical condition may also be mechanical failure that results in unpleasant inconvenience. On the other hand, a conceptual problem simply has the condition of not knowing something, and the

---

[6] Booth et al., 53.
[7] This chart is a modification of one found in Booth et al., 51.
[8] Booth et al., 52.

248   THE METHOD OF CHRISTIAN THEOLOGY

consequence is that we do not understand something.[9] But conceptual problems often address practical problems. The work of the scientist in a lab simply trying to understand how things work may result in applications for medicine or technology.

Theological inquiries may begin *only* as conceptual problems of academic interest, but for theology to accomplish its task as *critical and organized reflection on God's self-revelation for the purposes of growing in Christ and making disciples*, the academic problem needs to be related back to a practical one. You may want to understand what the church has taught about divine simplicity, the doctrine that God as a perfect being is not an aggregate of his attributes, composed of parts. This conceptual problem can have practical consequences for our worship and our overall understanding of God.[10] You may explore the differences between the revivalist postmillennialism taught by the Puritans and the reconstructionist postmillennialism often associated with dominion theology today. Both eschatologies have real-world consequences for how we practice Christian spirituality, become involved in politics, and understand our role in government.

Of course, all conceptual problems in doctrine relate to two key practical problems: (1) Is the doctrine faithful to the Word of God? (2) How do we as faithful disciples "live out" the doctrine? If the answer to (1) is no, we must explore an alternative that is faithful to the norming norm of Scripture. Once you have established the "problem" of your research, you can proceed to using a method of theological research like that described in chapter 11.

Make Good Arguments

Writing strong papers involves making **arguments**. We often associate arguments with heated disputes or disagreements over things like politics, religion, or sports. But that is not what I mean by arguments here.

---

[9] Booth et al., 54–55.

[10] James E. Dolezal, *All That Is in God: Evangelical Theology and the Challenge of Classical Christian Theism* (Grand Rapids: Reformed Heritage, 2017), 37–58; cf. Dolezal, *God without Parts: Divine Simplicity and the Metaphysics of God's Absoluteness* (Eugene, OR: Pickwick, 2011).

Instead, the use I have in mind is closer to the original Latin verb, *arguere*, which means "to make clear," to "make known," or to "prove" something. An argument is "any set of assertions that is intended to support some conclusion or influence a person's beliefs."[11] When we make an argument, we are trying to clearly state what we believe or demonstrate what we believe is true. When you write a paper, you are trying to (1) explain a concept or concepts, and (2) provide reasonable support for believing what you believe about the concept(s).

There are two basic ways of crafting the argument and structure of your paper: a **deductive approach** and an **inductive approach**.[12] A deductive approach to paper writing involves setting out to *prove a claim*. You are trying to make a case for something. In an inductive paper, you are not setting out to prove something as much as you are setting out to *explore an issue*. You have a set of questions you would like answered as you approach the material, and you draw conclusions from your investigation.

The Deductive Approach

The deductive approach gets its name from deductive logic, a way of reasoning from generally accepted premises to more specific conclusions. Deductive arguments are either valid or invalid. What gives an argument a valid form? Every argument has two essential components: at least two **premises** and a **conclusion**. Premises are propositions or statements of fact. Conclusions, located at the end of an argument, are statements of fact for which someone argues. A deductive argument is valid only when its premises *necessarily* lead to its conclusion. An argument necessarily leads to its conclusion when "it is *impossible* for the conclusion to be false assuming that the premises are true."[13] The following argument is a valid argument because its premises necessarily lead to the conclusion:

---

[11] Raymond S. Nickerson, *Reflections on Reasoning* (Hillsdale, NJ: Lawrence Erlbaum, 1986), 68.

[12] See Yaghjian, *Writing Theology Well*, 42–46.

[13] C. Stephen Layman, *The Power of Logic*, 3rd ed. (New York: McGraw-Hill, 2005), 3.

> Major Premise: God is truthful and trustworthy in everything
>   he does.
> Minor Premise: God inspired all of Scripture.
> Conclusion: All of Scripture is trustworthy and true.

The argument has what we may call a major premise, a minor premise, and a conclusion. Deductive arguments make explicit what is implicit in the major and minor premises of the argument. The argument here makes explicit the idea that is implicit in the major and minor premises, namely the idea that all Scripture is trustworthy and true.

Valid arguments with all true premises that guarantee true conclusions are **sound arguments**. The conclusion is only true if all the valid argument's premises are true. If it is true that God is trustworthy in everything he does and true that he inspired every word of Scripture, then it is necessarily true that every word of Scripture is trustworthy and true.

Like a deductive argument, a deductive paper begins with a **claim** or a hypothesis the author is trying to prove throughout the course of the paper. The claim of the paper is "All Scripture is trustworthy and true or inerrant." Every section of the paper that follows this claim provides another line of support for it. A section based on the major premise would talk about God's character. A section based on the minor premise would talk about the process of inspiration. Each of these sections would help support the claim put forward at the beginning about the inerrancy of Scripture.

The following **abstract** (or thesis paragraph) from Dr. Stephen Wellum provides another helpful example of how a deductive approach to paper writing can be structured.

> In this paper, *I argue that* Scripture rightly read, from beginning to end, is Christocentric and Christotelic, and that Scripture presents our Lord Jesus Christ as God the Son incarnate. My argument proceeds in three steps. First, I *discuss how* a right reading of Scripture is dependent on a theology of Scripture. Before we can ask how Christ is revealed in all of Scripture, *we must first* think through how to approach and read Scripture on its own terms. *Second, I argue that* Christ is not revealed in all of Scripture

in hidden verses or hidden codes, but by tracing out God's redemptive plan, rooted in eternity, enacted in time, and unveiled for us by the progression of the biblical covenants. In fact, it is the Bible's covenantal storyline that serves as the background, framework, and theology to the New Testament's presentation of Jesus, and how all Scripture reveals Christ's identity as the eternal Word/Son made flesh (John 1:1, 14). *Third, I contend that* the Church's later confessions, namely the Nicene Creed and the Chalcedonian definition, are not a distortion of Scripture but a faithful confession of the biblical teaching regarding the person and work of Christ. No doubt the later Creeds utilize theological language that is not directly found in Scripture. However, the language the Creeds employ and the theological judgments they make correctly grasp and put together the biblical data in a way that faithfully renders who Jesus is from the entirety of what Scripture teaches.[14]

Wellum begins with a main claim, signaled by "In this paper, I argue that . . ." He then lists three steps he will take to support his claim that "Scripture . . . is . . . Christocentric and Christotelic." The first section on the doctrine of Scripture comes with a subclaim: we must read Scripture on its own terms. The second section is about how Christ is revealed in Scripture, and the author makes another claim about how interpreters of Scripture are to discover him in the text. The third section deals with creeds and confessions. Each of these sections contains lines of support for the subclaim of the section, which ultimately supports the main claim of the article.

In a deductive approach, every element of the paper should reinforce the central claim of the author. *Information not directly relevant to or supportive of the main claim should be excised from the paper or moved to an appendix or footnote.*

---

[14] Stephen Wellum, "From Alpha to Omega: A Biblical-Theological Approach to God the Son Incarnate," *JETS* 63.1 (2020): 71, emphases mine.

The Inductive Approach

Whereas deductive arguments move from general statements to a specific case, inductive arguments move from specific data to general statements. Inductive arguments, like deductive arguments, use premises to support their claims or conclusions. Unlike the deductive approach, the inductive approach is more exploratory than defensive in its posture. Inductive papers begin with the observation of a problem and form a research question. Throughout the course of the paper, the writer will evaluate evidence that helps answer the question and will conclude with generalizations based on this examination of the evidence.

The next abstract shows what an inductive approach to a theological paper would look like.

> *This article explores* the definition of the NT "autographs" as articulated in various inerrancy doctrinal statements. *It begins by sketching* the history of the doctrine of the inerrancy of the "autographs," *followed by some modern criticisms* of the doctrine. Greco-Roman composition and publication practices are surveyed by investigating three figures from the beginning of the Roman imperial age through to its height: Cicero, Pliny the Younger, and Galen. Four extant examples of ancient papyrus "autographs" are examined, illustrating the draft and rewriting stages of composition. *After analyzing* Greco-Roman publication, a definition is *proposed*: in reference to the NT, the "autograph," as often discussed in biblical inerrancy doctrinal statements, should be defined as the completed authorial work which was released by the author for circulation and copying, not earlier draft versions or layers of composition.[15]

This paragraph begins with a general statement of purpose "to explore" rather than a claim it sets out to prove. The statement of purpose—"This

---

[15] Timothy N. Mitchell, "What Are the NT Autographs? An Examination of the Doctrine of Inspiration and Inerrancy in Light of Greco-Roman Publication," *JETS* 59.2 (2016): 287, emphases mine.

article explores the definition of 'NT autographs' as articulated in various inerrancy doctrinal statements"—could also be posed as a question or a problem to solve: "Why are 'NT autographs' inerrant?" All the sections that follow lay out a different approach to the research question: a history of the doctrine, criticism of the doctrine, and analysis of ancient compositional practices. Having combed through the data and analyzed it, the author of this article ends with general conclusions and a definition of the "NT autograph."

Inductive papers end with general conclusions derived from the research. This section can briefly *summarize your research*, but it should *also provide clear answers to the questions you asked* at the beginning of the paper. In your analysis of the material, write about its significance (i.e., why your discovery was important).[16] You can also state ways in which the problem requires more research, introducing other avenues that could be explored in a future paper or article.[17] General conclusions can also include the element of practice addressed in our discussion of worldviews and the theological spiral: What are the practical consequences of this study for disciples?

How Thomas Aquinas Made Arguments

Thomas Aquinas's *Summa Theologica* (written between 1265 and his death in 1274) is the epitome of scholastic theology and philosophy, with questions and thoughtful, clearly written answers. Whether the overall approach for your paper is deductive or inductive, the *Summa* provides a helpful model for *structuring your arguments*.

The *Summa* is a systematic and philosophical treatment of major theological questions pertinent to Thomas in his context. The work is divided into three larger parts (with the second part divided into two parts and the third part being supplemented by the writing he never finished). Each part is divided into a series of "questions" that mark off

---

[16] Booth et al., *The Craft of Research*, 245–46.
[17] Booth et al., 246.

sections or chapters. Each of these chapters centered around a larger question are divided into "articles" based on smaller questions. The "questions" here are more like titles for the article or chapter. The "articles" contained with the "question" are more like actual questions. Take for example part 1, question 23 on predestination, which is divided into eight articles or sub-questions. These articles include subquestions like, Is predestination suitably attributed to God? What is predestination, and does it place anything in the predestined? Does the reprobation of some men belong to God?

Each article contains a question, objections, a rebuttal, an answer to the question, and replies to the various objections. To see how this works, read part 1, question 23, article 4, which I have provided here in its entirety. Do not get hung up on the content of his argument right now, but pay close attention to the way he makes an argument.

Article 4. Whether the predestined are chosen by God?

Objection 1. It seems that the predestined are not chosen by God. For Dionysius says (Div. Nom. iv, 1) that as the corporeal sun sends his rays upon all without selection, so does God His goodness. But the goodness of God is communicated to some in an especial manner through a participation of grace and glory. Therefore God without any selection communicates His grace and glory; and this belongs to predestination.

Objection 2. Further, election is of things that exist. But predestination from all eternity is also of things which do not exist. Therefore, some are predestined without election.

Objection 3. Further, election implies some discrimination. Now God "wills all men to be saved" (1 Timothy 2:4). Therefore, predestination which ordains men towards eternal salvation, is without election.

On the contrary, It is said (Ephesians 1:4): "He chose us in Him before the foundation of the world."

I answer that, Predestination presupposes election in the order of reason; and election presupposes love. The reason of this is that predestination, as stated above (Article 1), is a part of providence. Now providence, as also prudence, is the plan existing in the intellect directing the ordering of some things towards an end; as was proved above (I:22:2). But nothing is directed towards an end unless the will for that end already exists. Whence the predestination of some to eternal salvation presupposes, in the order of reason, that God wills their salvation; and to this belong both election and love:—love, inasmuch as He wills them this particular good of eternal salvation; since to love is to wish well to anyone, as stated above (I:20:2 and I:20:3):—election, inasmuch as He wills this good to some in preference to others; since He reprobates some, as stated above (Article 3).

Election and love, however, are differently ordered in God, and in ourselves: because in us the will in loving does not cause good, but we are incited to love by the good which already exists; and therefore we choose someone to love, and so election in us precedes love. In God, however, it is the reverse. For His will, by which in loving He wishes good to someone, is the cause of that good possessed by some in preference to others. Thus it is clear that love precedes election in the order of reason, and election precedes predestination. Whence all the predestinate are objects of election and love.

Reply to Objection 1. If the communication of the divine goodness in general be considered, God communicates His goodness without election; inasmuch as there is nothing which does not in some way share in His goodness, as we said above (I:6:4). But if we consider the communication of this or that particular good, He does not allot it without election; since He gives certain goods to some men, which He does not give to others. Thus in the conferring of grace and glory election is implied.

Reply to Objection 2. When the will of the person choosing is incited to make a choice by the good already pre-existing in the object chosen, the choice must needs be of those things which already exist, as happens in our choice. In God it is otherwise; as was said above (I:20:2). Thus, as Augustine says (De Verb. Ap. Serm. 11): "Those are chosen by God, who do not exist; yet He does not err in His choice."

Reply to Objection 3. God wills all men to be saved by His antecedent will, which is to will not simply but relatively; and not by His consequent will, which is to will simply.

While students may not want to follow the exact style of Thomas's writing, they can imitate the way he works through a research question.

- First, he begins his article by *providing objections* (or "no" answers given to the question). He either knows these objections from other sources or anticipates these objections being raised. Thinking through how people will oppose your ideas is crucial to strong arguments.
- Second, he provides a *counterpoint to the objections* (usually labeled "On the Contrary") provided from the Bible or another source in philosophy or theology.
- Third, Thomas *provides his own answer to the question* (the affirmative, "yes" answer) and provides an explanation for why he answers the question the way he does. These "I answer that" statements contain clear definitions, biblical support, and cogent support from other doctrines.
- Finally, *Thomas answers each objection individually.*

Your paper may not follow this pattern exactly or use these subheadings, but when making good arguments, use objections and their counterpoints, clear definitions, support from your sources, and critical responses to the objections that other sources raise.

Outline the Paper

Once you have assembled and worked through the resources you need to address in your paper from Scripture and other sources in theology, history, or philosophy, you will need to sketch an outline of your paper. This sketch is somewhat tentative and subject to change, but if you have an outline, it will help you follow an orderly process in research and writing. Lucretia Yaghjian has provided an excellent model for mapping deductive and inductive papers, which I have adapted here.[18] Both the following outlines are general treatments of the doctrine of biblical inerrancy that can look very different depending on the approach taken for the paper.

---

[18] See Yaghjian, *Writing Theology Well*, 53–55.

A Deductive Outline	An Inductive Outline
Introduction (Deductive) • Set up the problem to readers with an attention-grabbing introduction. In this introduction, make a brief case for why they should care about the problem (the "so what"). 　When the doctrine of inerrancy is ignored or rejected . . . • Make a **claim** or **hypothesis** statement that you will set out to prove over the course of the paper. 　The Bible is inerrant—true and trustworthy in everything its authors affirm to be true. • State the **assertions** you will make that lead to this conclusion. These assertions will provide the rough outline for the body of your paper. 　In the first section, I will argue that the character of God supports the doctrine of biblical inerrancy. Second, I will demonstrate how the nature of Scripture supports the doctrine of inerrancy. In the final section, I will draw general conclusions about how God's character and the nature of Scripture come together in a doctrine of inerrancy.	**Introduction (Inductive)** • Set up the problem to readers with an attention-grabbing introduction. In this introduction, make a brief case for why they should care about the problem (the "so what"). 　When the doctrine of inerrancy is ignored or rejected . . . • State the primary **research question** you hope to investigate throughout the paper. 　This paper explores the question, Is the notion of biblical inerrancy still a tenable theological position for evangelical Christians today? • Sketch your plan for answering the question. This can include **purpose statements** for each section of the paper or **sub-questions** that will help you answer the primary research question. These questions will shape the outline of the paper. 　• Does the Bible support the doctrine of inerrancy? 　• Does the teaching of the church throughout history support the doctrine of inerrancy? 　• Does reason buttress the doctrine of inerrancy?

A Deductive Outline	An Inductive Outline
Body of the Paper (Deductive)	**Body of the Paper (Inductive)**
• The body of the paper in a deductive approach contains sections that support the main claim of the paper.	• The body of the paper in an inductive approach contains sections that explore possible answers to the question.
• This section contains the assertions that support the main claim and evidence that supports the assertions.	• This section weighs evidence for different sides of the debate.
— *Section 1:* The Character of God	— *Section 1*: The Biblical Evidence
o *Assertion*: God is truthful and trustworthy in everything he does.	o *Question:* Does the Bible support the doctrine of inerrancy?
o *Evidence* (can be in subsections):	o *Objections* used against inerrancy from Scripture
◊ Biblical evidence	o *Evidence* from Scripture for inerrancy
◊ Historical support	o Draw *conclusions* from evidence.
◊ Philosophical support/arguments	— *Section 2*: Historical Arguments
— *Section 2*: The Nature of Scripture	o *Question:* Has the church throughout history affirmed biblical inerrancy?
o *Assertion*: God inspired all Scripture.	o *Objections* to inerrancy from church history
◊ Biblical evidence	o *Support* for inerrancy from church history
◊ Historical support	o Draw *conclusions*.
◊ Philosophical support/arguments	— *Section 3*: The Philosophical Arguments
— *Section 3*: The Inerrancy of Scripture	o *Question:* What arguments are employed for and against inerrancy?
o *Assertion*: God's act of inspiring Scripture guarantees a fully truthful and trustworthy Bible.	o *Arguments* against inerrancy
◊ Biblical evidence	o *Arguments* for inerrancy
◊ Historical support	o Draw *conclusions*.
◊ Philosophical support/arguments	

A Deductive Outline	An Inductive Outline
Conclusion (Deductive) • Restate the claim and summarize the support you have given throughout the paper for it. • Briefly draw out implications of your argument. • Leave the reader with a challenge that fosters his or her further discipleship in Christ.	**Conclusion (Inductive)** • Draw conclusions from your research, making general statements that help answer the primary research question and the sub-questions stated in the introduction. • Briefly draw out implications for your argument. • Leave the reader with a challenge that fosters his or her further discipleship in Christ.

Four Other Important Things to Remember (and Four Things to Avoid)

There are many more things that could be said about the process of writing theological papers. I want to leave you with four things to remember (and four things to avoid).

First, remember to manage your time well. Do not put off reading or writing. Calendar your research time and writing time. Make notes while reading, but don't write your papers while you are reading. Students who are reading and writing at the same time often present incoherent, half-baked thoughts rather than fully formed arguments that connect the materials. Most importantly, know when to quit researching and start writing!

Second, remember to cite sources properly. Do not plagiarize—on purpose or by accident. Few things bother me more than seminary or Bible college students cutting corners on assignments designed to make them more effective ministers of the gospel. Plagiarism is theft of intellectual properties and a violation of the eighth commandment (Exod 20:15).

Third, remember the importance of grammar and style. Do not write long, awkward sentences with grammatical errors. If your campus has a writing center, submit paper samples to it for revision and correction. Become familiar with the most common mistakes in your writing and work to become a better writer with each and every assignment submitted.

To strengthen the quality of your writing, I recommend students visit writersdiet.com and use the free test available for writing samples. This test can assess the fitness of prose by weeding out excessive adjectives, adverbs, and technical terms.

Finally, remember to review and revise your paper. On behalf of all teachers and graders everywhere, I beg you, please do not submit the first draft! The best way to review your paper is to find a quiet place and slowly read it aloud to yourself. Reading the paper is the best way to catch common grammatical or stylistic mistakes. Newer versions of Microsoft Word even have a "read aloud" option under the "Review" tab. Make use of it! Listen to your paper as it is read to you, and you will likely pick up on many of the errors your eye skips over when reading quietly to yourself.

KEY TERMS

abstract

argument

arguments, sound

arguments, valid

claim

conclusion

deductive approach

inductive approach

premises

problems, practical

problems, conceptual

GO DEEPER

Eco, Umberto. *How to Write a Thesis*. Translated by Caterina Mongiat Farina and Geoff Farina. Cambridge, MA: The MIT Press, 2015.

Kibbe, Michael. *From Topic to Thesis: A Guide to Theological Research*. Downers Grove, IL: InterVarsity Press, 2016.

Sword, Helen. *Stylish Academic Writing*. Cambridge, MA: Harvard University Press, 2012.

Yaghjian, Lucretia B. *Writing Theology Well: A Rhetoric for Theological and Biblical Writers*. 2nd ed. New York: Bloomsbury T&T Clark, 2015.

14

Preaching a Doctrinal Sermon

Preach the word; be ready in season and out of season; correct,
rebuke, and encourage with great patience and teaching.
—2 TIMOTHY 4:2

Theological reflection should result in disciple-making doctrine.
Those of us who are blessed with the opportunity of studying theology academically must remember that we are not called to be theological cul-de-sacs—dead ends where doctrine goes nowhere—but tributaries whose study of sacred doctrine flows into the larger body of Christ. Most Christians in the pew will never read a systematic theology textbook or an advanced monograph about the relations within the Godhead. The primary way they will receive the content of theology is through doctrinal preaching and teaching. So, we are given a crucial and important task: to preach and teach Christian truth faithfully (1 Tim 4:13; 2 Tim 4:2).

What distinguishes doctrinal preaching from conventional preaching? In the sense that it is authoritative teaching meant to shape the worldviews of its hearers, all preaching is doctrinal.[1] All biblical preaching fits the definition of doctrine as *faithful and true teaching derived from Scripture and used to grow God's people in knowledge, spiritual maturity, and obedience*. Yet there is another sense in which doctrinal preaching is reserved to describe a special kind of preaching focused on Christian doctrine derived from the Bible. Faithful doctrinal preaching, like faithful doctrine, is more than a presentation of cognitive information. It shapes worldviews by drawing hearers into the grand narrative of Scripture, teaching truths about God and his world, stirring our affections, and directing us to obedience.

This chapter serves as both a defense of doctrinal preaching and a starting point for prepping doctrinal sermons. As whole volumes dedicated to doctrinal preaching would indicate, much more can be written on the subject than I have written here. (I am a preacher but not a scholar of preaching.) However, I am convinced that many of the skills taught throughout our discussion of theological method are directly applicable to preaching doctrine.

Advantages and Drawbacks of Book-by-Book Exposition

Evangelicals who affirm the inspiration and truthfulness of every word of Scripture give the Bible primacy in their preaching and teaching. The conventional approach to preaching celebrated by evangelicals is **expository preaching**. This style of preaching gets its name from the word *exposition*, which means "a comprehensive explanation of an idea or a theory." Expository preachers strive to let the written Word of God speak for itself by explaining the meaning of the biblical text as its authorship intended.

Preachers and scholars of **homiletics** (i.e., "the study of sermon preparation"[2]) are not uniform in their understanding of what makes a

---

[1] William J. Carl, *Preaching Christian Doctrine* (Philadelphia: Fortress, 1984), 5.

[2] Jerry Vines and Jim Shaddix, *Power in the Pulpit: How to Prepare and Deliver Expository Sermons* (Chicago: Moody, 1999), 28.

sermon expository.[3] Some relate expository preaching to a certain *style* of preaching, relating the style of the sermon to a lecture or a "deep" message with lots of information. Some relate expository preaching to a *form* of preaching, such as the idea that an expository sermon is any sermon where the main idea comes from "a Bible passage longer than two or three consecutive verses."[4] Others, such as Harold T. Bryson or John MacArthur, relate expository preaching to a *process*, like a series through a single book of Scripture.[5]

For our purposes here, I take expository preaching to be a philosophy of preaching defined by its *subject matter*.[6] An expository sermon is any sermon that faithfully communicates the purpose and meaning of biblical texts for the purpose of making Christian disciples. As my preaching professor, Tony Merida, has defined it, the expository sermon is "explaining what God has said in his Word, declaring what God has done in his Son, and applying this message to the hearts of people."[7] An expository sermon accounts for the intended purpose of a biblical text (its illocutionary act) so hearers of the text experience its intended effects (its perlocutionary act).

The book-by-book exposition of biblical texts should be the primary instrument in the toolbox of the preacher. There are many reasons why expository preaching should be the regular, go-to mode of preaching. *First, expository preaching is a way of putting into practice what we believe*

---

[3] For a fuller evaluation of these categories, see Tony Merida, *The Christ-Centered Expositor: A Field Guide for Word-Driven Expositors* (Nashville: B&H Academic, 2016), 12–17; cf. Millard L. Erickson and James L. Heflin, *Old Wine in New Wineskins: Doctrinal Preaching in a Changing World* (Grand Rapids: Baker, 1997), 167–72.

[4] Andrew Blackwood, *Expository Preaching Today* (Grand Rapids: Baker, 1975), 13.

[5] Harold T. Bryson, *Expository Preaching* (Nashville: B&H, 1995), 39. It only took forty-two years (1969–2011), but John MacArthur preached through every single verse of the New Testament at Grace Community Church in Sun Valley, California.

[6] Haddon W. Robinson, *Biblical Preaching: The Development and Delivery of Expository Messages*, 2nd ed. (Grand Rapids: Baker, 2001), 22.

[7] Merida, *The Christ-Centered Expositor*, 9.

about biblical inspiration: every word in the Bible is inspired by God and "is profitable for teaching, for rebuking, for correcting, for training in righteousness" (2 Tim 3:16). When we draw our claims directly from the text, we model our trust in the Bible for our congregations.[8]

Second, expository preaching gives controls over the message proclaimed in the local church.[9] The theological content of the Bible often gets overlooked in some topical messages that have more in common with pop psychology than the divinely inspired Word delivered to ancient Israelites and the early church. Expository preaching rescues us from this consumeristic pragmatism and "enables God to set the agenda for your Christian community."[10] The whole counsel of God, not the agenda or pet issue of the pastor, becomes the primary focus of preaching.[11]

Third, expository preaching gives the "voice of God" in the text primacy over the sermon. Steven W. Smith has argued for "text-driven preaching . . . that re-presents the substance, structure, and the spirit of the text."[12] The main point of the text becomes the main point of the sermon.[13] The preacher is merely the messenger who speaks with the voice of God to the degree he accurately expresses what God's Word says in its many genres and forms.

Finally, expository preaching models for our people a way to read the Bible in their personal studies. It demonstrates the importance of reading the Bible systematically and interpreting passages in their proper literary and historical contexts. Expository preaching can train people how to have a better understanding of the way themes connect across a book of the Bible and across the canon. Expository preaching also shows readers how to see Christ exalted in every text they read.

While book-driven expository preaching should have pride of place in the pulpit of a local church, there are good reasons to deviate from this

---

[8] Keller, *Preaching*, 33 (see chap. 12, n. 29).

[9] Merida, *The Christ-Centered Expositor*, 17.

[10] Keller, *Preaching*, 36.

[11] Keller, 37.

[12] Steven W. Smith, *Recapturing the Voice of God: Shaping Sermons Like Scripture* (Nashville: B&H Academic, 2015), 17.

[13] Mark Dever and Greg Gilbert, *Preach* (Nashville: B&H, 2012), 36.

pattern on occasion. *First, as Timothy Keller has noted, our society is more mobile than any other point in human history.*[14] In the churches where I have pastored in south Louisiana, I have seen a lot of people come and go with industries like the oil industry and film industry, which are always in flux. I am conscious of the fact that people moving into the area to take a job may be part of our fellowship for a season and then go where the economy takes their family in another season. For this reason, I decided I would not spend an excessively long time (over one year) in one book of the Bible. Over three or four years, I could help people become experts in a single Pauline epistle, or I could help them become more biblically literate by helping them develop an understanding and an appreciation for the grand narrative of Scripture.

Second, some forms of serial preaching can discourage congregants from reading the Bible for themselves. If their preacher spends years preaching through 1 Corinthians, unpacking hours of content on individual verses, congregants may grow insecure in their own reading when they cannot produce the same level of information. Furthermore, they may become dependent on the preacher's exposition rather than the text itself. For this reason, I encourage young preachers going through books of the Bible to provide reading guides for their congregations to follow along with during the week. Even if the pastor elects to skip a section of the text in his sermons, he can rest assured in having led them through reading the text on their own time.

Third, some expository preaching can overlook key doctrines addressed throughout Scripture. Centuries ago, Bernard of Clairvaux (1090–1153) spent eighteen years preaching verse-by-verse through the Song of Songs and only got through the first verse of chapter 3! Millard Erickson and James Heflin ask appropriate questions about the effectiveness of this kind of preaching: "How long would a minister preach in the Song of Solomon before getting to a doctrine? To ask it another way: Would a pastor wish to preach for eighteen years and only discuss the doctrines found in the Song of Solomon?"[15]

---

[14] Keller, *Preaching*, 33.
[15] Erickson and Heflin, *Old Wine in New Wineskins*, 169.

Fourth, some forms of expository preaching can be theologically redundant. Of course, redundancy in discipleship isn't always a bad thing, unless it is to the neglect of other pertinent issues. A few years ago, I planned a year-long sermon series through the book of Isaiah. Isaiah is one of the longest and most theologically rich books of the Old Testament, covering a wide gamut of issues like the sovereignty of God, the holiness of God, the judgment of God, the salvation of God, and the Suffering Servant. I chose not to cover every chapter of Isaiah, in part because of the mobility of my congregation but also because many of the themes in Isaiah are repeated across several texts. Had I covered every verse and every chapter of the book, it would have taken much longer to work through the book, and the "big idea" of my sermons would often have been the same several weeks in a row. Instead of covering all sixty-six chapters, I took a "greatest hits" or a thematic-theological approach to Isaiah that touched on most of the major historical, theological, and practical issues raised by the book.

Fifth, sometimes major events or life situations require the pastor to give a faithful, biblical response that may deviate from his normal pattern of book-by-book exposition. For example, as I write this book in the year 2020, I have been required to preach sermons that responded to the coronavirus pandemic and racial reconciliation spurred by contemporary events. In addition, special ceremonies like weddings or funerals often require a more systematic or doctrinal-topical sermon (e.g., what the Bible says about marriage, death, etc.).

Finally, and most importantly for the present topic, some theological themes in Scripture require a more systematic explanation than verse-by-verse, book-by-book preaching can offer. In some ways, expository preaching in this manner meets with some of the same shortcomings of a purely biblical theology. While the doctrine of the Trinity is one of the most foundational doctrines of the Christian faith, it cannot be explained adequately with a single unit of text. This doctrine requires an overview of several passages. Other debated theological issues, such as the doctrines of perseverance/apostasy, require complex arguments that take into consideration multiple passages. To demonstrate the consistency of these passages, they need to be explained in relationship to one another and harmonized.

Two Types of Doctrinal Sermons

All preaching may be doctrinal in that it is authoritative teaching used to make disciples, but doctrinal preaching in a more specific sense focuses on teaching doctrines and theological themes from the Bible. We will consider two forms of doctrinal preaching in this section: (1) **expository-theological sermons**, which begin with a biblical text and draw out doctrinal themes in the text, and (2) **doctrinal-topical sermons**, which begin with a doctrinal topic or question that must be addressed through the exploration of relevant biblical data.[16] Approach (1) closely resembles biblical theology, and approach (2) more closely conforms to systematic theology. Both approaches have their place and occasion in the preaching ministry of the local church.

The Expository-Theological Sermon

The expository-theological sermon is a text-driven sermon that camps out in a single unit of text and draws special attention to the doctrinal truths of that passage. Expository-theological sermons can be preached in a series through a book of Scripture or in a series of other expository-theological sermons drawn from various biblical passages that speak to the given topic (e.g., a series on the attributes of God, spiritual gifts). If preaching through Ephesians, one could prepare expository-theological sermons focused on predestination in 1:3–14, spiritual death and regeneration from 2:1–5, union with Christ in 2:6–7, and salvation apart from works in 2:8–10. In a thematic series on Christ's penal-substitutionary atonement on our behalf, expository-theological sermons primarily camp out in one of a number of biblical texts: Isa 53:5–6; Gal 3:10–14; 1 Pet 2:21–25, and many others. When preaching through a series on ecclesiology, a pastor can preach several expository sermons from different

---

[16] Erickson and Heflin, *Old Wine in New Wineskins*, 167–82; 183–99. To these two categories, Erickson and Heflin add narrative and dramatic doctrinal preaching.

passages across the New Testament that are relevant to topics like the nature of the church, the government of the church, the ordinances of the church, and church discipline.

Like the procedure described in chapter 11, the expository-theological sermon works to (1) present the *main idea* of the text, (2) relate the text to the *grand narrative* of Scripture, (3) isolate *theological truths* found in the text, (4) identify *practices* the author demands of his readers, and (5) draw out the ways the text shapes Christian *affections*.

In the expository-theological sermon, the preacher preaches the text in its historical, literary, and canonical contexts. Questions like these might help form the content of the sermon: What is the author doing with the text (i.e., his speech-act)? How does this passage point back to God's dealings with Israel? How does God address the church in it?

The text I have chosen for my example of an expository-theological sermon is Isa 43:1–13. Here, the prophet comforts fretful Israel by reminding them God is their only Savior. Just as he saved them in the past, he will save them again in the future. This original idea of the text has direct application to people today who are wrestling with basic world-view questions like, What's the problem? and What's the solution? Our ultimate hope is in God as our Savior, and Christ is the only name under heaven capable of saving us from our plight.

Once we have identified the place in the story of Scripture where the text resides, we need to seek the connection it makes to the climax of the story in Christ. What does the text say about God—his attributes and his activity in the world? What does the text say about humanity—our nature, our sin, and our hope? What does the text say about redemption? Isa 43:1–13 is in Act 2 of the divine drama of Scripture, but it anticipates God's future salvation through the Messiah. God ultimately fulfilled his promise to save Israel and protect them through Christ.

Expository-theological sermons are not content-heavy lectures but sermons that direct hearers to obedience; it must address the practices of disciples. Homiletics scholars observe the important connection between **indicatives** and **imperatives** in the sermon. Indicatives are statements of fact. In the case of the expository-theological sermon, indicatives are the theological truths taught by a text. Imperatives are commands, requests, or calls to action. A sermon made up only of indicatives never draws the implications of theological truths. Sermons made up only of imperatives never give hearers the reasons for why they should act in obedience.[17] The theological indicatives of the text lead to the imperatives of the sermon. As Daniel Overdorf noted, "Truth has implications. Sermons, consequently, need applications."[18]

The theological indicatives of Isa 43:1–13 serve as a foundation for the imperatives or direct commands of the text:

- v. 1: "Do not fear," (imperative) "for I have redeemed you" (indicative).
- v. 5: "Do not fear," (imperative) "for I am with you" (indicative).
- v. 12: "I alone declared, saved, and proclaimed—and not some foreign god among you" (indicative) "so you are [or you should be] my witnesses" (imperative).

When formulating application from the biblical texts, look first at the explicit directions of the text that are still directly applicable today. Then "translate" instructions specific to the ancient setting into principled instruction for a twenty-first-century context.

Effective doctrinal preaching also stirs the affections. We should draw the attention of our hearers to direct biblical statements about our affections, like the call to "rejoice" (Ps 5:11; 33:1; Phil 4:4). In Isa 43:1–13, the prophet calls us to replace fear with *trust*. We should also work to understand how the author of a text himself is feeling as he writes the passage (e.g., joy, sorrow, anger, etc.). Also, spend time in prayer to ensure your emotions are in line with the text and the needs of your hearers. It is disingenuous to preach about the need for joy when you are not experiencing it yourself. Ask the Lord to stir your own heart before entering the pulpit. The rich use of illustrations

---

[17] Daniel Overdorf, *Applying the Sermon: How to Balance Biblical Integrity and Cultural Relevance* (Grand Rapids: Kregel, 2008), 55–60.

[18] Overdorf, *Applying the Sermon*, 60.

and stories can connect with affections more than direct propositional statements ever will.

Every expository sermon is different in its style, presentation, and context. Some preach deductive sermons that begin by stating the main idea from the text and then offer subpoints that support it. Others preach inductive sermons that work through the text, make general statements about it, and offer its central idea at the conclusion of the message. What is important is not uniformity in the outline but conformity to the message of the author. The following sample is only one way of drafting an expository-theological sermon from one unit of text that calls attention to the story, the truths, the practices, and the pathos of the text.

Sample Outline of an
Expository-Theological Sermon
Isaiah 43:1–13

Introduction: Where do people look for salvation in this world? Anxious people are always looking for more security. Progressives believe the world needs to make more drastic social changes so we can live in a utopia. Hedonists search for salvation in pleasure. Consumerists think they need more stuff in order to find happiness.[19] But for the people of God, we see a very different problem with the world—human sin—and a very different solution: the salvation only God can bring. Only God can give us relief from this broken world. Only God can save us!

What the Author Is Doing with This Text: The Lord comforts Israel by reminding them he is their only savior.

How the Text Fits in the Story of Scripture: This passage is set in the story of Israel (Act 2 of the divine drama of Scripture). Isaiah writes during the eighth century BC, close to two hundred years after the united monarchy of Israel under Saul, David, and Solomon split into

---

[19] See Wax, *Eschatological Discipleship*, 96–187 (see chap. 3, n. 16).

the northern kingdom of Israel and the southern kingdom of Judah, and a little over a century before the southern kingdom of Judah would fall to Babylon (586 BC). Through the prophet, God promises captivity in Babylon, but also promises he will deliver them through the judgments he pours out on the nations. Ultimately, this story points us to Israel's Savior—Jesus Christ—who would, through his cross, make a way for all men to be saved from God's judgment on sin.

Theological Truths:

1. **We are comforted because God has <u>created</u> a people for himself (v. 1a).** We exist for God, not God for us. We were created to bring God glory!

2. **We are comforted because God has <u>redeemed</u> a people for himself (vv. 1b, 3).** Old Testament authors speak regularly about the "kinsman redeemer" (*gō-'ēl*) who acts on behalf of his family to rescue them from trouble or danger (Exod 6:6; Ruth 3–4). The Lord has acted to redeem us from danger.

3. **We are comforted because God will <u>protect</u> his people in times of suffering (v. 2).** Difficulty is inevitable. The children of Israel and Judah knew this in their time of exile and suffering. But the Lord God never allowed the suffering of his people to overwhelm them.

4. **We are comforted because God is always <u>present</u> with his people (vv. 2a; 5a).** Twice in this text, the Lord reminds us he is with us. This speaks of what Christian theologians call God's omnipresence and immensity. God is present to every point in space and present with us in his entirety. We could never get away from God's presence even if we tried (Ps 139:7–10).

5. **We are comforted because God <u>cherishes</u> his people (v. 4).** God tells Israel they are precious in his sight. God also extends a special love to his elect people in the church today (Eph 2:4–7).

6. **We are comforted because God will <u>deliver</u> his people (v. 5b–6).** God promised to deliver his children from exile, a promise he

fulfilled through the Persian King Cyrus (2 Chron 36:22–23; Ezra 1:1–8; Isa 44:24–28). But this deliverance was only temporary. The lasting deliverance he gave his people was through Jesus Christ. As Paul stated, God "has rescued us from the domain of darkness and transferred us into the kingdom of the Son he loves. In him we have redemption, the forgiveness of sins" (Col 1:13–14).

7. **We are comforted because God will be <u>glorified</u> through his people (v. 7).** We are saved by grace through faith, not by our own works or accomplishments (Eph 2:8–9). This is to remind us we cannot save ourselves or take credit for our redemption. God has created us and saved us to bring attention to himself.

8. **We are comforted because God is the only <u>true God</u> (v. 10).** As they went into exile and were tempted by foreign gods, Israel needed the reminder that there is only one true God. Contrary to cultic teaching like Mormonism, there was no god formed before our God, nor will there be a god formed after our God.

9. **We are comforted because God alone can <u>save</u> us from sin and destruction (v. 11–12).** Just as there is only one God, there is only one Savior. Many in our culture today shout things like, "There are many ways to God!" Scripture, however, teaches *absolute truth about an exclusive Savior.*

10. **We are comforted because God is limitless in his <u>power</u> (v. 13).** God is, as Christian theologians observe, omnipotent. This does not mean God can do absolutely anything. For instance, he cannot lie. But God can do anything that does not involve a contradiction with his nature. Because God is limitless in his power, he was able to redeem Israel from their plight.

Practical Takeaways:

1. We must not give into **<u>fear</u>**, for our God is with us and cares for us (vv. 1b).

2. We must **<u>place our trust</u>** in Israel's Savior (v. 3).

3. We must **proclaim the truth** that there is only one God who can save people (vv. 8–9). Jesus Christ, Israel's true Savior, is still the only means to salvation in this dark and sinful world (John 14:6; Acts 4:12).

Conclusion and Invitation: Do not let these theological and practical truths from Scripture go in one ear and out the other. We must respond with our minds, our affections, and our actions. Quit turning your heart toward things that cannot save or satisfy, and look to Christ Jesus, our Savior and our only hope. Don't be overcome with fear and anxiety. God has been faithful before, and he will be faithful again. If you have never responded in repentance and faith to the good news of the God who has saved us in Christ Jesus, I plead with you to "seek the LORD while he may be found; call to him while he is near" (Isa 55:6).

The Doctrinal-Topical Sermon

Seminary students are often trained to disdain topical preaching, in no small part because topical preaching is often poorly executed. We should reject topical sermons that do not relate to the biblical text or only use the biblical text as proof texts for the opinions of the preacher. I have heard many topical sermons that ignore the intent of the biblical author and his worldview. But doctrinal-topical sermons faithful to the theological framework of biblical authors are occasionally warranted. We may need to address a life situation or a hot-button cultural issue, or we may feel led to teach doctrine systematically from the pulpit. These sermons do not begin with a text (as in serial, book-by-book preaching) but with a topical or doctrinal question that the preacher takes to the biblical text in search of an answer. The faithful doctrinal-topical sermon allows biblical authors to answer the question on their own terms rather than forcing the preacher's viewpoint on the texts.

The first approach is driven by a topic or pressing cultural issue the pastor must shepherd his people through. Topics such as abortion, transgenderism, and racial reconciliation are controversial but in need of a clear biblical voice. Even if the Bible does not directly address every contemporary issue, we know God's Word provides the disciple with the primary "filter" or "guide" for which all beliefs are formed and decisions are made. We may address a topic like abortion with biblical texts that prohibit the murder of humans made in the image of God (Gen 9:5–6) or God's work in creating us in the womb (Ps 139:13–14; Jer 1:4). The Bible does not speak about transgenderism in the contemporary sense of the word, but it does have much to say about the creation of men and women in the image of God (Gen 1:27; 1 Cor 11:7). Many of these issues can be addressed by presenting the biblical doctrine of humanity.

The second approach is more like systematic theology, addressing the doctrinal topics of the Bible in an organized manner. The systematic-doctrinal sermon begins with a doctrinal question or topic and brings together several biblical texts to answer the question, What does the Bible say about . . . ? (the topic). Instead of having a narrow focus on one text (as in biblical-expository and expository-theological sermons), a *systematic-doctrinal sermon brings together multiple texts that help answer the theological question posed to Scripture.*

As we have noted, we cannot paint a full picture of the biblical doctrine of the Trinity from the exposition of any *single* biblical text, so we must resort to a number of texts in order to explain it. But this work can only be done *after we have understood the texts in question* in their historical, literary, and larger canonical contexts.

With the doctrinal-topical sermon, the preacher harmonizes the theological and practical truths of the passage with other theological statements and ideas throughout Scripture. God's Word will not contradict itself, and it is your job as the preacher to present what the voice of the whole canon says on the matter at hand. If there are texts that appear to be contradictory, it benefits your hearers for you to address them and explain why there is no genuine contradiction.

The following sermon outline unpacks the doctrine of the Trinity, a doctrine that requires a more systematic presentation. It is a deductive outline that begins with the main idea: we can believe three things the Bible teaches about the Trinity. This basic outline could be preached superficially in one sermon or in greater detail across several sermons.

Sample of a Doctrinal-Topical Sermon "Grasping the Doctrine of the Trinity"

Introduction: There is a fascinating legend about Augustine of Hippo (354–430). According to this tale, Augustine was walking along the beach one day mulling over the doctrine of the Trinity. As he walked, he pondered questions like, How can God be both one and three? How do I comprehend the relationship between the Father, the Son, and the Holy Spirit?

Somewhere down the shoreline, Augustine encountered a little boy who was frantically running back and forth between the ocean and a little hole he had dug out of the sand.

The theologian stopped to watch the curious sight for a moment.

The little boy was clasping his hands together to form a bowl shape, running to the water, and scooping up as much as he could carry. He would then run back to the tiny hole he had dug in the ground and dump the water in it.

The boy did this several times before Augustine had the nerve to ask why, but when he did, the little boy replied, "I'm trying to move the ocean into this hole."

Augustine snickered and said, "Little boy, you know you will never be able to fit that big ocean in that tiny little hole! The ocean is great, and your little pit is too small."

The boy stopped what he was doing. He looked up at Augustine and said, "Yes, but it is far more likely I will be able to move the whole ocean into this tiny hole than you will be able to understand the mystery of the Trinity in your tiny little brain. The Trinity is much larger than the ocean, and your understanding is smaller than this hole in the ground."

As soon as he said these words, the little boy disappeared from Augustine's sight. (Cue the *Twilight Zone* theme song.) The famous theologian was left on the beach with the realization he would never be able to capture answers to all the questions he was asking.[20] While the

---

[20] See Alberic de Meijer, "Saint Augustine and the Conversation with the Child on the Shore: The History behind the Legend," *Augustinian Heritage* 39 (1993): 21–34.

event described in this legend is undoubtedly fictitious, it serves as an important warning. As the real Augustine said, "When we are speaking of God, why should it surprise you if you do not fully comprehend it? If you can comprehend it, you are not talking about God."[21] As much as we try to rationalize the things God has revealed to us in Scripture, they are beyond what our minds can fully fathom or process.

We will never fully *comprehend* a precious doctrine like the Trinity, but we must be able to *believe* what God's Word says about it! The doctrine of the Trinity is one of the most precious biblical doctrines—a truth that is foundational to everything else we believe about God, his Word, and his salvific plan for us. Though it is mysterious, I suggest there are *three things the Bible teaches about the Trinity we can all affirm*, even if we do not fully understand how all these things relate.

1. **The Bible teaches us that there is only one God (Deut 6:4; Isa 44:6–8; 1 Cor 8:4).**

    1.1. **The Old Testament consistently teaches <u>monotheism</u>—the belief in one God.** The Bible repeatedly stresses this theme: there is only one God. Though they frequently rebelled and violated God's commandment, the people of Israel were called to worship the one true God.

    1.2. **The New Testament authors reinforce monotheism as well.** The predominantly Jewish authorship of the New Testament did not see a contradiction between their monotheism and their belief in their affirmation of the Father, the Son, and the Holy Spirit as God.

2. **The Bible teaches us that the Father, the Son, and the Holy Spirit are truly God.**

    2.1. **The Father is truly God (1 Cor 8:6).** Scripture is plain about the deity of the Father: "yet for us there is one God, the Father. All things are from him, and we exist for him."

---

[21] I have taken the liberty of updating the language here. See Augustine *Sermons* 67.5 [117.3.5]; *NPNF*[1] 6:459.

2.2. **The Son is truly God (John 1:1–18; Phil 2:5–11; Col 1:15–20; Heb 1:1–4).** There are numerous biblical texts we could point to that teach the deity of the Lord Jesus, but these four are among the most quoted. John described Jesus as the "Word" of God who "was God" (John 1:1). Paul declared Jesus existed "in the form of God" (Phil 2:6). The author of Hebrews wrote, "The Son is the radiance of God's glory and the exact expression of his nature" (Heb 1:3a). Jesus also carried out the activities of God: *creating* (John 1:3; Col 1:16; Heb 1:2b), *revealing* (John 1:14, 18; Col 1:15; Heb 1:2), *sustaining creation* (Col 1:17; Heb 1:3), and *redeeming sinners* (John 1:4; Phil 2:8–9; Col 1:19–20; Heb 1:3).

2.3. **The Spirit is truly God (Acts 5:3–4; 1 Cor 3:16–17; 6:19–20).** There are places in Scripture where "Holy Spirit" is interchangeable with God. The Holy Spirit possesses the attributes or qualities of God.

3. **The Bible teaches us that the Father, the Son, and the Holy Spirit are distinct, eternal persons (Matt 3:16–17; Luke 4:1–2; Acts 10:38).**

   3.1. **During the incarnation, the Son displayed perfect submission to the will of the Father (John 5:17; 26–27).**

   3.2. **The Spirit testifies about the Son (John 15:26–27).**

   3.3. **The Father glorifies the Son (John 17:5).**

   3.4. **All three persons of the Godhead work together in the same external works (what theologians call the "inseparable operations" of the Trinity).**

      3.4.1. All three persons of the Trinity were involved in creation.

      3.4.2. All three persons of the Trinity are involved in revelation.

      3.4.3. All three persons of the Trinity were involved in salvation.

Practical Takeaways:

1. We do not have to fully comprehend the biblical teaching of the Trinity in order to believe it.

2. It is biblically appropriate to worship and pray to all three persons of the Godhead.

3. All three persons of the Trinity have acted to save us from sin.

Conclusion and Invitation:

The triune God of the Bible has revealed himself to us as Father, Son, and Holy Spirit. All three persons of the Trinity were involved in creation. All three persons of the Trinity have acted to save us from our sins. And we can have fellowship with the Father, the Son, and the Holy Spirit through what God has done for us in Christ Jesus.

Planning Doctrinal Sermons

There are numerous opportunities to preach and teach doctrine in the local church. Here are just a sample of strategies that may be used.

First, Erickson and Heflin recommend pastors surveying congregations to discover what theological questions they may have, either by using questionnaires, focus groups, or a "question box" (or in our digital era, a form on our church websites) to discover what doctrinal topics they would like or need to hear.[22] I have pastor friends who have dedicated their Sunday night or Wednesday night teaching times to answering doctrinal questions from people in the church.

Second, major news or cultural events can prompt a break from an expository series to focus on a relevant biblical or doctrinal theme.

Third, preachers should calendar their sermons for the year, working to ensure they have an appropriate balance of expository and doctrinal sermons. Holidays like Christmas or Easter can be great opportunities to preach Christological doctrines. Erickson and Heflin suggest the lectionary as one way of making these plans.[23]

---

[22] Erickson and Heflin, *Old Wine in New Wineskins*, 244–46.
[23] Erickson and Heflin, 248–59.

Fourth, Erickson and Heflin encourage pastors new to a congregation to consider beginning their preaching tenure with a series of doctrinal sermons that convey the pastor's beliefs and philosophy of ministry.

Finally, working with staff and lay teachers across the church, a pastor could provide a "university model" for midweek Bible studies. University models offer several different Bible study classes around different themes or topics. For years, I have worked to ensure my churches offer "story" classes focused on growing people in biblical literacy (e.g., classes on books of the Bible or biblical theology), "truth" classes concentrating on Christian doctrine (e.g., classes on the Trinity, church history, or apologetics), "practice" classes directed toward practical issues we face (e.g., classes on parenting, money, etc.), and "affections" courses focused on emotional and devotional health (e.g., classes on anxiety, worship). In order to promote holistic worldview formation, I encourage church members to take a class from all four sections throughout a calendar year.

KEY TERMS

doctrinal-topical sermon
expository preaching
expository-theological sermon

homiletics
imperatives
indicatives

GO DEEPER

Erickson, Millard J., and James L. Heflin. *Old Wine in New Wineskins: Doctrinal Preaching in a Changing World*. Grand Rapids: Baker, 1997.

Merida, Tony. *The Christ-Centered Expositor: A Field Guide for Word-Driven Disciple Makers*. Nashville: B&H Academic, 2016.

Smith, Robert, Jr. *Doctrine That Dances: Bringing Doctrinal Preaching and Teaching to Life*. Nashville: B&H Academic, 2008.

Smith, Steven W. *Recapturing the Voice of God: Shaping Sermons Like Scripture*. Nashville: B&H Academic, 2015.

CONCLUSION

Doctrine That Makes Disciples

*What you have heard from me in the presence of many witnesses,
commit to faithful men who will be able to teach others also.*

—2 Timothy 2:2

This is not the end, but a beginning. Theological method is *prolegom-ena*, critical words said before jumping into the tasks before us. In this volume, we have explored the nature of theology, spiritual preparation for it, its resources, its procedure, and its application. Faithful theology is always under the authority of Scripture, but it does not neglect tradition, reason, and experience. It begins with a clear understanding of the biblical message, both in its parts and the whole. Theologians seek to know the God disclosed in the text and make him known through doctrine.

We do not study theology merely to enhance our knowledge or understanding of the Bible or spiritual things. We endure in this labor because we face a task unfinished: to "make disciples of all nations, baptizing them in the name of the Father and of the Son and of the Holy Spirit, teaching them to observe everything" we have learned from God in Christ (Matt 28:19–20). We reflect *on God's self-revelation for the purposes of growing in Christ and making disciples.* Our aim is nothing less than changing the worlds of the people to whom we proclaim Christ.

Theology in the flesh divides people and seeks the accolades of others. By contrast, theology in the Spirit grows us in our love for God and our love for our neighbor. Augustine observed this as central to the theological task: "If it seems to you that you have understood the divine scriptures, or any part of them, in such a way that by this understanding you do not build up this twin love of God and neighbor, then you have not yet understood them."[1] This true love for neighbor and human flourishing will inevitably result in gospel proclamation and disciple-making. We seek to submit ourselves to the authority of Scripture and to allow its transforming effects to reshape our worldviews—our beliefs, our practices, and our affections.

We proclaim doctrine in disciple-making relationships and in the teaching ministry of the local church. We long to see our neighbors behold the beauty of the gospel and its power play out in their lives. The labor of theology should result in the fruit of doctrine: *faithful and true teachings derived from Scripture and used to grow God's people in knowledge, spiritual maturity, and obedience.*

Yet we do not carry out this momentous task alone. We wrestle with God's self-presentation in Scripture in the context of a community of Spirit-led believers called the local church. We also study Christian doctrine with the faithful community of believers across time—living and dead alike. We have been handed a gift in the tradition of the church we would be foolish to overlook or ignore, as faithful men and women of God have gone before us, interpreting and applying the Scripture in ways fitting to their ministry contexts. Most importantly, we study Christian doctrine in the presence of the living God. Through the Spirit of God, our Lord who tasked us with this Great Commission, remains ever present with us (Matt 28:20).

---

[1] Augustine, *On Christian Doctrine* 1.36.40, in *Teaching Christianity: De Doctrina Christiana,* ed. and trans. Edmund Hill (Hyde Park, NY: New City Press, 1996), 124.

BIBLIOGRAPHY

Abraham, William J. "Systematic Theology as Analytic Theology." In *Analytic Theology: New Essays in the Philosophy of Theology*, edited by Oliver D. Crisp and Michael C. Rea, 54–69. Oxford: Oxford University Press, 2009.

Akin, Daniel L., and R. Scott Pace. *Pastoral Theology: Theological Foundations for Who a Pastor Is and What He Does*. Nashville: B&H Academic, 2017.

Allen, Michael, and Scott R. Swain. *Reformed Catholicity: The Promise of Retrieval for Theology and Biblical Interpretation*. Grand Rapids: Baker, 2015.

Allen, R. Michael, and Scott R. Swain. "In Defense of Proof-Texting." *JETS* 54.3 (September 2011): 589–606.

Allison, Gregg R. *Historical Theology*. Grand Rapids: Zondervan, 2011.

———. "The Protestant Doctrine of the Perspicuity of Scripture: A Reformulation on the Basis of Biblical Teaching." PhD diss., Trinity Divinity School, 1995.

Alston, William P. "Functionalism and Theological Language." *American Philosophical Quarterly* 22.3 (July 1985): 221–30.

———. "Substance and the Trinity." In *The Trinity: An Interdisciplinary Symposium on the Trinity*, edited by Stephen T. Davis, Daniel Kendall, and Gerald O'Collins, 179–201. New York: Oxford University Press, 2000.

Anizor, Uche. *How to Read Theology: Engaging Doctrine Critically & Charitably*. Grand Rapids: Baker, 2018.

Anselm. *Proslogion*.

Aquinas, Thomas. *Summa Theologica*.

Arbour, Benjamin H. *Philosophical Essays against Open Theism*. New York: Routledge, 2018.

Aristotle. *Meteorologica*.

———. *Metaphysics*.

Ashford, Bruce Riley, and Heath A. Thomas. *The Gospel of Our King: Bible, Worldview, and the Mission of Every Christian*. Grand Rapids: Baker, 2019.

Ashford, Bruce Riley, and Keith Whitfield. "Theological Method: An Introduction to the Task of Theology." In *A Theology for the Church*. 2nd ed., edited by Daniel L. Akin, 3–65. Nashville: B&H Academic, 2014.

Augustine. *Letter 28*.

———. *On Christian Doctrine*.

———. *Sermons*.

———. *Teaching Christianity: De Doctrina Christiana*. Edited and translated by Edmund Hill. Hyde Park, NY: New City Press, 1996.

———. *Tractates on the Gospel of John*.

Austin, J. L. *How to Do Things with Words*. 2nd ed. Cambridge, MA: Harvard University Press, 1975.

Ayer, A. J. *Language, Truth, and Logic*. New York: Dover, 1992.

Bandy, Alan S., ed. *A Greek Reader's Apostolic Fathers*. Eugene, OR: Cascade, 2018.

Barr, James. *The Concept of Biblical Theology: An Old Testament Perspective*. Minneapolis: Fortress, 1999.

Barrett, Matthew. *God's Word Alone: The Authority of Scripture—What the Reformers Taught . . . and Why It Still Matters*. Grand Rapids: Zondervan, 2016.

Barth, Karl. *Protestant Theology in the Nineteenth Century*. Translated by Brian Cozens and John Bowden. Grand Rapids: Eerdmans, 2002.

Bartholomew, Craig G., and Michael W. Goheen. *The Drama of Scripture: Finding Our Place in the Biblical Story*. Grand Rapids: Baker, 2004.

Beilby, James K. "Introduction: The Contribution of Philosophy to Theology." In *For Faith and Clarity: Philosophical Contributions to Christian Theology*, edited by James K. Beilby. Grand Rapids: Baker, 2006.

Berger, Peter L. *The Sacred Canopy: Elements of a Sociological Theory of Religion*. New York: Anchor, 1990.

Bird, Michael F. *What Christians Ought to Believe: An Introduction to Christian Doctrine through the Apostles' Creed*. Grand Rapids: Zondervan, 2016.

Blackwood, Andrew. *Expository Preaching Today*. Grand Rapids: Baker, 1975.

Bloesch, Donald G. *A Theology of Word and Spirit: Authority and Method in Theology*. Downers Grove, IL: InterVarsity Press, 1992.

Bockmuehl, Markus, and Alan J. Torrance, eds. *Scripture's Doctrine and Theology's Bible: How the New Testament Shapes Christian Dogmatics*. Grand Rapids: Baker, 2008.

Booth, Wayne C., Gregory G. Colomb, Joseph M. Williams, Joseph Bizup, and William T. Fitzgerald. *The Craft of Research*. 4th ed. Chicago: University of Chicago Press, 2016.

Bosch, David J. *Transforming Mission: Paradigm Shifts in Theology of Mission*. Maryknoll, NY: Orbis, 1991.

Bowman, Robert M., Jr. *The Word-Faith Controversy: Understanding the Health and Wealth Gospel*. Grand Rapids: Baker, 2001.

Bradley, James E., and Richard A. Muller. *Church History: An Introduction to Research, Reference Works, and Methods*. Grand Rapids: Eerdmans, 1995.

Brown, Harold O. J. *Heresies: Heresy and Orthodoxy in the History of the Church*. Peabody, MA: Hendrickson, 2003.

————. "What Is Liberation Theology?" In *Liberation Theology*, edited by Ronald Nash, 1–16. Milford, MI: Mott Media, 1984.

Brown, Peter. *Augustine of Hippo*. Berkeley, CA: University of California Press, 1967.

Bruce, F. F. *The Epistle to the Galatians*. Grand Rapids: Eerdmans, 1982.

————. *Tradition: Old and New*. Eugene, OR: Wipf and Stock, 2006.

Bruner, F. Dale. *A Theology of the Holy Spirit*. Grand Rapids: Eerdmans, 1970.

Bryson, Harold T. *Expository Preaching*. Nashville: B&H, 1995.

Buschart, W. David, and Kent D. Eilers. *Theology as Retrieval: Receiving the Past, Renewing the Church*. Downers Grove, IL: InterVarsity Press, 2015.

Callender, Craig, ed. *The Oxford Handbook of Philosophy of Time*. New York: Oxford University Press, 2011.

Calvin, John. *Institutes of the Christian Religion*.

Carl, William J. *Preaching Christian Doctrine*. Philadelphia: Fortress, 1984.

Carson, D. A. "Unity and Diversity in the New Testament: The Possibility of Systematic Theology." In *Scripture and Truth*, edited by D. A. Carson and John D. Woodbridge, 65–95. Grand Rapids: Baker, 1983.

Carter, Joe. *The Life & Faith Field Guide for Parents*. Eugene, OR: Harvest House, 2019.

Catechism of the Catholic Church. 2nd ed. New York: Doubleday, 2012.

Childs, Brevard S. *Biblical Theology of OT and NT: Theological Reflection of the Christian Bible.* Minneapolis: Fortress, 1993.

———. *Introduction to the Old Testament as Scripture.* Philadelphia: Fortress, 1979.

———. *Old Testament Theology in a Canonical Context.* Minneapolis: Fortress, 1990.

Clark, David K. *To Know and Love God: Method for Theology.* Wheaton, IL: Crossway, 2003.

Clement of Alexandria. *Stromata.*

Cole, Graham. *Faithful Theology: An Introduction.* Wheaton, IL: Crossway, 2020.

Cone, James. *A Black Theology of Liberation.* Maryknoll, NY: Orbis, 2012.

Congar, Yves. *The Meaning of Tradition.* Translated by A. N. Woodrow. San Francisco: Ignatius, 2004.

———. *Tradition and Traditions: A Historical and Theological Essay.* New York: Macmillan, 1966.

Cooper, John W. *Body, Soul, and Life Everlasting: Biblical Anthropology and the Monism-Dualism Debate.* Grand Rapids: Eerdmans, 2006.

Copan, Paul. *Loving Wisdom: A Guide to Philosophy and Christian Faith.* 2nd ed. Grand Rapids: Eerdmans, 2020.

Cowan, Steven B. *The Love of Wisdom: A Christian Introduction to Philosophy.* Nashville: B&H Academic, 2009.

———. ed. *Five Views on Apologetics.* Grand Rapids: Zondervan, 2000.

Craig, William Lane. *Reasonable Faith: Christian Truth and Apologetics.* 3rd ed. Wheaton, IL: Crossway, 2008.

Crisp, Oliver D. *Analyzing Doctrine: Toward a Systematic Theology.* Waco, TX: Baylor University Press, 2019.

———. *Approaching the Atonement.* Downers Grove, IL: InterVarsity Press, 2020.

———. *Divinity and Humanity.* New York: Cambridge University Press, 2007.

———. *God Incarnate.* New York: T&T Clark, 2009.

Descartes, René. *Oeuvres de Descartes.* Vols. 1–12. Rev. ed., edited by Charles Adam and Paul Tannery. Paris: J. Vrin/C.N.R.S., 1964–1976.

Dever, Mark, and Greg Gilbert. *Preach.* Nashville: B&H, 2012.

Dew, James K., Jr., and Mark W. Foreman. *How Do We Know? An Introduction to Epistemology.* Downers Grove, IL: InterVarsity Press, 2014.

Dew, James K., Jr., and Paul M. Gould. *Philosophy: A Christian Introduction.* Downers Grove, IL: InterVarsity Press, 2019.

Dockery, David S. *Christian Scripture: An Evangelical Perspective on Inspiration, Authority, and Interpretation.* Nashville: B&H, 1995.

Dolezal, James E. *All That Is in God: Evangelical Theology and the Challenge of Classical Christian Theism.* Grand Rapids: Reformed Heritage, 2017.

———. *God without Parts: Divine Simplicity and the Metaphysics of God's Absoluteness.* Eugene, OR: Pickwick, 2011.

Dorrien, Gary. *The Making of American Liberal Theology: Imagining Progressive Religion 1805–1900.* Louisville: Westminster John Knox, 2001.

Duesing, Jason G., and Nathan A. Finn, eds. *Historical Theology for the Church.* Nashville: B&H Academic, 2021.

Dunn, James D. G. *The Epistle to the Galatians.* Black's New Testament Commentary. Peabody, MA: Hendrickson, 1993.

———. *Jesus Remembered.* Christianity in the Making. Vol. 1. Grand Rapids: Eerdmans, 2003.

Eco, Umberto. *How to Write a Thesis.* Translated by Caterina Mongiat Farina and Geoff Farina. Cambridge, MA: The MIT Press, 2015.

Edwards, Mark J. "Quoting Aratus: Acts 17,28." *Zeitschrift für die neutestamentliche Wissenschaft und die Kunde der älteren Kirche* 83.3 (1992): 266–69.

Ehrman, Bart D., ed. *The Apostolic Fathers.* Loeb Classical Library, vols. 1–2. Cambridge, MA: Harvard University Press, 2003.

Elwell, Walter A., ed. *Topical Analysis of the Bible: A Survey of Essential Christian Doctrines.* Peabody, MA: Hendrickson, 2012.

Emerson, Matthew Y. *"He Descended to the Dead": An Evangelical Theology of Holy Saturday.* Downers Grove, IL: InterVarsity Press, 2019.

Erickson, Millard J. *Christian Theology.* 3rd ed. Grand Rapids: Baker, 2013.

———. *What Does God Know and When Does He Know It?: The Current Controversy over Divine Foreknowledge.* Grand Rapids: Zondervan, 2006.

Erickson, Millard L., and James L. Heflin. *Old Wine in New Wineskins: Doctrinal Preaching in a Changing World.* Grand Rapids: Baker, 1997.

Evans, Craig A. "Mark 8:27–16:20." In *Word Biblical Commentary* 34B. Nashville: Thomas Nelson, 2000.

Farley, Edward. *Theologia: The Fragmentation and Unity of Theological Education.* Philadelphia: Fortress, 1983.

Fee, Gordon D., and Douglas Stuart. *How to Read the Bible for All Its Worth.* 4th ed. Grand Rapids: Zondervan, 2014.

Feinberg, Paul. "The Meaning of Inerrancy." In *Inerrancy*, edited by Norman
    L. Geisler. Grand Rapids: Zondervan, 1980.

Ferguson, Everett. *The Rule of Faith*. Eugene, OR: Cascade, 2015.

Flemming, Dean. "Paul the Contextualizer." In *Local Theology for the Global
    Church: Principles for an Evangelical Approach to Contextualization*, edited
    by Matthew Cook, Rob Haskell, Ruth Julian, and Natee Tachanpongs,
    1–20. Pasadena, CA: William Carey Library, 2010.

Foster, Paul, ed. *Early Christian Thinkers: The Lives and Legacies of Twelve Key
    Figures*. Downers Grove, IL: InterVarsity, Press 2011.

Frame, John. *Systematic Theology: An Introduction to Christian Belief*.
    Philipsburg, NJ: P&R, 2013.

Frame, John M. *The Doctrine of the Knowledge of God*. A Theology of
    Lordship, vol. 1. Phillipsburg, NJ: P&R, 1987.

Franke, John R. "Missional Theology." In *Evangelical Theological Method:
    Five Views*, edited by Stanley E. Porter and Steven M. Studebaker, 60.
    Downers Grove, IL: InterVarsity Press, 2018.

Gabler, Johann Philipp. "An Oration on the Proper Distinction between
    Biblical and Dogmatic Theology and the Specific Objectives of Each." In
    *The Flowering of Old Testament Theology: A Reader in Twentieth-Century
    Old Testament Theology, 1930–1990*, edited by Ben C. Ollenburger,
    E. A. Martens, and Gerhard F. Hasel, 493–502. Winona Lake, IN:
    Eisenbrauns, 1992.

Gale, Richard M. "McTaggart's Analysis of Time." *American Philosophical
    Quarterly* 3.2 (1966): 145–52.

Galli, Mark. "What to Make of Karl Barth's Steadfast Adultery?" *Christianity
    Today*, October 20, 2017. https://www.christianitytoday.com/ct/2017
    /october-web-only/what-to-make-of-karl-barths-steadfast-adultery
    .html.

Ganssle, Gregory E., ed. *God and Time: Four Views*. Downers Grove, IL:
    InterVarsity Press, 2001.

Gaon, Saadia. *The Book of Doctrines and Beliefs*. Translated by Alexander
    Altmann. Indianapolis: Hackett, 2002.

Garrett, James Leo. *Systematic Theology*. Vol. 1. 3rd ed. North Richland Hills,
    TX: B.I.B.A.L., 2007.

Gärtner, Betril. *The Areopagus Speech and Natural Revelation*. Acta Seminarii
    Neotestamentici Upsaliensis 21. Translated by Carolyn Hannay King.
    Uppsala: Almquist & Wiksells, 1955.

Geertz, Clifford. *The Interpretation of Cultures*. New York: Basic Books, 1973.

Geiger, Eric, Michael Kelley, and Philip Nation. *Transformational Discipleship: How People Really Grow*. Nashville: B&H, 2012.

Geisler, Norman. *Systematic Theology*. Vol. 1. Minneapolis: Bethany House, 2002.

Gentry, Peter J., and Stephen J. Wellum. *God's Kingdom through God's Covenants: A Concise Biblical Theology*. Wheaton, IL: Crossway, 2015.

George, Timothy. "An Evangelical Reflection on Scripture and Tradition." *Pro Ecclesia* 9 (Spring 2000): 184–207.

Gonzales, Justo L. *A History of Christian Thought*. Rev. ed. Nashville: Abingdon, 2014.

Gould, Paul M., and Richard Brian Davis, eds. *Four Views on Christianity and Philosophy*. Grand Rapids: Zondervan, 2016.

Green, Joel B., and Max Turner. *Between Two Horizons: Spanning New Testament Studies and Systematic Theology*. Grand Rapids: Eerdmans, 1999.

Grenz, Stanley J., and Roger E. Olson. *20th-Century Theology: God and the World in a Transitional Age*. Downers Grove, IL: InterVarsity Press, 1992.

———. *Who Needs Theology? An Invitation to the Study of God*. Downers Grove: InterVarsity Press, 1996.

Griffin, David Ray. *The Christian Gospel for Americans: A Systematic Theology*. Anoka, MN: Process Century, 2019.

Grudem, Wayne. *Christian Ethics: An Introduction to Biblical Moral Reasoning*. Wheaton, IL: Crossway, 2018.

———. *The Gift of Prophecy in 1 Corinthians*. Eugene, OR: Wipf and Stock, 2000.

———. *The Gift of Prophecy in the New Testament and Today*. Wheaton, IL: Crossway, 2000.

———. *Systematic Theology*. Grand Rapids: Zondervan, 2000.

Gutiérrez, Gustavo. *A Theology of Liberation*. Translated by Caridad Inda and John Eagleson. Maryknoll, NY: Orbis, 1973.

Habermas, Gary, and J. P. Moreland. *Beyond Death: Exploring the Evidence for Immortality*. Eugene, OR: Wipf & Stock, 2004.

Hamilton, David. *The Inward Testimony of the Spirit of Christ to His Outward Revelation*. London, 1701.

Hamilton, James M. *God's Glory in Salvation through Judgment: A Biblical Theology*. Wheaton, IL: Crossway, 2010.

Hanegraaff, Hank. *Counterfeit Revival: Looking for God in All the Wrong Places*. Rev. ed. Nashville: Word, 2001.

Hanson, R. P. C. *The Search for the Christian Doctrine of God: The Arian Controversy, 318–381*. New York: T&T Clark, 1988.

Harrison, Patricia. "Bridging Theory and Training." In *Local Theology for the Global Church*, edited by Matthew Cook, Rob Haskell, Ruth Julian, and Natee Tanchanpongs, 210–12. Pasadena, CA: William Carey Library, 2013.

Hasker, William. *God, Time, and Knowledge*. Ithaca, NY: Cornell University, 1989.

Helm, Paul. *Eternal God: A Study of God without Time*. 2nd ed. New York: Oxford University Press, 2011.

———, ed. *Faith and Reason*. Oxford Readers. New York: Oxford University Press, 1999.

Henrichs, Albert. "Philosophy, the Handmaiden of Theology." *Greek, Roman, and Byzantine Studies* 9.4 (1968): 437–50.

Henry, Carl F. H. *God, Revelation, and Authority*. 6 vols. Wheaton, IL: Crossway, 1999.

Hesselgrave, David J. "Syncretism: Mission and Missionary Induced?" In *Contextualization and Syncretism: Navigating Cultural Currents*, Evangelical Missiological Society 13, edited by Gaylin Van Rheenen, 71–97. Pasadena, CA: William Carey Library, 2006.

Hesselgrave, David J., and Edward Rommen. *Contextualization: Meanings, Methods, and Models*. Grand Rapids: Baker, 1989.

Heyduck, Richard. *The Recovery of Doctrine in the Contemporary Church:An Essay in Philosophical Ecclesiology*. Waco, TX: Baylor University Press, 2001.

Hick, John. *An Interpretation of Religion: Human Responses to the Transcendent*. 2nd ed. New Haven, CT: Yale University Press, 2005.

———. *The Metaphor of God Incarnate: Christology in a Pluralistic Age*. 2nd ed. Louisville: Westminster/John Knox, 2006.

Hiebert, Paul G. *Anthropological Reflections on Missiological Issues*. Grand Rapids: Baker, 1994.

———. *Transforming Worldviews: An Anthropological Understanding of How People Change*. Grand Rapids: Baker, 2008.

Hodge, Charles. *Systematic Theology*. 3 vols. Peabody, MA: Hendrickson, 2003.

Holmes, Arthur F. *Contours of a World View*. Grand Rapids: Eerdmans, 1983.

Holmes, Michael W., ed. *The Apostolic Fathers: Greek Texts and English Translations*. 3rd ed. Grand Rapids: Baker, 2007.

Hooper, Walter, ed. *The Collected Letters of C. S. Lewis*. Vol. 1. San Francisco: Harper, 2005.

Hordern, William. *New Directions in Theology Today*. Vol. 1. Philadelphia: Westminster, 1966.

Horton, Michael. *The Christian Faith: A Systematic Theology for Pilgrims on the Way*. Grand Rapids: Zondervan, 2011.

Hume, David. *An Enquiry Concerning Human Understanding*.

Hunter, Trent, and Stephen Wellum. *Christ from Beginning to End: How the Full Story of Scripture Reveals the Full Glory of Christ*. Grand Rapids: Zondervan, 2018.

Ibrahim, Ayman S., and Ant Greenham, eds. *Muslim Conversions to Christ: A Critique of Insider Movements in Islamic Contexts*. New York: Peter Lang, 2018.

Irenaeus. *Against Heresies*.

Jacobs, A. J. *The Year of Living Biblically: One Man's Humble Quest to Follow the Bible as Literally as Possible*. New York: Simon and Schuster, 2007.

Jacobs, Alan. *A Theology of Reading: The Hermeneutics of Love*. New York: Routledge, 2001.

James, William. *The Varieties of Religious Experience: A Study in Human Nature*. New York, 1902.

Johnson, Luke Timothy, and Eve Tushnet. "Homosexuality and the Church: Two Views." *Commonweal*, June 15, 2007. http://commonwealmagazine.org/homosexuality-church-1.

Johnston, Robert K. "Experience, Theology Of." In *Evangelical Dictionary of Theology*. 2nd ed., edited by Daniel J. Treier and Walter A. Elwell, 428. Grand Rapids: Baker, 2001.

Jones, Beth Felker. *Practicing Christian Doctrine: An Introduction to Thinking and Living Theologically*. Grand Rapids: Zondervan, 2014.

Kapic, Kelly M. *A Little Book for New Theologians: Why and How to Study Theology*. Downers Grove, IL: InterVarsity Press, 2012.

Keener, Craig S. *Miracles: The Credibility of the New Testament Accounts*. Grand Rapids: Baker, 2011.

Keller, Timothy. *Center Church: Doing Balanced, Gospel-Centered Ministry in Your City*. Grand Rapids: Zondervan, 2012.

———. *Preaching: Communicating Faith in an Age of Skepticism.* New York: Viking, 2015.

Kelly, J. N. D. *Early Christian Creeds.* London: Longmans, 1950.

Kelsey, David. *Proving Doctrine: The Uses of Scripture in Modern Theology.* Harrisburg, PA: Trinity Press International, 1999.

Kibbe, Michael. *From Topic to Thesis: A Guide to Theological Research.* Downers Grove, IL: InterVarsity Press, 2016.

Kim, Matthew D. *Preaching with Cultural Intelligence: Understanding the People Who Hear Our Sermons.* Grand Rapids: Baker, 2017.

Kirkham, Richard L. *Theories of Truth: A Critical Introduction.* Cambridge, MA: The MIT Press, 1995.

Klein, William, Craig Blomberg, and Robert Hubbard. *Introduction to Biblical Interpretation.* 3rd ed. Grand Rapids: Zondervan, 2017.

Klink, Edward W., III, and Darian R. Lockett. *Understanding Biblical Theology: A Comparison of Theory and Practice.* Grand Rapids: Zondervan, 2012.

Kreider, Glenn R., and Swigel, Michael J. *A Practical Primer on Theological Method: Table Manners for Discussing God, His Works, and His Ways.* Grand Rapids: Zondervan, 2019.

Kuyper, Abraham. *Principles of Sacred Theology.* Translated by J. Hendrik DeVries. New York, 1898.

La Croix, Richard R. "The Hidden Assumption in the Paradox of Omnipotence." *Philosophy and Phenomenological Research* 38, no. 1 (September 1977): 125–27.

Layman, C. Stephen. *The Power of Logic.* 3rd ed. New York: McGraw-Hill, 2005.

Levering, Matthew. *Proofs of God: Classical Arguments from Tertullian to Barth.* Grand Rapids: Baker, 2016.

Lewis, C. S. Introduction to *On the Incarnation*, by Athanasius. Translated and edited by a Religious of the C.S.M.V. [Sister Penelope] Yonkers, NY: St. Vladimir's Seminary Press, 1977.

———. *The Last Battle.* The Chronicles of Narnia 7. New York: HarperCollins, 2000.

———. *Miracles.* San Francisco: HarperCollins, 2000.

———. *The Weight of Glory and Other Addresses.* San Francisco: HarperCollins, 2001.

Lindbeck, George A. *The Nature of Doctrine*. Louisville: Westminster John Knox, 1984.

Locke, John. *An Essay Concerning Human Understanding*.

Lonergan, Bernard. *Method in Theology*. Collected Works of Bernard Lonergan 14. Toronto: University of Toronto Press, 2017.

Lovejoy, Arthur O. *Essays in the History of Ideas*. Baltimore: John Hopkins University Press, 1948.

Lundgaard, Kris. *The Enemy Within: Straight Talk about the Power and Defeat of Sin*. Phillipsburg, NJ: P&R, 1998.

Luther, Martin. Dr. Martin Luther's *s.mmtliche Werke* Erlangen Ausgabe Erlangen 16. Enlangen, 1828.

———. "On the Councils and the Church." In *Luther's Works*. Vol. 41. Translated by Charles M. Jacobs and Eric W. Gritsch. Edited by Jaroslav Pelikan, 3–178. Philadelphia: Fortress Press, 1966.

MacGregor, Kirk R. *Contemporary Theology: An Introduction: Classical, Evangelical, Philosophical, and Global Perspectives*. Grand Rapids: Zondervan, 2019.

MacIntyre, Alasdair. *Whose Justice? Which Rationality?* Notre Dame: University of Notre Dame Press, 1988.

Manser, Martin H., Alister McGrath, J. I. Packer, and Donald J. Wiseman. *The Complete Topical Guide to the Bible*. Grand Rapids: Baker, 2017.

Marsden, George. *Jonathan Edwards: A Life*. New Haven, CT: Yale University Press, 2003.

Marshall, Bruce D. "Introduction: *The Nature of Doctrine* After 25 Years." In George A. Lindbeck, *The Nature of Doctrine: Religion and Theology in a Postliberal Age*. 2nd ed., xii–xviii. Louisville: Westminster John Knox, 2009.

Martin, Richard C., Mark R. Woodward, and Dwi S. Atmaja. *Defenders of Reason in Islam: Mu'tazilism from Medieval School to Modern Symbol*. London: Oneworld, 1997.

Mathison, Keith A. *The Shape of Sola Scriptura*. Moscow, ID: Canon, 2001.

Mavrodes, George I. "Miracles and the Laws of Nature." *Faith and Philosophy* 2.4 (October 1985): 333–46.

———. "Some Puzzles Concerning Omnipotence." *The Philosophical Review* 72.2 (April 1963): 221–23.

McCall, Thomas H. *An Invitation to Analytic Theology*. Downers Grove, IL: InterVarsity Press, 2015.

McClendon, James Wm., Jr. *Ethics: Systematic Theology*. Vol. 1. 2nd. ed. Nashville: Abingdon, 2002.

McClymond, Michael J. *The Devil's Redemption: A New History and Interpretation of Christian Universalism*. 2 vols. Grand Rapids: Baker, 2018.

McConnell, D. R. *A Different Gospel: Biblical and Historical Insights into the Word of Faith Movement*. Peabody, MA: Hendrickson, 1994.

McDonald, Lee M. *The Formation of the Christian Biblical Canon*. Rev. ed. Peabody, MA: Hendrickson, 1995.

McGrath, Alister E. *Christian Theology*. 5th ed. Malden, MA: Wiley-Blackwell, 2011.

———. *The Genesis of Doctrine: A Study in the Foundation of Doctrinal Criticism*. Grand Rapids: Eerdmans, 1997.

———. *Iustitia Dei: A History of the Christian Doctrine of Justification*. 4th ed. Cambridge: Cambridge University Press, 2020.

———. *A Passion for Truth: The Intellectual Coherence of Evangelicalism*. Downers Grove, IL: InterVarsity Press, 1996.

———. *The Passionate Intellect: Christian Faith and the Discipleship of the Mind*. Downers Grove, IL: InterVarsity Press, 2014.

———. *Reformation Thought*. 3rd ed. Malden, MA: Blackwell, 1999.

———. *A Scientific Theology*. Vols. 1–3. Grand Rapids: Eerdmans, 2001–2003.

McTaggart, J. M. E. *The Nature of Existence*. Vol. 2. Cambridge: Cambridge University Press, 1927.

———. "The Unreality of Time." *Mind* 17 (1908): 457–74.

Meijer, Alberic de. "Saint Augustine and the Conversation with the Child on the Shore: The History Behind the Legend." *Augustinian Heritage* 39 (1993): 21–34.

Merida, Tony. *The Christ-Centered Expositor: A Field Guide for Word-Driven Expositors*. Nashville: B&H Academic, 2016.

Metzger, Bruce M. *The Canon of the New Testament: Its Origin, Development, and Significance*. New York: Oxford University Press, 1987.

Michener, Ronald T. *Postliberal Theology: A Guide for the Perplexed*. New York: Bloomsbury, 2013.

Mitchell, Timothy N. "What Are the NT Autographs? An Examination of the Doctrine of Inspiration and Inerrancy in Light of Greco-Roman Publication." *JETS* 59.2 (2016): 287–308.

Moody, Josh, and Robin Weekes. *Burning Hearts: Preaching to the Affections*. Ross-shire, UK: Christian Focus, 2014.

Moreau, Scott. "Contextualization, Syncretism, and Spiritual Warfare: Identifying the Issues." In *Contextualization and Syncretism: Navigating Cultural Currents*, edited by Gaylin Van Rheenen, 47–70. Pasadena, CA: William Carey Library, 2006.

———. *Contextualization in World Missions: Mapping and Assessing Evangelical Models*. Grand Rapids: Kregel, 2012.

———. "Evangelical Models of Contextualization." In *Local Theology for the Global Church*, edited by Matthew Cook, Rob Haskell, Ruth Julian, and Natee Tanchanpongs, 165–93. Pasadena, CA: William Carey Library, 2013.

Moreland, J. P. *Kingdom Triangle: Recover the Christian Mind, Renovate the Soul, Restore the Spirit's Power*. Grand Rapids: Zondervan, 2007.

Moreland, J. P., and William Lane Craig. *Philosophical Foundations for a Christian Worldview*. 2nd ed. Downers Grove, IL: InterVarsity Press, 2017.

Morgan, Christopher W., and Robert A. Peterson. *Christian Theology: The Biblical Story and Our Faith*. Nashville: B&H Academic, 2020.

Mouw, Richard J. *Called to the Life of the Mind: Some Advice for Evangelical Scholars*. Grand Rapids: Eerdmans, 2014.

Muller, Richard A. *The Study of Theology: From Biblical Interpretation to Contemporary Formation*. Grand Rapids: Zondervan, 1990.

Naselli, Andrew David. *How to Understand and Apply the New Testament: Twelve Steps from Exegesis to Theology*. Phillipsburg, NJ: P&R, 2017.

Nash, Ronald H. *The Concept of God: An Exploration of the Contemporary Difficulties with the Attributes of God*. Grand Rapids: Zondervan, 1983.

Naugle, David. *Worldview: The History of a Concept*. Grand Rapids: Eerdmans, 2002.

Neufeld, Vernon H. *The Earliest Christian Confessions*. New Testament Tools and Studies 5. Leiden: Brill, 1963.

Nichols, Tom. *The Death of Expertise: The Campaign against Established Knowledge and Why It Matters*. New York: Oxford University Press, 2018.

Nickerson, Raymond S. *Reflections on Reasoning*. Hillsdale, NJ: Lawrence Erlbaum, 1986.

Nicole, Roger. "The Biblical Concept of Truth." In *Scripture and Truth*, edited by D. A. Carson and John D. Woodbridge, 287–302. Grand Rapids: Baker, 1983.

Oberman, Heiko A. *Forerunners of the Reformation: The Shape of Late Medieval Thought*. New York: Holt, Rhinehart and Winston, 1966.

Oden, Thomas C. *John Wesley's Teachings*. Vols. 1–4. Grand Rapids: Zondervan, 2014.

Oden, Thomas C., gen ed. *Ancient Christian Commentary on Scripture*. 29 vols. Downers Grove, IL: InterVarsity Press: 2001–2010.

———. *Pastoral Theology: Essentials of Ministry*. San Francisco: Harper & Row, 1983.

Olson, Roger E. *The Journey of Modern Theology: From Reconstruction to Deconstruction*. Downers Grove, IL: InterVarsity Press, 2013.

Ortlund, Gavin. *Finding the Right Hills to Die On: The Case for Theological Triage*. Wheaton, IL: Crossway, 2020.

———. *Theological Retrieval for Evangelicals: Why We Need Our Past to Have a Future*. Wheaton, IL: Crossway, 2019.

Osborne, Grant. *The Hermeneutical Spiral*. Rev. ed. Downers Grove, IL: InterVarsity Press, 2006.

Osborne, Thomas M. "Ockham as Divine-Command Theorist." *Religious Studies* 41.1 (March 2005): 1–22.

Overdorf, Daniel. *Applying the Sermon: How to Balance Biblical Integrity and Cultural Relevance*. Grand Rapids: Kregel, 2008.

Packer, J. I. *Knowing God*. Downers Grove, IL: InterVarsity Press, 1993.

Parshall, Phil. "Danger! New Directions in Contextualization." *Evangelical Missions Quarterly* 34, no. 4 (1998): 404–10.

Pascal, Blaise. *Pensées and Other Writings*. Translated by Honor Levi. New York: Oxford University Press, 1992.

Pelikan, Jaroslav. *The Christian Tradition: A History of the Development of Doctrine*. 5 vols. Chicago: University of Chicago Press, 1975–1991.

———. *The Vindication of Tradition*. New Haven, CT: Yale University Press, 1984.

Peterson, Michael, William Hasker, Bruce Riechenbach, and David Basinger. *Reason & Religious Belief: An Introduction to the Philosophy of Religion*. 3rd ed. New York: Oxford University Press, 2003.

Places, Edouard Des. "'Ipsius enim et genus sumus' (Act 17,28)." *Biblica* 43.3 (1962): 388–95.

Plato. *Meno.*

————. *The Republic.*

Preus, Robert D. "The View of the Bible Held by the Church: The Early Church through Luther." In *Inerrancy*, edited by Norman L. Geisler, 357–84. Grand Rapids: Zondervan, 1982.

Putman, Rhyne R. *In Defense of Doctrine: Evangelicalism, Theology, and Scripture.* Minneapolis: Fortress, 2015.

————. *When Doctrine Divides the People of God: An Evangelical Approach to Theological Diversity.* Wheaton, IL: Crossway, 2020.

Rae, Scott B. *Moral Choices: An Introduction to Christian Ethics.* 2nd ed. Grand Rapids: Zondervan, 2000.

Rainer, Thom S. *The Unchurched Next Door: Understanding Faith Stages as Keys to Sharing Your Faith.* Grand Rapids: Zondervan, 2003.

Ramm, Bernard. "Liberalism." In *Baker's Dictionary of Theology*, edited by Everett F. Harrison, Geoffrey W. Bromiley, and Carl F. H. Henry, 322–23. Grand Rapids: Baker, 1960.

Reeves, Michael. *Theologians You Should Know: An Introduction: From the Apostolic Fathers to the 21st Century.* Wheaton, IL: Crossway, 2006.

Rice, John R. *Our God-Breathed Book—The Bible.* Murfreesboro, TN: Sword of the Lord, 1969.

Richards, E. Randolph. *Paul and First-Century Letter Writing: Secretaries, Composition, and Collection.* Downers Grove, IL: InterVarsity Press, 2004.

Roberts, Alexander, James Donaldson, Philip Schaff, and Henry Wace, eds. *Nicene and Post-Nicene Fathers.* Series 1. 14 vols. Peabody, MA: Hendrickson, 1994.

Roberts, Robert C., and W. Jay Wood. *Intellectual Virtues: An Essay in Regulative Epistemology.* New York: Oxford University Press, 2007.

Robinson, Haddon W. *Biblical Preaching: The Development and Delivery of Expository Messages.* 2nd ed. Grand Rapids: Baker, 2001.

Rogers, Jack B., and Donald K. McKim. *The Authority and Interpretation of the Bible: A Historical Approach.* San Francisco: Harper & Row, 1979.

Rooker, Mark F. *The Ten Commandments: Ethics for the Twenty-First Century.* Nashville: B&H Academic, 2010.

Ryken, Philip Graham. *Christian Worldview: A Student's Guide.* Wheaton, IL: Crossway, 2013.

Samples, Kenneth Richard. *Classic Christian Thinkers: An Introduction.* Covina, CA: Reasons to Believe, 2019.

Sawyer, M. James. *The Survivor's Guide to Theology*. Rev. ed. Eugene, OR: Wipf & Stock, 2016.

Schnabel, Eckhard J. *Early Christian Mission*. Vol. 2. Downers Grove, IL: InterVarsity Press, 2004.

———. *Paul the Missionary: Realities, Strategies, and Methods*. Downers Grove, IL: InterVarsity Press, 2008.

Schleiermacher, Friedrich D. E. *Hermeneutics: The Handwritten Manuscripts*. Translated and edited by James Duke and Jack Forstman. Atlanta: Scholars Press, 1977.

Schreiner, Thomas R. *The King in His Beauty: A Biblical Theology of the Old and New Testaments*. Grand Rapids: Baker, 2013.

———. *Spiritual Gifts: What They Are and Why They Matter*. Nashville: B&H, 2018.

Schreiter, Robert J. *Constructing Local Theologies*. Maryknoll, NY: Orbis, 1985.

Scientific American. *A Question of Time: The Ultimate Paradox*. New York: Scientific American, 2017. eBook.

Searle, John. *Speech Acts: An Essay in the Philosophy of Language*. New York: Cambridge University Press, 1969.

Silva, Moisés, ed. *New International Dictionary of New Testament Theology and Exegesis*. 2nd ed. 5 vols. Grand Rapids: Zondervan, 2014.

Sire, James W. *Naming the Elephant: Worldview as a Concept*. 2nd ed. Downers Grove, IL: InterVarsity Press, 2015.

Smith, James K. A. *Desiring the Kingdom: Worship, Worldview, and Cultural Formation*. Cultural Liturgies. Vol. 1. Grand Rapids: Baker, 2009.

———. *How (Not) to Be Secular: Reading Charles Taylor*. Grand Rapids: Eerdmans, 2014.

Smith, Robert, Jr. *Doctrine That Dances: Bringing Doctrinal Preaching and Teaching to Life*. Nashville: B&H Academic, 2008.

Smith, Steven W. *Recapturing the Voice of God: Shaping Sermons Like Scripture*. Nashville: B&H Academic, 2015.

Spinoza, Benedict de [Baruch]. *Tractatus Theologico-Politicus*. London, 1682.

Spong, John Shelby. *Why Christianity Must Change or Die: A Bishop Speaks to Believers in Exile—A New Reformation of the Church's Faith and Practice*. San Francisco: HarperCollins, 1998.

Spykman, Gordon. *Reformational Theology: A New Paradigm for Doing Dogmatics*. Grand Rapids: Eerdmans, 1992.

Stendahl, Krister. "Biblical Theology, Contemporary." In *The Interpreter's Dictionary of the Bible*, vol. 1, edited by George Buttrick, 148–32. New York: Abingdon, 1962.

Stewart, Robert B. "The Insufficiency of Naturalism: A Worldview Critique." In *Come Let Us Reason: New Essays in Christian Apologetics*, edited by Paul Copan and William Lane Craig, 81–96. Nashville: B&H Academic, 2012.

Storms, C. Samuel. "A Third Wave View." In *Are the Miraculous Gifts for Today? Four Views*, edited by Wayne Grudem, 173–223. Grand Rapids: Zondervan, 1996.

Swain, Scott R. "Dogmatics as Systematic Theology." In *The Task of Dogmatics: Explorations in Theological Method*, edited by Oliver D. Crisp and Fred Sanders, 49–69. Grand Rapids: Zondervan, 2017.

Swinburne, Richard. *The Concept of Miracle*. New York: MacMillan, 1970.

———. "Miracles." *Philosophical Quarterly* 18 (1968): 320–28.

Sword, Helen. *Stylish Academic Writing*. Cambridge, MA: Harvard University Press, 2012.

Talman, Travis, ed. *Understanding Insider Movements: Disciples of Jesus within Diverse Religious Communities*. Pasadena, CA: William Carey Library, 2015.

Taylor, Charles. *A Secular Age*. Cambridge, MA: Belknap, 2007.

Tennent, Timothy C. *Theology in the Context of World Christianity*. Grand Rapids: Zondervan, 2007.

Tertullian. *On the Flesh of Christ*.

———. *On the Prescription of Heretics*.

———. *The Prescriptions against the Heretics 7*. In *Faith and Reason*, Oxford Readers, edited by Paul Helm. New York: Oxford University Press, 1999.

Thacker, Jason. *The Age of AI: Artificial Intelligence and the Future of Humanity*. Grand Rapids: Zondervan, 2020.

Thielicke, Helmut. *A Little Exercise for Young Theologians*. Translated by Charles L. Taylor. Grand Rapids: Eerdmans, 1962.

Thiselton, Anthony C. "Knowledge, Myth, and Corporate Memory." In *Believing in the Church: The Corporate Nature of Faith*, compiled by the Doctrine Commission of the Church of England, 45–78. Wilton, CT: Morehouse-Barlow, 1981.

———. *New Horizons in Hermeneutics: The Theory and Practice of Transforming Biblical Reading*. Grand Rapids: Zondervan, 1992.

————. *Systematic Theology*. Grand Rapids: Eerdmans, 2015.

Thompson, Mark D. *A Clear and Present Word: The Clarity of Scripture*. Downers Grove, IL: InterVarsity Press, 2006.

Thornbury, Gregory Alan. *Recovering Classical Evangelicalism: Applying the Wisdom and Vision of Carl F. H. Henry*. Wheaton, IL: Crossway, 2013.

Thorsen, Donald A. D. *The Wesleyan Quadrilateral: Scripture, Tradition, Reason, and Experience as a Model of Evangelical Theology*. Grand Rapids: Zondervan, 1990.

Tietz, Christiane. "Karl Barth and Charlotte von Kirschbaum." *Theology Today* 74 (July 2017): 86–111.

Tillich, Paul. *Systematic Theology*. Vol. 1. Chicago: University of Chicago Press, 1951.

Tolkien, J. R. R. "On Fairy-Stories." In *Essays Presented to Charles Williams*, edited by C. S. Lewis. Grand Rapids: Eerdmans, 1966.

Toon, Peter. *The Development of Doctrine in the Church*. Grand Rapids: Eerdmans, 1979.

Treier, Daniel J. "The Freedom of God's Word: Toward an 'Evangelical' Dogmatics of Scripture." In *The Voice of God in the Text of Scripture*, edited by Oliver D. Crisp and Fred Sanders, 21–40. Grand Rapids: Zondervan, 2016.

————. *Virtue and the Voice of God: Toward Theology as Wisdom*. Grand Rapids: Eerdmans, 2006.

Treier, Daniel J., and Walter A. Elwell, eds. *Evangelical Dictionary of Theology*. 3rd ed. Grand Rapids: Baker, 2017.

Treloar, Geoffrey R. *The Disruption of Evangelicalism: The Age of Torrey, Mott, McPherson, and Hammond*. A History of Evangelicalism. Vol. 4. Downers Grove, IL: InterVarsity Press, 2017.

Ukpong, Justin. "What Is Contextualization?" *Neue Zeitschrift für Missionswissenschaft* 43 (1987): 161–68.

Vanhoozer, Kevin J. "Augustinian Inerrancy: Literary Meaning, Literal Truth, and Literate Interpretation in the Economy of Biblical Discourse." In *Five Views on Biblical Inerrancy*, edited by J. Merrick and Stephen M. Garrett, 199–235. Grand Rapids: Zondervan, 2013.

————. *The Drama of Doctrine*. Louisville: Westminster John Knox, 2006.

————. "A Drama-of-Redemption Model." In *Four Views on Moving beyond the Bible to Theology*, edited by Gary T. Meadors, 151–99. Grand Rapids: Zondervan, 2009.

———. *Faith Speaking Understanding: Performing the Drama of Doctrine.* Louisville: Westminster John Knox, 2014.

———. *First Theology: God, Scripture, and Hermeneutics.* Downers Grove, IL: InterVarsity Press, 2002.

———. *Hearers and Doers: A Pastor's Guide to Making Disciples through Scripture and Doctrine.* Bellingham, WA: Lexham, 2019.

———. "Letter to an Aspiring Theologian: How to Speak of God Truly." *First Things*, August 2018. https://www.firstthings.com/article/2018/08/letter-to-an-aspiring-theologian.

———. *Remythologizing Theology: Divine Action, Passion, and Authorship.* New York: Cambridge University Press, 2010.

Van Rheenen, Gailyn. "Syncretism and Contextualization: The Church on a Journey Defining Itself." In *Contextualization and Syncretism: Navigating Cultural Currents*, edited by Gaylin Van Rheenen, 1–30. Pasadena, CA: William Carey Library, 2006.

Vincent of Lérins. *Commonitory.*

Vines, Jerry, and Jim Shaddix. *Power in the Pulpit: How to Prepare and Deliver Expository Sermons.* Chicago: Moody, 1999.

Vines, Matthew J. *God and the Gay Christian: The Biblical Case in Support of Same-Sex Relationships.* New York: Convergent, 2015.

Wagner, C. Peter. *The Third Wave of the Holy Spirit.* Ann Arbor: Vine, 1988.

Walls, Andrew. *The Missionary Movement in Christian History: Studies in the Transmission of the Faith.* Maryknoll, NY: Orbis, 1996.

Walsh, Brian J., and J. Richard Middleton. *The Transforming Vision: Shaping a Christian Worldview.* Downers Grove, IL: InterVarsity Press, 1984.

Ware, Bruce A. *God's Lesser Glory: The Diminished God of Open Theism.* Wheaton, IL: Crossway, 2000.

Wax, Trevin K. *Eschatological Discipleship: Leading Christians to Understand Their Historical and Cultural Context.* Nashville: B&H Academic, 2018.

Webster, John. *Holiness.* London: SCM, 2003.

———. *Holy Scripture: A Dogmatic Sketch.* New York: Cambridge University Press, 2003.

———. "Theologies of Retrieval." In *The Oxford Handbook of Systematic Theology*, edited by John Webster, Kathryn Tanner, and Iain Torrance, 583–99. New York: Oxford University Press, 2007.

———. "What Makes Theology Theological?" *Journal of Analytic Theology* 3 (May 2015): 17–28.

Wells, Samuel. *Improvisation: The Drama of Christian Ethics*. Grand Rapids: Brazos, 2004.

Wellum, Stephen. "From Alpha to Omega: A Biblical-Theological Approach to God the Son Incarnate." *JETS* 63.1 (2020): 71–94.

Wesley, John. *The Works of John Wesley*. 3rd ed. 14 vols. Edited by Thomas Jackson. Grand Rapids: 1979.

Westminster Confession of Faith.

Whaling, Frank. "The Development of the Word 'Theology.'" *Scottish Journal of Theology* 34 (1981): 289–312.

Wheeler, Ray. "The Legacy of Shoki Coe." *International Bulletin of Missionary Research* 26.2 (2002): 77–80.

Whitney, Donald S. *Spiritual Disciplines for the Christian Life*. Rev. ed. Colorado Springs, CO: NavPress, 2014.

Wilkens, Steve, ed. *Faith and Reason: Three Views*. Downers Grove, IL: InterVarsity Press, 2014.

Williams, J. Rodman. *Renewal Theology: Systematic Theology from a Charismatic Perspective*. 3 vols. Grand Rapids: Zondervan, 1996.

Witherington, Ben, III. *The Acts of the Apostles: A Socio-Rhetorical Commentary*. Grand Rapids: Eerdmans, 1997.

———. *Grace in Galatia: A Commentary on Paul's Letter to the Galatians*. Grand Rapids: Eerdmans, 1998.

Wittmer, Michael E. *Don't Stop Believing: Why Living Like Jesus Is Not Enough*. Grand Rapids: Zondervan, 2008.

Wolterstorff, Nicholas. *Divine Discourse: Philosophical Reflections on the Claim That God Speaks*. New York: Cambridge University Press, 1995.

———. "The Migration of the Theistic Arguments: From Natural Theology to Evidentialist Apologetics." In *Rationality, Religious Belief, and Moral Commitment: New Essays in the Philosophy of Religion*, edited by Robert Audi and William J. Wainright, 38–81. Ithaca, NY: Cornell University Press, 1986.

———. "Unqualified Divine Temporality." In *God and Time: Four Views*, edited by Gregory E. Ganssle, 187–213. Downers Grove, IL: InterVarsity Press, 2001.

Wood, W. Jay. *Epistemology: Becoming Intellectually Virtuous*. Downers Grove, IL: InterVarsity Press, 1998.

Woods, Robert, and Brian Walrath, eds. *The Message in the Music: Studying Contemporary Praise and Worship*. Nashville: Abingdon, 2007.

Wright, Christopher J. H. *The Mission of God: Unlocking the Bible's Grand Narrative*. Downers Grove, IL: InterVarsity Press, 2006.

Wright, Christopher J. H., and Jonathan Lamb, eds. *Understanding and Using the Bible*. Minneapolis: Fortress, 2015.

Wright, N. T. "How Can the Bible Be Authoritative?" *Vox Evangelica* 21 (1991): 7–32.

———. *Jesus and the Victory of God*. Minneapolis: Fortress, 1997.

———. *The New Testament and the People of God*. Minneapolis: Fortress, 1992.

———. *Paul and the Faithfulness of God*. 2 vols. Minneapolis: Fortress, 2013.

———. "Reading Paul, Thinking Scripture." In *Scripture's Doctrine and Theology's Bible: How the New Testament Shapes Christian Dogmatics*, edited by Markus Bockmuehl and Alan J. Torrance, 59–74. Grand Rapids: Baker, 2008.

———. *Scripture and the Authority of God: How to Read the Bible Today*. New York: HarperCollins, 2013.

Yaghjian, Lucretia B. *Writing Theology Well: A Rhetoric for Theological and Biblical Writers*. 2nd. ed. New York: Bloomsbury T&T Clark, 2015.

Yeago, David S. "The New Testament and Nicene Dogma: A Contribution to the Recovery of Theological Exegesis." In *Theological Interpretation of Scripture: Classic and Contemporary Readings*, edited by Stephen E. Fowl, 87–100. Cambridge, MA: Blackwell, 1997.

Zagzebski, Linda Trinkaus. *Virtues of the Mind: An Inquiry into the Nature of Virtue and the Ethical Foundations of Knowledge*. Cambridge: Cambridge University Press, 1996.

Zahl, Simeon. *The Holy Spirit and Christian Experience*. New York: Oxford University Press, 2020.

GENERAL INDEX

A

abortion, 75, 199, 275–76
Abstract of Principles, 144
affections
    courses on, 281
    doctrine and, 34, 51, 62–64, 218–20,
      264, 270–72
    in worldview, 47, 49, 174
Allison, Gregg, 72, 131, 149–50
analogical language, 37
analogy of faith, 212–13
analytic theology, 170–74
*Ancient Christian Commentary on
    Scripture* (Oden), 214
Anizor, Uche, 94, 152–53
Anselm of Canterbury, 21, 68, 73, 102,
    107, 139, 159
anti-intellectualism, 101, 104
Apollinarianism, 41, 144
apologetics, 14, 23, 67, 74–75, 82, 171
Apostles' Creed, 143, 158
Apostolic Fathers, The, 155
Aratus, 232
arguments
    cosmological, 166
    deductive approach to, 249–51,
      258–60
    inductive approach to, 249, 252–53,
      258–60
    moral law, 166
    ontological, 107, 166
    polemic, 75
    sound, 250

    teleological, 166
Arianism, 41, 142, 144, 151
Aristotle, 11, 97
Arius, 3, 60
Arminius, Jacob, 159, 246
artificial intelligence, 28, 41
Ashford, Bruce, 11
Athanasius, 139
atheism, 30, 75, 106, 122–23, 166–67,
    175, 199
atonement, 79, 149, 171, 212–13,
    245–46, 269
Augsburg Confession, 144
Augustine, 68, 72, 102, 107, 128, 139,
    146, 155, 159, 173, 246, 256, 277–
    78, 284
Austin, J. L., 135–36
Azusa Street Revival, 185

B

Baptist Faith & Message 2000, 144
Barrett, Matthew, 129, 133
Barth, Karl, 90, 146
behavior, 49
    justification of, 76, 101
    prohibited, 189, 238
    shaping of, 20
    worldview and, 49, 60
Beilby, James K., 67
Belgic Confession, 144
beliefs
    coherence of, 166–67
    exercising of, 88–89

four stages of, 114–16
three types of, 108
Berdyaev, Nikolay, 159
Bernard of Clairvaux, 267
Bible. *See* Scripture
biblical authority, 17, 128, 142, 157, 229
    See also Scripture: authority of
biblical theology, 14, 69–72, 82, 206–8, 238
    canonical approach to, 71
    descriptive vs. prescriptive, 70–71
bibliolatry, 17
Bloesch, Donald, 102
blog posts, 145, 239
Blomberg, Craig, 98
Bondurant, Diana, 164
Bradley, James, 149, 153
Brainiac Theology, 28
Brownsville Revival, 185
Bruce, F. F., 95
Bryson, Harold T., 265
Buschart, David, 80
Butler, Joseph, 159

C

Calvin, John, 68, 139, 145–46, 155–56, 159
Carson, D. A., 80–81
catechumens, 158
Chalcedonian Definition, 144, 251
charismatic theology, 182, 184–86
Christology, 19, 59, 209, 245
City of God (Augustine), 155
Civil Rights Movement, 199
Clark, David, 34, 79
Clement of Alexandria, 12
climate change, 238
cloning, 75
commentaries, 147, 204, 214
community, faith, 30–34, 38, 61, 266, 284
Complete Topical Guide to the Bible, The (Manser et al.), 201
concordances, 200
Cone, James, 189
consequentialist ethics, 76–77, 211
contextualization, 224–30
coronavirus, 268
Council at Chalcedon, 144
Council of Constantinople, 144

Council of Nicaea, 144, 169
Craft of Research, The (Booth et al.), 246
Craig, William Lane, 112, 165, 191
crises, 62, 116
culture
    of audience, 234
    global, 3
    other, 215, 234
    post-truth, 178
    Western, 20, 62, 147, 153, 178, 236–37

D

Darwinism, 20
decision-making, 116, 177, 196
Deism, 122–23
deontological ethics, 76
Descartes, René, 106, 109
Devil's Redemption, The (McClymond), 150
devotional reading, 82, 122
dictionaries, 200–201, 205
Dionysius, 254
disciple-making, 22, 44, 47, 78, 223
    doctrine in, 50–65, 283–84
    tradition in, 158–60
divine command ethics, 75–76, 211
divine revelation, 77, 103, 105, 122, 145, 188–89, 197, 208
Dockery, David, 130
doctrine
    abstract, 28
    branches of study, 14
    cognitive-propositional, 25–29, 34
    correction of, 39–40
    cultural-linguistic theory, 30–34
    defined, 39, 264
    descriptive and prescriptive, 28–29
    development of, 40–41, 147, 150–51, 246
    distinct from theology, 23–25
    error in vs. false, 40
    experiential-expressive, 29–30, 34, 188
    false, 2–4, 24, 33, 38, 143
    function of, 25
    origin of term, 24, 35
    ranking, 215–18
    sound, 24, 36

doctrine of biblical inerrancy, 128–31, 217, 252, 257–59
doctrine of Christ, 59, 144, 209
doctrine of God, 12, 19, 209
doctrine of humanity, 19, 58, 209, 276
doctrine of inspiration, 125
doctrine of justification, 72, 150
doctrine of last things, 19, 59, 209
doctrine of revelation, 19, 245
doctrine of salvation, 19, 59, 151, 209
doctrine of Scripture, 142, 245, 251
doctrine of sin, 19, 59, 72
doctrine of the church, 19, 58, 78, 155, 209
doctrine of the clarity of Scripture, 131–32
doctrine of the Holy Spirit, 19, 151, 182, 209
doctrine of the incarnation, 2, 12, 29, 171
doctrine of the Trinity, 2, 18, 40, 104, 144, 147, 151, 169, 184, 217, 229, 268, 276–79
dogmatics, 14
doubt, 109–10, 113
     vs. unbelief, 109–10

E

ecclesiology, 19, 58, 78, 209, 218, 245, 269
Eilers, Kent, 80
emotional wellness, 220
emotivism, 29
engaging
     the biblical text, tradition, and culture, 198
     with other academic disciplines, 21–22
     in polemics, 94–95
     public, 152
     in theological debates, reasons for the early church's, 60
     your ministry context, 236
Enlightenment, 68, 106, 128, 167–68, 187, 189
enthusiasts, 105, 184, 192
Epimenides, 232
epistemology, 74, 111, 113–14, 165
equivocal language, 37

Erickson, Millard, 15, 225, 267, 280–81
eschatology, 19, 55, 59, 200, 209, 245
ethics, 14, 29, 60, 74, 75–77, 82, 135, 211
     approaches to, 75–76
     guidance in, 61–62
Eutychianism, 144
Evangelical Dictionary of Theology (Treier and Elwell), 201
exegesis, 72, 81–82, 91, 122, 134, 169, 201, 234–38
experiences, 30, 194, 199
     empirical, 179–80
     existential, 180–81
     learning from, 146, 178–79, 190
     near-death, 180
     of others, 190–91, 199
     religious, 112, 178–94
     role of in traditions, 179–90
     senseless, 48

F

faith, 97
     blind, 104, 108, 112
     confessions of, 30, 33, 38, 144, 201
     and reason, 102, 105–7
     without understanding, 103–5
"faith seeking understanding," 102, 107–8, 115
Father-sufferers, 2
feelings, 62–64. *See* affections
Feinberg, Paul, 129–30
Felker Jones, Beth, 15
fideism, 102, 103–5, 109
Frame, John M., 15, 156–57
Franke, John, 15
Freytag, Gustav, 55–56

G

Gaon, Saadia, 16
Garrett, James Leo, 132
Geertz, Clifford, 31
general revelation, 17, 22, 123–24, 133, 164, 166, 232, 245
gentleness, 92, 97
George, Timothy, 140
glossolalia. *See* tongues
Gnosticism, 2, 12, 142, 153
God
     failure to love, 102

knowledge of, 16, 21, 35, 63–64, 91,
112–13, 132–33, 200
omnipotence of, 166–67
self-disclosure by, 17, 124, 129
grand narrative, 36, 47, 51–58, 72, 109,
135, 143, 147, 174, 197, 206–8, 212,
236, 264, 267, 270
Great Commission, 4, 22, 50, 57, 60, 78,
98, 207, 284
Grotius, Hugo, 246
Grudem, Wayne, 14–15, 131, 186
gun control, 75, 238
Gutiérrez, Gustavo, 188–89

H

Habermas, Gary, 180
habits, 49, 60–61, 64, 116
hamartiology, 19, 59, 245
Hamilton, David, 191–92
Hanson, R. P. C., 142
"health and wealth" gospel, 175
hearts, 21, 46–47, 50–51, 62–64, 89, 91,
93, 96, 109–10, 178–79, 192–94, 265
Heflin, James, 267, 280–81
Heidelberg Catechism, 144
Henry, Carl F. H., 104
heresies, 2, 12, 20, 144, 229
hermeneutical circle, 81
hermeneutics, 70, 74, 134, 199, 202–6,
211
Hick, John, 29, 105
Hiebert, Paul G., 47–48, 218
historical theology, 14, 72–73, 82, 140,
146–47, 158, 214–15
biographical approach to, 149
courses in, 158
diachronic approach to, 149–51
resources in, 152–57, 214–15
synchronic approach to, 150–51
theology of retrieval approach to,
151
Hodge, Charles, 29
Holmes, Arthur, 13
holy living, 61, 226
Holy Spirit
illumination of, 98, 131–32
indwelling of, 17
homiletics, 264–65, 270
homosexuality, 189–90

Hooker, Richard, 159
Hordern, William, 225, 230
Horton, Michael, 28
hot-button issues, 1, 75, 92, 275–76
Hubbard, Robert, 98
humanity, 19–20, 41, 52–53, 58–59, 107,
144, 207, 209, 213, 232, 245, 270,
276
Hume, David, 167–68
hymnody, 62

I

illocutionary acts, 136, 206, 265
immigration, 75
Irenaeus, 12, 128
irenic theology, 95
Islam, 75, 104, 228–29
Iustitia Dei (McGrath), 150

J

Jacobs, A. J., 225–26
James, William, 180–81
Jesus Christ
divinity and humanity of, 20,
144
study of person and work of, 19
John Smyth's Short Confession, 144
Johnson, Luke Timothy, 189–90
Jones, Jim, 192
joy, 33, 55, 92–95, 220, 246, 271
Justin Martyr, 12

K

Kant, Immanuel, 46
Keener, Craig, 180
Keller, Timothy, 159, 224, 235, 267
Kelsey, David, 121
kindness, 92–93, 97
Klein, William, 98
knowledge, 44, 68, 108, 111, 133, 179,
264
by acquaintance, 111–12
competence, 111–12
God as ultimate source of, 111–12
propositional, 111–13
Koresh, David, 192

L

Lamb, Jonathan, 135, 203

language, 30–33, 36–37, 140, 142–43, 223
  imagery in, 41
  philosophy of, 74
laypersons, 159, 203, 215, 235
legalism, 20
Lewis, C. S., 48, 108–9, 159–60, 167–68
liberal theology, 187–89, 229
liberation theology, 188–89
  black, 189
  Latin American, 188–89
Lindbeck, George, 25–34
liturgy, 62
Locke, John, 105–6
locutionary acts, 136, 205
Loeb Classical Library, 154
logic, 74, 165, 249
Lonergan, Bernard, 195
love, 37–38, 64, 76, 92–94, 204
  ultimate, 49–50
Luther, Martin, 68, 72, 103, 128, 139–40, 145–46, 159

M

MacArthur, John, 265
Majority World churches, 234
Marcionite, 12
Maritain, Jacques, 159
marriage, 2, 41, 90, 236–37, 268
  same-sex, 75
McCall, Thomas, 171
McClymond, Michael J., 150
McGrath, Alister, 15, 79, 150, 182
McTaggart, John, 172
meditation, 63–64, 197, 219–20
Merida, Tony, 265
metaphysics, 165
Middleton, Richard, 48
ministry, 35, 43, 77, 217–18, 236–38
  shaping of, 20
miracles, 123, 165, 167–69, 180, 191
missiologists, 224
Modalism, 2, 12, 151
Mohler, R. Albert, Jr., 215
monographs, 154, 215, 263
Montanism, 2
Montanus, 2
Moody, Josh, 49
moral relativism, 189–90

Moreland, J. P., 112–13, 165, 180
morphology, 204
Muller, Richard, 149, 153
Muslims, 191, 228–29
Mu'tazila, 16
mysticism, 180
myths, 11, 47–48

N

Naselli, Andrew David, 72
Nash, Ronald, 167
Nave's Topical Bible, 201
Nestorianism, 144
New Hampshire Confession of Faith, 144
New International Dictionary of New Testament Theology and Exegesis, 200
New International Dictionary of Old Testament Theology and Exegesis, 200
Nicene Council, 60
Nicene Creed, 144, 158
Niceno-Constantinopolitan Creed, 144
Niebuhr, Reinhold, 159

O

Oberman, Heiko, 145
Office, The, 56–57
orthodoxy, 29, 40, 60, 63, 72, 170, 179, 181, 229
orthopathy, 63, 179
orthopraxy, 60, 63, 179
Ortlund, Gavin, 216, 218
Osborne, Grant, 81, 205
Overdorf, Daniel, 271

P

Packer, J. I., 219
pantheism, 122–23, 167
Parham, Charles Fox, 184
pastoral theology, 14, 77–78
patience, 92–93, 95–96, 116
patripassianists, 2
peace, 92–95, 220
Pelikan, Jaroslav, 147
Pennyworth, Alfred, 92
Pensacola Outpouring, 185
Pentecostalism, 184–86
perlocutionary acts, 136, 206, 265

philosophical theology, 14, 73–74, 82,
   170–71, 215
philosophy
   apologetic dimension of, 165–68
   defined, 164
   key concepts of, 74, 169–70
   as second-order discipline, 165
philosophy of religion, 12–13, 68, 73,
   165
Piper, John, 159
Plato, 11, 179
pluralism, 105, 188
pneumatology, 19, 209, 245
polemics, 75, 95
postmodernity, 25, 29
practical theology, 14
prayer, 62, 91–92, 190
preaching. *See* sermons
progressive revelation, 207
prolegomena, 1–3, 19, 74, 283
proof-texting, 201
prophecy, 185–86, 246
propositional acts, 136, 205
Protestantism, 186–88
Protestant Reformers, 30, 108, 145, 147

Q

quadrilateral method, 133
questions, 1, 21, 51, 238
   life, 31, 41, 48–49, 51, 57–60, 165,
      224, 238
   theological, 18–19, 24, 40, 74, 78,
      111, 142, 163–64, 170, 174, 188,
      190, 198–200, 207, 209, 213,
      236–37

R

rationalism, 102–3, 105–7, 109
reason, 20, 101, 103
   and faith, 102
   gift of, 17
Reformation Commentary on Scripture, 214
Reid, Andrew, 134–35
research papers
   citing sources for, 260
   creating interest in, 246–47
   good arguments in, 248–56
   grammar and style in, 260–61
   outlining, 257–60

reviewing and revising of, 261
time spent on, 260
topic of, 242
resources
   biblical fidelity of, 157
   close reading of, 155–56
   contextual dimensions of, 152–53
   evaluation of, 156
   familiarity with, 196
   primary, 153, 158
   prioritizing, 200–202
   secondary, 153, 214
   tertiary, 153
Richards, E. Randolph, 87
romanticism, 187
rule of faith, 143

S

salvation, 31, 36, 217, 245–46, 272
same-sex relationships, 75, 189, 238
Santayana, George, 147
Sayers, Dorothy, 159
Schleiermacher, Friedrich, 81, 146,
   187–88
science of speech, 16
Scott, Michael, 56–57
Scripture
   academic study of, 67–69
   "acts" in, 55–56, 206–7
   authority of, 126, 170
   authorship of, 208–11
   clarity of, 131–33
   context of, 203–6
   contradictions in, 213
   cultural background of, 204–5
   genre of, 203–4, 210
   as God's communication, 135–37
   inerrancy of, 127–31
   inspiration of, 124–26
   instruction in, 210–12
   intended audience of, 210–11
   interpretation of, 20, 98, 134–35, 142
   nonnegotiables in, 237–38
   organization of, 18–20, 212
   in original language, 204
   personal view of, 121–22
   reading plans for, 197–98
   sufficiency of, 132–34
   truths across, 212–13

Second London Confession, 144
Second Temple Judaism, 205–6
semantics, 204
sermons
    audience of, 234–39
    doctrinal, 263–81
    doctrinal-topical, 269, 275–80
    expository, 264–69
    expository-theological, 269–75
    indicatives and imperatives in, 270
    life effects on, 268, 280
    preparation of, 158, 280–81
    vocabulary of, 235
sex change, 62, 75
sexual revolution, 20, 189–90, 236
Seymour, William J., 184
Shakespeare, William, 54–55
sin, 194
    confronting, 219–20
    noetic effects of, 106
    original, 246
    theology used to justify, 90–91
Sire, James, 47
skepticism, 101, 108, 156–57, 179
Smith, James K. A., 49–50
Smith, Joseph, Jr., 192
Smith, Steven W., 266
sola Scriptura, 35, 132–33, 140, 213
soteriology, 19, 59, 209, 245
special revelation, 17, 68, 108, 122–24,
    164, 166, 170, 185, 245
speech-act theory, 135–37, 205–6, 210,
    270
Spinoza, Baruch, 167–68
Spurgeon, Charles, 139
Spykman, Gordon, 2
Standard Confession, 144
Stewart, Robert, 45, 164, 174–75
Summa Theologica (Aquinas), 253–54
Swedenborg, Emanuel, 184
Swinburne, Richard, 168
syntax, 204–5
systematic theology, 20–21
    apologetics and, 75
    biblical theology and, 72
    categories of, 19–20, 209
    critical reflection in, 16–17
    defined, 14–16, 22, 44
    as distinctively Christian, 16, 21
    features of, 15–22
    and other disciplines, 21, 78–83
    primary subject of, 17

T

Taylor, Charles, 45, 153
teachers
    false, 16, 24, 40, 89, 142, 192
    virtues of, 115–16
Tennent, Timothy, 237
Tertullian, 12, 103
theism, 106, 166–67, 170, 173
theologia, 11–12, 68
theologians
    aim of, 20–21, 44
    everyone as, 13
    virtues of student, 114–15
theological anthropology, 19, 58, 209
theological encyclopedia, 68
theological syncretism, 228–29
theological, use of word, 13–14
theology
    as both science and art, 195–96
    defined, 9–22, 10–14
    distinct from doctrine, 23–25
    experiential, 190
    faithful, 97–99
    in the flesh, 89–92
    in the Spirit, 92–99
    way to study, 196–20
    See also specific type of theology
theology proper, 12, 19, 209, 245
third-wave evangelicalism, 186
Thiselton, Anthony, 107
Thomas Aquinas, 10, 68, 73, 128, 139,
    146, 159, 166–67
    arguments by, 253–56
time, 171–72
Tolkien, J. R. R., 34, 55
tongues, 181, 184–85, 198
Toon, Peter, 40
Topical Analysis of the Bible (Elwell), 201
Toronto Blessing, 185
tradition, 20
    apostolic, 141–42
    defined, 140–46
    extremes with, 139–40
    learning from another, 148–49
    magisterial authority of, 146

ministerial authority of, 146
    research of, 152–57
    study of, 146–49
Tradition I, 145
Tradition II, 145
transformers, 225, 227–30, 237
transgenderism, 189, 275
translators, 230–38
transplanters, 225–27, 237
truth
    coherence theory of, 32
    communication of, 223–24
    correspondence theory of, 26–29, 36
    pragmatic theory of, 29–30
    ultimate, 57–60
    vocabulary of, 27

U

ultimate truths, 51
unbelief, 109–10, 194
univocal language, 37

V

Vanhoozer, Kevin, 28, 45, 54, 56, 123,
    130, 148
Van Rheenen, Gailyn, 228
Varieties of Religious Experience (James),
    180
verbal-plenary inspiration, 126
vices, 89–92
Vincent of Lérins, 142
virtue epistemology, 113
virtue ethics, 77, 211
virtues, 115
    pedagogical, 115
    required in belief, 114
    of steadfast faith, 115–16

W

Walls, Andrew, 237
Walsh, Brian, 48

Wax, Trevin, 51, 59
Webster, John, 21, 108, 123
Weekes, Robin, 49
Wells, Samuel, 54–56
Wellum, Stephen, 135, 250–51
Wesley, John, 133–34, 139, 159, 192
    Aldersgate experience of, 183
    on role of experience, 182–84
Westminster Confession of Faith, 144
Whitfield, Keith, 11
Wilkin, Jen, 159
William of Ockham, 73, 104
Williams, J. Rodman, 185
wisdom, 3, 35–36, 61, 64, 106, 196
Witherington, Ben, III, 92
Wittgenstein, Ludwig, 31
Wittmer, Michael, 217
Wolterstorff, Nicholas, 173
Wood, W. Jay, 114–15
Word of God, threefold, 111–12
worldview
    alternative terms for, 45
    analysis of, 174–75
    defined, 45–47
    elements of, 47
    grand narrative of, 47–48
    presuppositional, 46
    pre-theoretical, 46
worship, 15, 49, 51, 62, 241
    shaping of, 20
Wright, Christopher J. H., 135, 203
Wright, N. T., 47–48, 54–56, 127, 168

Y

Yaghjian, Lucretia, 155–56, 243, 257
Yeago, David, 169
Year of Living Biblically, The (Jacobs),
    225–26

Z

Zahl, Simeon, 182

SCRIPTURE INDEX

Genesis
1:3 *58, 136*
1:9 *58*
1:12 *58*
1:18 *58*
1:21 *58*
1:24 *58*
1:26–28 *61*
1:27 *147, 276*
1:27–28 *58, 234*
1:31 *58*
2:7 *125*
6:9 *77*
9:5–6 *276*
9:6 *61*
17:17–22 *109*
18:10–15 *109*
42:16 *27*
49:24 *38*

Exodus
4:22 *125*
6:6 *273*
15:12 *41*
20:3 *229*
20:7 *76*
20:11 *232*
20:15 *260*
20:16 *27*
23:13 *229*
34:27 *125*

Leviticus
11:44–45 *61*
19:2 *61*
19:19 *225*
19:27 *226*
20:7 *61*
20:26 *61*
21:5 *226*

Numbers
15:32–36 *226*
23:19 *128, 167*

Deuteronomy
4:1–14 *35*
5:7 *229*
5:16 *211*
6:4 *278*
6:14 *229*
7:9 *97, 219*
11:16 *229*
13:14 *27*
17:4 *27*
22:20 *27*
32:1–2 *124*
33:27 *171*

Joshua
24:2 *125*

Judges
6:8 *125*

6:36–40 *109*
21:25 *29*

Ruth
3–4 *273*

1 Samuel
2:2 *38*

2 Samuel
7:28 *27*
22:24 *77*

1 Kings
8:36 *35*
19:1–22 *109*

2 Kings
17:14–15 *110*
17:41 *229*

2 Chronicles
36:22–23 *274*

Ezra
1:1–8 *274*

Nehemiah
9:16 *110*

Job
4:1–5:27 *129*

8:1–22 *129*
9:10 *163*
9:21 *77*
11:1–20 *129*
15:1–35 *129*
18:1–21 *129*
20:1–29 *129*
22:1–30 *129*
25:1–6 *129*
38:1–41:34 *129*
41:11 *64*

Psalms

5:11 *271*
8:1–8 *58*
8:5b *206*
10:4 *128*
14:1 *128*
18:2 *38*
18:31 *38*
19:1–4 *123*
19:1–6 *17*
33:1 *271*
34:19 *95*
51:5 *234*
53:1 *128*
78:6–7 *39*
78:17–22 *110*
90:2 *171*
103:13 *38*
110:1 *54*
119:18 *195*
119:105 *163*
139:7–10 *273*
139:13–14 *276*
139:23–24 *193*
146:6 *232*
150:2 *218*

Proverbs

1:7 *21, 111, 114, 196*
3:1 *35*
3:5–6 *116*
4:2 *35*
4:20 *114*
8:7 *27*
9:10 *111*
10:17 *196*

12:1 *114*
14:12 *107*
15:2 *116*
18:15 *114*
18:24 *99*
21:25 *116*
22:17 *114*
27:17 *99*
28:26 *193*

Ecclesiastes

1:9b *242*
3:8 *95*
7:20 *234*
7:29 *234*

Isaiah

5:20 *90*
8:12 *110*
29:13 *109*
40:13 *64*
43:1 *271*
43:1–13 *270–72*
43:1a *273*
43:1b *273–74*
43:2 *273*
43:2a *273*
43:3 *273–74*
43:4 *273*
43:5 *271*
43:5a *273*
43:5b–6 *273*
43:7 *234–74*
43:8–9 *275*
43:10 *274*
43:11–12 *274*
43:12 *271*
43:13 *274*
44:6–8 *278*
44:24–28 *274*
45:5 *124*
53:5–6 *269*
55:6 *275*
63:16 *38*

Jeremiah

1:4 *276*
6:19 *114*
7:26 *110*

9:5 *27*
9:20 *114*
17:9 *63, 193*
23:18 *64*
30:2 *126*
32:17 *41*

Lamentations

3:22–23 *97*

Zechariah

8:16 *27*

Matthew

3:2 *219*
3:16–17 *279*
4:1–11 *213*
4:17 *219*
4:23 *35*
5:9 *95*
5:43–45a *76*
7:28–29 *35*
9:35 *35*
11:1–3 *109*
11:20 *219*
14:30–32 *109*
22:36–40 *50, 78*
22:37 *93*
22:37–40 *64*
22:39 *93*
22:44 *54*
23:27–28 *179*
24:12 *91*
24:36 *213*
25:14–23 *98*
27:18 *141*
27:26 *141*
28:17 *109*
28:18–20 *4, 78*
28:19 *60*
28:19–20 *50, 98, 284*
28:20 *21, 284*

Mark

1:12–13 *213*
1:15 *219*
1:22 *35*
1:27 *35*

3:28–30 *198*
9:14–29 *110*
9:19 *110*
9:24 *110*
12:30 *93, 102*
15:10 *141*
15:15 *141*

Luke
1:1–4 *126*
2:52 *213*
4:1–2 *279*
4:1–13 *213*
4:32 *35*
9:23–24 *175*
11:28 *124*
13:3 *219*
14:28 *116*
18:7 *96*
24:27 *137*
24:37–39 *109*

John
1:1 *251, 279*
1:1–18 *202, 279*
1:3 *279*
1:4 *279*
1:12–13 *38*
1:14 *123, 239, 251,*
  279
1:18 *17, 123–24,*
  279
3:16–17 *58*
3:18–19 *110*
5:17 *279*
5:26–27 *279*
5:39 *137*
6:35–40 *202*
7:14-18 *102*
7:17 *27*
8:6 *107*
8:47 *124*
10:27–30 *202*
12:43 *91*
12:48 *110*
13:1–16:33 *205*
14:6 *275*
14:26 *98, 132*
15:9–17 *204–5*

15:9a *204*
15:9b–10 *204*
15:13 *204*
15:14 *204*
15:16 *204*
15:16a *204*
15:17 *204*
15:26 *191*
15:26–27 *279*
16:8 *91*
16:12–15 *98*
16:13 *123, 132*
17:5 *279*
17:8 *123*
17:17 *121*
17:20 *147*
19:16 *141*
20:24–29 *109*
20:29 *106*
29:6 *21*

Acts
1:1 *126*
1:9–11 *124*
3:19–20 *52*
4:12 *275*
5:1–4 *27*
5:3–4 *279*
7:51 *110*
7:57–8:1a *46*
8:31 *148*
9:1–31 *46*
10:9–15 *226*
10:38 *279*
13:16 *231*
13:16–41 *231*
13:17 *231*
13:18–19 *231*
13:20–22 *231*
13:23–25 *231*
13:26–38 *231*
13:38–41 *231*
14:8–12 *232*
14:15 *232*
14:15–17 *231*
14:16 *232*
14:17 *232*
14:21 *52*
14:21–23 *233*

15:7 *52*
17:1–3 *231*
17:2 *110*
17:10–11 *231*
17:11 *17, 110*
17:17 *110*
17:22 *232*
17:22–31 *232*
17:23 *232*
17:24–27 *123*
17:24a *232*
17:24b–29 *233*
17:26 *57*
17:28 *169, 232*
17:28–29 *38*
17:28a *232*
17:30 *233*
17:31 *233*
17:32–33 *233*
17:34 *233*
18:3 *236*
18:4 *110, 236*
22:1-21 *46*
24:11 *27*

Romans
1:16 *239*
1:18–19 *124*
1:19–20 *17, 123*
1:20 *123*
1:21 *107*
1:24–27 *189*
2:14–16 *123*
2:15 *123*
4:1–5 *213*
5:1 *109, 234*
5:8 *58*
5:12 *234*
7:18–24 *59*
8:2 *91*
8:7 *193*
8:15 *191*
8:16 *191*
8:29–30 *77*
9:1–5 *63*
9:6–29 *63*
9–11 *63*
9:22 *96*
9:30–33 *63*

10:1–13 *63*
10:2 *91*
10:3 *91*
10:9 *50, 217*
10:9–13 *52*
10:10 *46*
10:13 *50*
10:14–21 *63*
10:17 *52, 124*
11:1–32 *63*
11:22 *97*
11:33–36 *63*
12:1–2 *64, 115*
12:2 *16, 43, 60, 91, 229*
12:18 *95*
14:19 *95*
16:26 *171*

1 Corinthians
1:4–9 *88*
1:9 *219*
1:22 *106*
1:25 *106*
2:10–13 *98*
2:14–16 *132*
3:16–17 *279*
5:1 *237*
5:9 *237*
6:9 *237*
6:9–11 *189*
6:19–20 *279*
7:2 *237*
8:4 *278*
8:6 *38, 278*
9:20–23 *231*
9:22 *223*
10:23–33 *76*
10:25–27 *76*
10:27–28 *77*
10:28 *76*
10:31 *76*
11:2 *115, 141*
11:7 *276*
12:5–6 *69*
12:12 *78*
12–14 *198*
13:2 *94*
13:4–7 *94*

13:12 *132*
15:1–8 *52*
15:3–4 *142*
15:6 *168*
15:20 *207*
15:33 *169*

2 Corinthians
2:17 *89*
3:18 *77*
4:4 *107*
5:7 *106*
5:20 *58*
5:21 *198*
10:1 *97*
10:4b–5 *200*
11:3–4 *115*

Galatians
1:6 *88*
1:6–7 *20*
1:6–9 *115*
1:8 *88, 95*
1:10 *92*
1:14–18 *233*
2:11–14 *20*
2:14 *88*
2:16 *98*
3:1 *88*
3:10–14 *269*
3:16 *54*
4:4–5 *17*
4:8–20 *20*
5:1–5 *202*
5:1–15 *88*
5:16 *88*
5:17 *88*
5:19 *237*
5:19–21 *89*
5:22 *92, 95, 97*
5:22–23 *77, 92*
5:24 *219*
6:11 *126*

Ephesians
1:3–14 *269*
1:4 *254*
1:17 *9*
1:17–18 *98*

2:1–3 *234*
2:1–5 *269*
2:4–7 *273*
2:6–7 *269*
2:7 *97*
2:8–9 *109, 274*
2:8–10 *269*
4:2 *96*
4:12 *16, 89*
4:12–13 *4*
4:13 *16, 94–95*
4:14 *4, 16, 24, 115*
4:15 *4, 97*
4:15–16 *239*
4:31 *97*
4:32 *97*
6:1 *211*
6:1–3 *211*
6:2–3 *211*

Philippians
1:27 *58*
2:5–11 *143, 202, 279*
2:6 *170, 279*
2:8–9 *279*
3:20 *58*
4:4 *94, 271*
4:8 *64*
4:9 *64*
4:11–12 *94*

Colossians
1:13–14 *219, 274*
1:15 *3, 17, 124, 279*
1:15–20 *279*
1:15–23 *202*
1:16 *279*
1:17 *279*
1:19–20 *279*
2:2 *24*
2:8 *230*
2:18 *230*
3:10 *16*
3:12–13 *97*
3:16 *62*
4:1 *226*
4:5–6 *239*

1 Thessalonians

2:13 *125*
4:3 *237*
4:14 *143*
5:19–22 *186*
5:21 *16, 110*
5:26 *211*

2 Thessalonians

2:10 *93*
2:11–12 *110*
2:15 *141*

1 Timothy

1:5 *23*
1:6–7 *89*
1:10 *24, 35*
1:17 *171*
2:4 *254*
3:3 *92*
3:16 *143*
4:1 *24, 35*
4:6 *35*
4:11 *35*
4:13 *35, 263*
4:16 *24, 91*
5:23 *211, 226*
6:3 *35–36*
6:3–4 *89*
6:4b–5 *89*
6:10 *89*
6:20 *105*
6:20–21 *27*

2 Timothy

1:12 *202*
1:13–14 *141*
2:2 *35, 233, 283*
2:13 *98*
2:15 *3*
2:17 *35*
2:24 *35*
3:5 *89*
3:7 *230*
3:10 *24*
3:13 *230*
3:15 *36*
3:16 *82, 121, 124, 266*

3:16–17 *38, 127*
3:16a *36*
4:2 *263*
4:3 *24, 35–36, 90*

Titus

1:2 *128, 167*
1:9 *24, 35*
1:12 *169, 232*
2:1 *24, 35*
2:1–8 *36*
2:7 *35*
2:10 *35*
3:4 *97*

Hebrews

1:1 *208*
1:1–3 *124*
1:1–4 *202, 279*
1:2 *279*
1:2–3 *12*
1:2b *279*
1:3 *17, 279*
1:3a *279*
2:1 *114*
3:12 *110*
4:12 *28, 91, 125, 193*
4:14 *115*
5:14 *16*
6:4–6 *202*
6:18 *128, 167*
9:11–12 *226*
10:23a *98*
10:23b *98*
11:39 *109*
12:1 *109*
12:14 *95*

James

1:8 *90*
1:12 *99*
1:13 *167, 213*
1:14 *193*
1:22 *124*
2:14–26 *60*
2:19 *108*
2:20–24 *213*
3:1 *35*

3:9–10 *61*
3:17 *95*
4:4 *96*

1 Peter

1:3 *38*
1:16 *61*
2:21–25 *269*
3:15 *109*
3:20b–22 *54*

2 Peter

1:21 *125*
2:1–3 *27, 115*
2:3 *89*
2:20–22 *202*
3:15–16 *131*
3:16 *126*

1 John

1:8–10 *234*
2:21 *27*
2:27 *27*
3:2b *132*
4:1 *17*
4:1–3 *27*
4:1–6 *20*
4:6 *27*
4:19 *62*
4:21 *76*
5:6 *191*
5:9–11 *191*

2 John

12 *126*

3 John

13 *126*

Jude

1:3 *39, 229*
1:22 *109*

Revelation

1:19 *126*
2:4 *89*
4:9 *171*
20:1–6 *198*
22:1–5 *207*